THE ROAD TO BLUE HEAVEN

THE ROAD TO BLUE HEAVEN

AN INSIDER'S DIARY OF NORTH CAROLINA'S 2007 BASKETBALL SEASON

WES MILLER

WITH A FOREWORD BY ROY WILLIAMS

PEGASUS BOOKS
NEW YORK

THE ROAD TO BLUE HEAVEN

Pegasus Books LLC
45 Wall Street, Suite 1021
New York, NY 10005

First Pegasus Books edition 2007

Library of Congress Cataloging-in-Publication Data is available.

ISBN: 978-1-933648-57-6

10 9 8 7 8 6 5 4 3 2 1

Interior design by Maria Fernandez

Printed in the United States of America
Distributed by Consortium

To my parents, Ken and Susan Miller,
for their unwavering love and support
over the last twenty-four years.

The publisher fondly dedicates *The Road to Blue Heaven*
to B. A., one of our greatest Tar Heels,
and without whose support this book would not exist.

FOREWORD

FOR MOST CAROLINA FANS, the play they'll remember most from Wes Miller's Tar Heel career is a three-pointer. He made so many big ones for us over the last two seasons.

But that's not what stands out to me the most. For me, the play I'll always remember from Wes's career is the charge he took against Arizona this past season. We had built a big lead, but Arizona is always tough at home and they were starting to close the gap. They had some momentum and were on a fast break, and it looked like they might have an easy basket.

Jordan Hill, who goes about 6-foot-9, 211 pounds, came blasting down the lane with the ball. I looked up and there stood Wes, feet planted, in perfect position, ready to take the charge.

Hill was called for an offensive foul and that play really turned the momentum of the game. His knees hit Wes right in the sternum, and of course Wes being Wes he had to bounce right back up and act like it didn't hurt. We scored the next 11 points of the game, and I don't think we would have been able to do that without that defensive play. Watching the film gave me an even better appreciation for that play, and I told him in front of the team that it was one of the two best charges any of my players had ever taken.

I was kidding around with the media after that game and said it took either a lot of stupidity or a lot of courage to stand in there and take that charge. Any Carolina fan who watched Wes's career knows it wasn't stupidity—it was courage and toughness. That's been the trademark of his Tar Heel career. When you look down our roster, he is probably not as gifted and talented as anyone else we have. He doesn't have great jumping ability or exceptional quickness. In most cases, especially in today's game and playing the way we like to play, those are assets you have to have to play in the Atlantic Coast Conference.

But here's what he does have, and this is what enabled him to be a big-time contributor for us: a desire to work harder than anyone else.

When I met with him for the first time in my office, I honestly didn't know how much he would be able to play at North Carolina. I told him exactly that. At that point, I didn't know him—all I had to go on was what a few people had told me and the impressions I gathered from that initial meeting.

What I soon learned was that he was completely devoted to the game of basketball. As a coach, it's so rewarding to work with someone like that. We asked him to do a lot of things during his senior season. He began the year mostly playing the two-guard, and then we had to ask him to play some point guard—and the point guard is a very demanding position at Carolina—because of injuries. He never complained once about it to me. We were asking him to fill a lot of roles, and in some ways I think that probably impacted his shot and explains why his shooting percentages went down from his junior year.

When I think back on Wes Miller, I'm going to think of a player who I am as proud of as anyone I ever coached. I can't imagine any player who has ever worked harder than he worked to fulfill every single bit of his potential. That's endearing to a basketball coach, because our job is to help players maximize their potential, and when they're willing to work with you to achieve that some very special things can happen.

Short on height, long on intensity, long on dedication and competitiveness, great big heart—that is how I describe Wes Miller. I would simply love for every player I coach the rest of my career to have "Wes Miller" qualities.

—ROY WILLIAMS

PROLOGUE

RIGHT BEFORE SCHOOL STARTED, I went with my girlfriend to her family's place in the Bahamas. There was no one in Chapel Hill because everybody on the team goes home after the second session of summer school, so all the pickup games and workouts are done for a few days. As basketball players, it's basically the last chance we have to get away and clear our minds.

But I still had to play basketball. Abaco is very remote, and there aren't a lot of people there. We had been to the Bahamas for a couple of exhibitions before my junior season, so I knew the basketball competition would be a little different from home, but I was still hoping to get some work in. Going a few days without picking up a basketball just isn't an option for me. The first day we were there, I found a court that was about a 10-minute car ride from where we were staying. It wasn't the same kind of court we're used to in the United States. It was an outdoor court, and it had wooden backboards. It looked like the court in that movie *The Air Up There*.

On the first day I was there, everyone else who was playing was a native. As I was about to start playing, they asked me if I played college basketball.

"Yeah, I play at North Carolina," I said.

They couldn't believe it. They kept saying, "You mean the Tar Heels?" Then they started asking me questions. They asked me if I knew David Noel and if I knew Reyshawn Terry. There was one guy who really surprised me because he knew a lot about college basketball. Then he said, "What about that white guy who can shoot it? You know, number 22."

When I told him he was talking about me, that I was Wes Miller, he was really surprised. It seemed to really shock them that someone they had watched on TV was on their court hoping to get into their game.

When you're a Carolina basketball player, you realize pretty quickly that there are people all over the state and all over the country who watch you and know who you are. I think I'm pretty recognizable around Chapel Hill because people here love their basketball, but my size and stature usually mean that when I leave town I'm more unrecognizable. But I've traveled with teammates like Sean May and Jawad Williams, and those guys can't go anywhere without people stopping them.

Having people recognize me in Abaco really drove home the point that being a Carolina basketball player isn't just a Chapel Hill thing. It's a nationwide—and sometimes worldwide—thing. Wherever I go, whoever I meet, I'm always going to be Wes Miller, the former Carolina basketball player.

The 2006–07 season was my last chance to live that excitement first-hand. People will be talking to me about my career in Chapel Hill for the rest of my life. I wanted to make sure I remembered every second.

PRESEASON

I DON'T READ ANY of the preseason magazines. I try to pay as little attention as possible.

That might sound strange, because I'm a big college basketball fan and have been since I was a little kid. I like to know what's going on with other teams and who is predicted to be good. But when it comes to our team, I try to stay as far away from it as I can.

That's been tough to do so far this year because the name North Carolina comes up any time someone is talking about college basketball. Tyler Hansbrough and Reyshawn Terry have already taken a cover picture for the preview issue of *Sports Illustrated*. Dick Vitale picked us as his choice to win the national championship as early as last April.

Actually, I think I paid more attention to the preseason talk last year. That's because at that point, it was locker room material and motivation. We'd lost Sean May, Raymond Felton, Rashad McCants, and Marvin Williams, plus a great senior class, and we replaced them with a bunch of freshmen. One magazine picked us to miss the NCAA Tournament. The ACC's preseason poll put us in sixth place, just barely ahead of Miami.

In some ways, I guess I understand it. No one had really seen the players we had. They didn't see the things we saw all summer. We knew how good the freshmen were, and how important David Noel was going to be to us. They didn't. They definitely didn't expect anything from me. If I was mentioned at all, it was usually as a potential option at point guard.

We cherished that underdog role. We paid attention to the fact that no one wanted to pay attention to us. When we played, you could see that chip on our shoulder. When you come to North Carolina to play basketball, you expect people to have high expectations. That can create some pressure, and sometimes you start to think you're better than you really are. We never had that opportunity last year because everyone was telling us what we *couldn't* do rather than what we could do.

This year, we're the favorites. We have to remember that the same people building us up this year are the same ones talking about how bad we were going to be last year. Preseason picks are something we can't control. And because football season hasn't gone very well, there's been a lot of buzz about basketball throughout the fall. Coach Williams is good at keeping us in our little bubble, though. I think people would be surprised at how little we talk about some of the things fans talk about. I don't want to say it's a job, because it's a lot of fun. But playing basketball is something we do every day. We live it. So as players, we don't spend all our free time talking about it the way some fans might.

But we do spend a lot of time getting ready for the season. During the summer, we lift weights four or five times per week. That's anywhere from 90 minutes to two hours per day. Some people might have misconceptions about it—you tell someone that you're lifting for two hours, and they think you're in the weight room that whole time. It's much more than that. It's 15 minutes warming up, it's running and agility workouts, it's explosiveness. Then there is also a strength aspect to it. One of our workouts with Jonas Sahratian works our entire body.

Almost everyone does something in addition to our usual team workouts. I like to come in 30 minutes before we lift and work on my shot. Some guys say they take a certain number of shots. I don't count shots. I only count made shots. In 30 minutes, I can usually get up around 200 or 300 makes. Eric Hoots, a former manager who now serves as our video coordinator, has been a big help to me in those workouts, and so has Jackie Manuel.

Jackie usually hangs around to play pickup in the afternoons. We usually play pickup around an hour after we lift, so I use that hour to get in a 45-minute workout on the basketball court. Then we play pickup, and that can go for anywhere from an hour to two hours. So by the time a typical offseason day is finished, I've worked out three or four times and spent around six hours at the Smith Center.

This is going to sound funny to people who think 23 is young, but I've had to learn to listen to my body. I take one day off per week, and that's usually a Saturday or Sunday. In my younger days—way back when I was 19 or 20—I didn't do that, and I noticed it was taking a toll on my body. My legs would get weary and that would create bad habits on my jump shot. You want your shot to feel really good in the summer because you're getting so many repetitions, and taking a day off enables me to make sure I feel like everything is in tune.

WEEK ONE

LATE NIGHT COUNTS AS a practice for NCAA purposes, but it's not really a practice. It's mostly just for fun, and it was my last chance to do my impersonation of Coach Williams. The first year they asked me to do it, I was pretty nervous about it. At first I told them I didn't want to do it. But they convinced me, and people seemed to like it. I put a lot of effort into it—I even watched tape of him to make sure I had all the mannerisms correct. This year I'm a senior, so I felt more comfortable giving him a hard time. I even added a cane to make fun of all the back problems he's had. It's funny—for that night only.

The real practice starts the next morning. I've heard about

other schools—Duke is one of them—where they actually practice during football games. We don't do that. Our practices are always scheduled around football games in the fall, because we're college students, too, and Coach Williams knows we want to see the games. We have a pregame tailgate party and sometimes recruits are in town, so it turns into a big social event.

In most cases, that's good. But when the football team plays at 12 noon, that usually means an early practice for us. Our first "real" practice of the year comes on Saturday morning after Late Night. We have to be at the Smith Center to eat fruit at 6:45 a.m. For a college student, that's really early. We've just had a late evening the night before, almost everyone has their families in town, and then we have to turn around and get ready to concentrate. It's a quick turnaround, and practice starts at 8 a.m.

As a senior, I'm less nervous for the first practice than I've been for any of my other first practices. It's familiar to me because I've done it for the past three years, but it's also the first real day with the new team. I know what to expect. I know I'm not in basketball shape yet, because we haven't had any practices. Running and playing pickup is different from the kind of running Coach Williams expects in practice. That's what makes me the most nervous—I want to get through the first couple of days, get in shape, and start feeling more comfortable on the court.

During the preseason, C.B. McGrath went through some of the basic things we do during practice with the freshman. We've got a lot of young guys this year—six new freshmen. He took them through the basics of the secondary break and defensive stations so when they saw it in practice, it wouldn't be their first time. They have to pick everything else up on the fly. Coach Williams hates to waste time, so it's not like we spend the first week with him spoon-feeding the freshmen everything they need to know. In many ways, our first practice is just like the practice we'll run in March. Coach tells the freshmen to get in the back of the line during drills and stay behind an upperclassman, but they're still expected to participate.

I remember exactly what it is like as a freshman. It's a whirlwind. Coach is so intense and focused and everyone else knows exactly what to do. Meanwhile, you're new and you're just trying to hang in there and stay with it.

The best thing about the first practice is that I feel like I completely know what's going on at all times. I've done everything before. But I also have more leadership responsibility this year, so I have to look out for everyone else. I try to be aware of balancing leading by example and leading with my voice. People notice if you're always talking but you're not really getting anything done. So I make a conscious effort to lead by example. If we're in defensive stations or running a 5-on-0 drill, I want my teammates to look at the way I do it as the standard for everyone else. I want them to see that I'm going as hard as I possibly can and I'm doing things the right way. But I also know Coach places a big emphasis on talking, especially on the defensive end of the floor. So I'm trying to be louder in drills this year.

I wouldn't say I'm trying to fill David Noel's shoes as far as leadership. Everyone knows he was a great leader for last year's team. Coach Williams has said he might have been the best leader he's ever been around. But it was a different situation for him because he knew—and the team knew—he would always be on the floor. That's not the case for me, and it's not even the case for Reyshawn. So we have to start with leading by example. I have to do what Coach tells me to do all the time, and I have to do it the absolute best I can. No matter where I am on the depth chart or how much raw talent I have, I can always do that.

Before every practice, we go to the basketball office and get a copy of that day's practice plan. It's unbelievably detailed. We know exactly what drill we'll be doing at, for example, 8:31 a.m. We know it will last 8 minutes and we know we'll be finished with practice at 9:36 a.m. The bottom of every practice plan includes the lineups for that day: the starters on the White team and the reserves on the Blue team.

On Saturday morning, the White team is all upperclassmen and the Blue team is all freshmen. That makes it very competitive, because the old guys want to prove to the new guys that they can beat them. It also makes the freshmen learn fast, because they have to learn very quickly how to play together. There's no one else to help them, no one to grab them and point them in the right direction. They have to pick it up very quickly. It's a big shock for the freshmen, because the game is so much faster at this level. You can take plays off in high school. If you do that here, you won't play much. Coach Williams is so intense on every possession in practice. You learn pretty quickly that you always have to sprint back on defense and you always have to stay in your defensive stance and you always have to run to offense. Our coaches don't let things like that slide, and that usually is jarring for the freshmen.

I noticed right away that our first couple of practices were going to be different. Coach still wants the freshmen to learn everything on the fly, but he's more understanding this year. Last year, even though we had lost our top seven players, we took a preseason trip to the Bahamas that enabled us to have a few practices and a couple games before the official start of the season. Everyone had a basic familiarity with what we were trying to do. This year, we have six players who have no idea what we are doing. We've had more teaching this year. There was more chaos this year than in other opening practices.

It's hard to believe that I'm doing all of this for the last time. It really hit me during conditioning milestones. I thought about it being my last 12-minute run and my last Carolina mile and my last conditioning test of 12 33's. Those are good feelings, because none of those things are fun. But when Late Night was over, I thought, "I'll never get to do that again." That's sad because I would stay and do this until I was 50 if they would let me—my teammates would probably tell you that's not long from now. It's so much fun, and it's a weird feeling to never be able to do it again. This has been the central part of my life for the last four years. In the bigger picture, basketball has been the central part of my life for my entire life. This is the first time I don't really know what I'll be doing with the game at this time next year. Everyone has hopes and dreams, but there's no guarantee. In the past, I've always known I'd be playing somewhere. Now that I'm a senior, I think I'm stepping back and analyzing the big picture more often. It's my last chance to do a lot of these things.

WEEK TWO

To a certain extent, college basketball players are just like everyone else. When you look at our roster, it's obvious we have a lot of talent. Right now, that's the biggest story about this team. I've been asked about it in almost every interview I've done so far. When you're talking to the media, you don't want to say, "Yeah, I'm worried about my playing time." That gives them the wrong idea. But let's be honest: you don't get to be an ACC-level athlete without being competitive. Everyone on this team wants to play all 40 minutes. There's only one thing everyone wants to do more than that—win. That's how you reconcile it if you're not playing as much as you might want. You have to be willing to commit to what is best for the team, and all of us believe that Roy Williams knows what is best for the team. Just look at his record. It's not exactly a debatable subject. Who knows more—a guy with almost 500 wins or some kid from Charlotte?

But to a certain extent, players act just like fans. We look at the roster and think about minutes. If you look around in practice and think, "Man, he's playing a lot better than me," it's only natural to think about how that will impact your playing time. As you get older, you do that less frequently. As my career has progressed, I've started to look at the way my teammates play as something that is beyond my control. When it comes to game time, it's out of my hands. Coach Williams will decide when he puts me in the game. I can give myself a better opportunity based on how I perform in practice, but you'll drive yourself crazy if you sit there with a pad and paper and try to figure out which players are going to play which minutes. By this point in my career, I've tried to use this theory: trust yourself, be confident, play as hard as you can, leave it on the floor, and be ready in game time when Coach calls your name.

I started 16 games last year. Ordinarily, I think a returning senior who had started 16 games would be looking at preseason practice as a chance to do the same things I did last year, be solid, and step right back into that same role. It's not like that for me this year. I'm looking at it as if I didn't play a single minute last year, as if I'm trying to prove everything all over again. We have so much talent and there is so much up in the air. Tyler probably knows he has an assured spot in the rotation, and so does Reyshawn. But everyone else is battling for playing time. I want to prove to Coach Williams I can bring something to this team. So I've had three goals for these first two weeks of practice: get in basketball shape, help the young guys get acclimated, and compete for playing time.

Coach talked to us in the locker room a couple days ago about the attitude everyone has to have this year. He emphasized how important it was that everyone focus on what was good for the team, and he used last year's team as an example. The freshmen fully bought into the idea of playing for the team. Marcus Ginyard was a perfect example of that. I hosted him on his recruiting visit. We've had a good relationship ever since then, and he was around a lot during his senior year of high school. He came to almost all our home games. We joke that this is actually his junior year, not his sophomore year, because he was around so much after he committed to play here.

So we had a great relationship . . . and then halfway through last year I moved into his place in the starting lineup. We never really sat down and talked about it point-blank, but the most impressive thing to me was that I never felt one bit of animosity from him. It was the exact opposite, actually. He gave me so much support. Of course he wanted to play over me. He didn't want to lose his starting spot. But once it happened, he accepted Coach's decision and made an effort to do the best he could in his new role. I always respected that about him. That could have been a very difficult situation for everybody involved. I never felt like I couldn't talk to Marcus or couldn't hang around with Marcus because of what was happening on the court, and that's a tribute to the way he handled it. Attitudes like that are why last year's team seemed to click so well.

Now we have to make sure this year's freshmen have those same attitudes. One thing you know about Coach Williams: he is going to bring in players with high character. And he also won't accept anyone not playing for the good of the team. Players have tried to battle him in past years, but he will always win in the end. We'll see how quickly this year's freshmen catch on to that. We have so many talented players who think they're going to play. It's not easy playing as much as you would like, and at any given time there will be some players sitting on the bench who are used to playing major minutes. The way they handle that will determine a whole lot about the kind of season we have. Coach Williams will not accept anyone bringing this team down because of their selfishness. It'll be interesting to watch the freshmen adapt to that and how they grow throughout the year.

I always used to laugh at older players who talked about their body breaking down. But now I'm 23 competing against 18- and 19-year-olds, and suddenly I understand what they were saying. Being 23 and 18 might not seem like a very big difference, but I've noticed some major differences in the way my body reacts to physical activity. I've already had some issues this year—nothing that is preventing me from practicing, but a lot of nagging injuries throughout my body. I've been seeing a chiropractor, getting massages, and doing all kinds of things to try and stay ready to practice every day. You don't recover the same way when you're 23 that you did when you were 19.

Fortunately, I don't have a crushing load academically this semester, so I have time to take care of myself physically. I have 12 hours this fall—three classes and an independent study. Because I transferred to Carolina, I've had five years to finish my degree and I've been able to spread it out a little bit. Next semester, I'll just have two classes—an elective and a PE.

That's exactly the kind of class load you want when you're playing two or three games a week. Because of having five years and taking classes in the summer, I've never felt overwhelmed with school work. I'm a political science major, so I've always had plenty of work. There have been a lot of papers, a lot of tests and a lot of long nights.

It's a matter of balancing your time. You have to find those windows when you can knock out some school work. On some days it might be in the morning before class, and on others it might be late at night. It gets tougher during the season because your body hurts and you're on a strange schedule, so when you get that free time you want to rest. Our academic advisor, Wayne Walden, and all the tutors do a great job of helping us succeed.

WEEK THREE

WHEN COACH WILLIAMS FIRST CAME to Carolina, I thought of him the same way a lot of casual fans think of him. I had seen the ESPN highlights and some of the interviews, and I pictured him in that same, "Gee, shucks," way a lot of people see him. I knew that probably wasn't how he really was, but that was the perception the media had given me.

I was right—to a certain extent. Off the court, he really is that easygoing, caring man who cares about his players. He is very charismatic and he is very easy to talk to. I think the public sees that about him and they're right. What they don't see is how competitive he can be. On the court, he can be very fiery. He is as intense as anyone I have ever been around in my life. When you step between the lines to practice for him, you have to be ready to compete in every possible way.

The amazing thing about it is the way he expresses that intensity. He can raise his voice for an entire practice, but he'll never curse us. I think that goes back to Coach Smith's days. He gets his point across and motivates his players without ever using a curse word. As a leader, that's the perfect way to do it because he makes you want to play to his level of intensity.

What he does so well is make his players feel like nothing is important other than impressing him and doing things the way he wants. We're at North Carolina, so we get a lot of attention. Somehow he's able to make us forget about all that stuff. We're not trying to impress the fans or our friends or our teammates. We're just trying to do things the way he taught us. That's pretty amazing, really. Thousands of people are watching and we're only worried about one person.

That can make you feel pretty good when you know you did something exactly the right way in practice or in a game. That's a feeling I didn't get much my first couple years, because I was still learning and I would still occasionally botch something. The worst he has ever gotten on me was during my redshirt year—this is a story C.B. McGrath still loves. In practice I was on the Blue team playing point guard against Raymond Felton. I think I had about four turnovers in five possessions. On the sixth possession, I bring the ball down the court and the White team is in their scramble defense. I cross Raymond over at halfcourt, and I think I see an opening. So I drive into the lane, jump into the air . . . and there's nothing there. I end up throwing the ball out of bounds on the baseline and the pass wasn't within five feet of any of my teammates. So that was five turnovers in six possessions.

But that's not why Coach got on me. I was frustrated, so I screamed the f-word as loud as I could. It was a reaction that happened before I could think about it. It just so happened that Quentin Thomas and his parents were on their official visit that weekend, and they were sitting courtside watching our practice. What a great way to impress a recruit. At some schools, a moment like that would have been pretty common. At Carolina, that's not how we conduct ourselves. Needless to say, Coach laid into me. The funny part was that he reamed me but never used a single curse word to do it. He can make you feel like you're getting cursed out without ever using that kind of language.

When Coach singles you out for something negative, it can be hard to handle, especially for younger players. It's especially tough when you feel like you're doing well generally, but he keeps getting on you for little things. Some guys let that stay in their head for too long. I know I let it bother me too much when I was younger. Sometimes I wouldn't be able to sleep at night because I was thinking about what had happened at practice. As I've gotten older, I've tried not to let it impact my confidence. I try to listen to what he says, improve on it, and keep a level head. Of course, it helps that I think as you get older—and especially when you're a senior—Coach is a little easier on you.

Already this season, Dean Smith has stopped by a couple of our practices. It's happened so much that it's almost routine to me. But during my first couple years, when he walked in the gym, I'd think, 'Wow, Dean Smith is watching us practice!' When you grow up in the state of North Carolina, Dean

Smith *is* basketball. Being at practice and having the best current coach in college basketball coaching us and the best coach in the history of college basketball watching from the sidelines is a special feeling. It makes you feel like you're truly in the mecca of college basketball.

It's indicative of the kind of people who surround this program. Dean Smith can just walk in at any time. That doesn't happen anywhere else. Over the course of my career, I've gotten to know him a little bit, which has really been special. To be able to go say hello to him after practice and shake his hand is the perfect example of what makes this program different.

Of course, I haven't mentioned to him that I grew up watching him at Wake Forest games. I used to go to games with my dad all the time, and we'd go to the ACC Tournament too. When I was a fan, though, I never yelled at Coach Smith. I'm not saying I didn't see some other people doing it, but I never did. I'm glad I didn't, because he has such a good memory he'd probably remember the exact game situation, score, and what I said.

I moved onto the White team with the starters the day before our first exhibition game against St. Augustine's. When that happens, we know there's a good chance we'll be a starter the next day. Ninety-five percent of the time, the White starters in practice the day before a game will start the game. But you never know for sure until 15 minutes before game time. When Coach Williams comes in for his last pregame talk, the opponent's five starters are written on the chalkboard. He writes each player's name beside the person they'll be guarding, and that's when we know the starters.

One exception was last year when I moved into the starting lineup against Florida State. He had put me on the White team a couple days before the game, but I didn't really expect him to make the change in the starting lineup. I was shooting around on the court in Tallahassee about 45 minutes before the game and he pulled me aside and told me I was starting. It wasn't a complete surprise, because we had lost two games in a row and I knew he was considering shaking things up, but it was still exciting to hear him say it.

Then I had to make sure I controlled my emotions. I've improved on that quite a bit as I've gotten older. This is a game of highs and lows, and it can change very quickly. When I first got to Carolina, I had trouble remembering that. My teammates those first couple of years would tell you I was very emotional on the floor. I had a tendency to lose it a little bit. As I've gotten older, I've tried to stay on a more even keel, and that has made me a better player. That helps in a situation like Florida State where I'm getting my first start in a big conference road game.

Obviously, St. Aug's wasn't as big a game as Florida State. But it was still our first chance to play in a real game environment. Coach made it clear he was going to play everybody, but I had no idea how much I would play or whether I would start. The first month or two of this season will be very unpredictable. On last year's team, I knew early in the season when I would go into the game. I knew I'd be replacing Marcus when he was tired and I'd get at least one rotation each half. As the season progressed, everyone had a very clear idea of their roles.

We don't have that yet this year. It's more unpredictable for me personally as far as how much I'm going to play. At this point even Coach would tell you he doesn't know how it will turn out. By the time we get to February or March, it will be more predictable. But right now, everyone sees how much talent we have and how hard it's going to be to earn minutes.

The St. Aug's game was a good learning experience. They really wanted to run, which enabled us to play the style we want to play. In the early season we run into a lot of teams that want to try and slow us down—they didn't want to do that. We used our 44 defense, which is a full-court trap, to speed them up even more. That forced them to take shots they didn't want to take.

We won, 110–79, but we also saw we need a lot of improvement. We didn't run 44 the way it should be run. We did one thing right—we sped up the tempo of the game—but other than that we weren't very sound fundamentally. Things we might have gotten away with against the Blue team in practice didn't work against St. Aug's, and if it doesn't work against them, it definitely won't work in the ACC. We have to improve at making the right rotations and the right reads. Coach wants to push the basketball more than he ever has before this year, which means the press could be a bigger part of our gameplan. Everybody is excited about that, because it's a fun style to play. Everyone gets to fly around the court and it takes advantage of our depth, because we get tired more quickly and Coach can substitute more often. But in order to use it more frequently, we're going to have to play it much better than we did against St. Aug's.

WEEK FOUR

I WOULDN'T SAY WE'VE HAD bad practices lately, but I wouldn't call them good, either. And on Sunday Coach Williams got tired of it.

Every basketball team in the country has days where practice isn't as crisp as the coaches would like. That especially happens in the preseason, when games seem so far away and players get tired of going against the same people every day. But we have fewer of those days at Carolina than anywhere else I've ever been. We have a sense of urgency here, and Coach was discouraged because he didn't feel that sense of urgency.

The past two Sundays we've had scrimmages. We do them right at the beginning of practice, and it's three 20-minute scrimmages with a game situation clock. Coach mixes up the teams for each period and we have real officials. The only difference from a real game is that Coach is on the floor coaching the whole time, and he can stop play any time he wants. The first Sunday we did it, the score in the first scrimmage was 65–59. That's incredible for a 20-minute scrimmage. That's when I realized either we're the most talented offensive team in the history of college basketball or we're not playing very well defensively. I think it's probably the latter.

This Sunday, things really got ugly in the second and third scrimmage. Guys were tired and started breaking down physically and mentally. Coach always talks to us about the point in the game when one team will give in. He doesn't want us to be that team. But in practice Sunday, our whole team gave in. Some guys weren't running hard, and we were forgetting plays we've been running since the first day of practice. A couple of the freshmen were having trouble running some basic secondary break offense, and Coach jumped on Deon Thompson pretty hard. Then he put the whole team on the line for some running.

That third scrimmage was really discouraging. I've been around long enough to know how we should practice almost a month into practice, and we weren't doing it. After we finished our post-practice stretching, I was sitting on the side of the court with Reyshawn Terry and Quentin Thomas. We knew the practice we'd just had wasn't acceptable, and we didn't think Coach should have to deal with it. We wanted to deal with it ourselves. We decided meeting as a team definitely wouldn't hurt and it would also enable us to communicate some expectations to the younger players. Reyshawn and I wanted to make sure everyone understood that we all had some responsibility for the way things had gone. It was

the fault of the upperclassmen for not holding guys accountable, and it was the fault of the underclassmen for not doing
things the right way.

So we met as a team at 2:45 on Monday, right before practice. No coaches were there, just players. We told them we
couldn't continue to have those kinds of letdowns. We told
them it was our fault for letting some little things slide, and
we committed to setting a better example—while at the same
time telling them we were going to be harder on them about
the little things.

Coach Williams was obviously feeling the same way. He
pulled me into his office Monday afternoon.

"What did you think of yesterday's practice?" he said.

I already knew the answer: it wasn't very good. Coach told
me it was the most discouraged he had been with this team all
year. He said it made him question how to motivate us. But he
told me he was going to come out with a positive attitude that
afternoon and hopefully we would pick it up a little bit.

Deon also met with Coach before practice on Monday. It's
always interesting to see how freshmen handle their first experience with failure. How you respond to Coach is a big part of
your freshman year. Deon handled it very well. Even on
Sunday, he responded by running harder and hitting a couple
shots in the post. He made a conscious effort to try harder, and
you can see that sense of urgency that was missing.

We have some very talented freshmen on this team. All of
them are adjusting in their own way to college basketball. I
think Ty Lawson probably had the most difficult adjustment
in terms of getting acclimated to college life. He went to Oak
Hill for high school, which is a very regimented environment.
Then he got to Carolina and had much more freedom, and
that's been tough for him. Both Reyshawn and I have pulled

him aside and emphasized how important the little things are for our team. Something simple like being on time is critical. He's a very laid-back guy, and he doesn't take many things seriously. That's fine, because he is 18 years old. You're not supposed to take many things seriously when you're 18. Even in the last week, I've noticed him taking basketball more seriously. And when he steps on the floor, the transformation is amazing. He might have had a tough adjustment to college off the court, but on the court he's a complete natural. He's talented enough to make the jump from high school to college without many struggles, and it's very rare to be able to do that. It's even more rare that we have two other freshmen—Wayne Ellington and Brandan Wright—who have been able to make the same smooth jump.

People look at our team this preseason and talk about how much talent we have, and that leads to some very high expectations. But they never think about things like blending personalities and creating chemistry. That's why Coach Williams is so impressive. For some coaches, when you have a bad practice it lingers for a couple of days. It never lingers for Coach. When I first got to Carolina, that shocked me. By now, though, it was no surprise that he came out Monday and had a great attitude, and that translated to the rest of us. He didn't hold a grudge against us. That's one of the little things that separate him from the rest of the coaches in the country.

We beat Pfeiffer 140–101 in our second exhibition game. They are a very uptempo team, so we were able to get some easy baskets. I didn't start, but I played almost twice as much as I did in the first exhibition game.

We play our first game in a couple days and I don't know what to expect from this team. This time of year is always difficult. I don't know how it will unfold or who will play which minutes or how we'll respond to certain situations. I just know we better play hard, or Coach won't be happy. Thinking back to his first year at Carolina, I remember him saying several times, "I shouldn't have to coach effort." We've made big improvements in that area. And if we put forth the effort he expects, and the same effort he and the rest of the coaches are putting in, this team has the potential to be special.

WEEK FIVE

As we started getting closer to our first game, I began to see a pattern in the way Coach Williams was putting certain people on certain teams in practice. During most of the preseason, he mixed it up every day. But all of a sudden when the Sacred Heart game got closer, it was noticeable that certain lineups were staying the same on the White team. It's hard to say for sure, because there are a lot of uncertainties around the first game, but the guys who are clearly in that starting group are Bobby Frasor, Wayne Ellington, Brandan Wright, Tyler Hansbrough, and Reyshawn Terry.

For me, the season opener was even more special because it was played in Charlotte, my hometown. I tried to treat it like any away game, and if anything it was a pain in the butt because of all the ticket requests. My parents had bought some tickets for the game, but of course no one wants to sit in those seats. They all want to sit in the seats that the basketball office gets, which are right behind our bench. I have to explain that all the players and coaches are pulling from that same pool. By trading tickets with other guys I ended up with 13 seats through the basketball office.

It's special for me to play in front of my family and friends—especially my family. My parents have been here throughout everything during my career. My mom hasn't missed a home game since I've been at Carolina, even during my redshirt year. She hasn't missed a home game, an exhibition game, or a Late Night. And especially since I started playing more, my dad has been there for everything. He's even made quite a few of our road trips. When some players get to be seniors you hear about how their parents have made it a priority to get to all their games. That won't be the case for me, because my parents have always been there. I'm lucky to have two parents who support me and care about everything I do.

Both of them are very basketball savvy. But, let's be honest—I'm still their son. My mom likes to ask a lot of questions, and she's not afraid to give you her opinion and analysis. She'll be the first to admit she doesn't know everything about the game, but she has picked up a lot by following my career all these years. Sometimes I have to clear some things up for her after games.

I always talk to my dad—whether in person or on the phone—after every game, and we usually talk for 30 or 45 minutes. We analyze the game, talk about specific situations, and discuss my play individually and the team's play. My dad has never coached and he never played above high school. But he's been around the game so much with both living in this area and with following my career that he has a very good understanding of college basketball. I really respect his opinion.

⊏◊⊐

Coach Williams doesn't like to spend much extra time on the road when we play away from home. We were scheduled to leave for Charlotte on Monday night before our Tuesday game. That gave us time to practice at the Smith Center on Monday.

Most of the time, practice the day before the game is more of a thinking practice. Usually, it's not that hard on your body. Coach just wants to see everyone making sharp cuts and being in the right place. If that happens, we can get through the practice quickly and we'll be well rested for the game.

We were close to making it on Monday. We were working on our free throw calls at the end of practice. That means the other team would be shooting free throws and we're making a call for what offense we want to run. Fans may not realize it, but during a free throw we call who will take the ball out of bounds, who catches the in-bounds pass, and who catches the next pass. It's quite a science. But for some reason we just couldn't get it. The first time we messed it up, Coach was able to smile about it. But then we messed it up two more times and it stopped being funny. It went from a calm day to a situation where Coach exploded. But you can be sure that after he exploded, we got it right.

So far, everybody has been treated pretty equally in practice. During the national championship season, some of the guys called Jackie Manuel "Jackie Williams" because Coach Williams complimented him so much it was like they were related. No one has reached Jackie Williams status yet on this team. We do still hear about Jackie quite a bit, though.

The other guys would probably say Reyshawn and I are closest to being like Jackie. As a senior, you definitely get better treatment than you get as an underclassman. Coach takes it a little easier on you. He asks how you're feeling and he cares about how your body is responding to all the work. If you do something wrong, he's more likely to get on you in a more subtle way—maybe pull you aside and talk to you instead of blistering you in front of everyone. So there are definitely some senior benefits in practice.

During Coach's first year, he talked about Kansas a lot in practice. Certain situations or plays would remind him of Kansas. For some guys, I think that got old. They would joke in the locker room about having to hear another Nick Collison or Kirk Hinrich story. We'd laugh about it. But now I turn on the TV and Hinrich is scoring 20 points or getting eight assists every night. So I guess there was a reason Coach talked about him so much.

I was never someone who minded hearing the Kansas stories. His first year, that was all Coach Williams had to relate to. He didn't have any of his own teams at Carolina, and he had an amazing record at Kansas with some incredible teams. But now when he's explaining a situation he's more likely to reference the national championship team or even last year's team that had to overcome the loss of seven very important players.

About 35 or 40 minutes before the Sacred Heart game, Coach had our head manager, Preston Puckett—who also happens to be my roommate—call me back into the coaches' locker room. Coach looked at me and said very softly, so no one else could hear him, "Wes, I just want you to know that you're not starting tonight. I want you to know I'm proud of everything you have accomplished. I'm proud of everything that you're going to continue to accomplish. You're going to play a lot, but you're not going to be in the starting lineup. I wanted you to hear it from me instead of just seeing it when I write the starters on the board." Then he patted me on the back and told me he loved me.

How could anyone be upset about not starting when it's presented that way? I had started the last 16 games of last season, but I can't tell you how good it made me feel inside to know that he cared enough to take time in the moments before a game to talk to me and think about how it would impact me mentally to look at the starters on the board and not see my name. It wasn't necessary for him to give me an explanation. It didn't surprise me that Wayne Ellington was going to start in my position. I had seen him in practice just like everyone else. He deserved it. But the fact that Coach Williams cared enough to let me know ahead of time and tell me he believed in me gave me a lot of confidence. It was another example of why I feel good about this team and why I think he's handling this team so well.

I was disappointed in the way we played in the first half against Sacred Heart. On our scouting report, it specifically mentioned that they had two shooters. Our goal was to make them put the ball on the floor instead of catching and shooting. What happens? We let them catch and shoot and they get hot. We didn't adjust to that very well in the first half. And even though we won by 22 points, the game was a good illustration of the fact that we're still learning how to play with each other offensively. We're not completely sure of how to move as a unit without the ball, and we don't have that ingrained sense of where everyone will be at all times on the floor. That's part of experience, and we'll learn. But right now, when everyone expects us to be a great team immediately, it's a little frustrating.

Game 1

#2/2 North Carolina 103
Sacred Heart 81
Nov. 14, 2006 • Charlotte Bobcats Arena, Charlotte, N.C.
Dick's Sporting Goods NIT Season Tip-Off

SHU	FG	3FG	FT	REB	PF	TP	A	TO	B	S	Min
Howard*	3-6	0-1	0-0	2-2-4	3	6	2	1	0	0	20
Shubik*	5-9	3-5	0-0	0-3-3	4	13	4	3	0	1	30
Potter*	1-1	0-0	2-4	3-3-6	3	4	0	3	0	0	17
Frye*	3-11	0-2	1-3	2-6-8	5	7	4	2	0	1	24
Hobson*	4-9	1-4	2-2	0-3-3	2	11	2	1	0	4	27
Litke	1-5	0-0	0-0	0-2-2	0	2	1	1	0	0	11
Hardy	2-8	0-2	0-0	2-3-5	0	4	8	2	0	2	28
Henley	3-3	0-0	2-3	1-0-1	1	8	0	1	1	0	10
Granato	8-16	8-14	0-0	0-0-0	3	24	0	0	1	0	23
Pettway	1-4	0-1	0-0	1-1-2	3	2	0	1	0	0	10
TEAM				2-1-3							
Totals	31-72	12-29	7-12	13-24-37	24	81	21	15	2	8	200
Pct.	.431	.414	.583	DB: 4							

FG: (1st half: 14-33, .424; 2nd half: 17-39, .436)
3FG: (1st half: 6-13, .462; 2nd half: 6-16, .375)
FT: (1st half: 3-4, .750; 2nd half: 4-8, .500)

UNC	FG	3FG	FT	REB	PF	TP	A	TO	B	S	Min
Terry*	6-9	0-1	6-8	3-5-8	3	18	1	3	1	2	18
Wright*	4-9	0-0	2-6	0-3-3	0	10	4	0	1	1	28
Hansbrough*	11-14	0-0	7-12	4-5-9	3	29	2	1	0	2	27
Ellington*	4-8	2-5	0-0	0-0-0	2	10	1	1	0	0	24
Frasor*	1-2	1-1	0-0	0-0-0	1	3	4	1	0	1	17
Ginyard	1-2	0-0	0-0	0-3-3	0	2	1	1	0	0	12
Lawson	4-7	0-1	2-2	1-3-4	2	10	3	0	0	0	18
Thomas	0-2	0-0	0-0	0-0-0	0	0	0	0	0	0	4
Green	3-4	0-1	0-0	2-5-7	1	6	2	0	0	0	17
Burke	0-0	0-0	0-0	0-0-0	0	0	0	0	0	0	1
Thompson	0-3	0-0	0-0	1-2-3	1	0	1	2	0	0	7
Miller	3-5	3-5	0-0	0-1-1	0	9	4	2	0	0	18
Wood	1-1	0-0	0-0	0-0-0	0	2	0	0	0	0	1
Stepheson	2-2	0-0	0-0	0-1-1	1	4	0	1	1	0	8
TEAM				1-0-1							
Totals	40-68	6-14	17-28	12-28-40	14	103	23	12	3	6	200
Pct.	.588	.429	.607	DB: 4							

FG: (1st half: 18-33, .545; 2nd half: 22-35, .629)
3FG: (1st half: 2-8, .250; 2nd half: 4-6, .667)
FT: (1st half: 4-7, .571; 2nd half: 13-21, .607)

Officials: Doug Shows, J.B. Caldwell, Tim Clougherty
Attendance: 7,060 • **Technical Fouls:** None

Score by Periods	1st	2nd	Total
Sacred Heart	37	44	81
North Carolina	42	61	103

The Winthrop game was different. We fell behind by 12 points in the first half, trailed 38–30 at halftime, and they hit eight 3-pointers in the first 20 minutes. We had 14 turnovers. The first thing Coach always mentions at halftime is points per possession. That's how he evaluates offensive and defensive efficiency—it's a methodology that was also used extensively by Coach Smith. The only other statistic he ever tells us is loss of ball, which measures how many times we've turned over the ball relative to our number of possessions. With 14 turnovers, I knew the loss of ball statistic wasn't going to be good.

Late in the first half, Coach was so frustrated that he subbed in a new set of five guys. I was in the new group of five. I've been on both ends of that situation. When you're watching from the bench and you see the mistakes piling up, you can see it building. You see Coach getting frustrated and you know it might be coming. And then he turns around, points at us, and says, "One, two, three, four, five." When you're in the new five, you know you can't come in the game and make the same mistakes the other group had made. Your job is to improve the energy and the tempo of the game.

We didn't do that job. As soon as we came in, they hit back-to-back three-pointers. After that, though, we made some improvements—we stopped making mistakes, stopped turning the ball over, and picked it up defensively over the last two minutes of the half.

Based on my three years of experience, I thought Coach was going to be very frustrated with us, which was going to lead to him being very fired up in the locker room. That was the exact opposite of what happened. He was completely calm. He was disappointed, but he wasn't mad. He told us,

"We're down, but all of you guys have been down before. In the first half, we didn't do the things we knew we needed to do. If we do those things in the second half, we'll win the game. Period." It was very straight to the point. We all knew what had gone wrong. We didn't do some of the things on the scouting report that had been very clear—like making sure Torrell Martin, Winthrop's best player, didn't get catch-and-shoot 3-pointers. If you're not making someone dribble the ball, that means you're not playing very intense defense. We weren't pressuring Martin and he was having a great game. Coach Williams made a couple of adjustments and then we ran back on the floor.

As we were going through warm-ups, I was thinking about how amazing it was that he had been so patient with us in our first two games. I think it's because he understands how young we are. But I also know how competitive he is, and it hurts him to watch one of his teams make so many mistakes. He demands perfection any time one of his teams is on the floor.

It paid off, because we played a much better second half and won the game 73–66. Even though we're 2–0, I'm not sure we know much more about this team than we knew before the games in Charlotte. It's something we can feel good about and it gives us a little confidence, but no one is satisfied.

As far as my role, I played 13 minutes against Winthrop. With so much talent on this team, it's going to be a dogfight all year. I'll be the first one to tell you that I'm a competitor. If I'm playing 15 minutes, I want to be playing 25. If I'm playing 35 minutes, I want to play 40. So I'm never going to be satisfied. But I also have to look at it from a team perspective. We're here for North Carolina to win basketball games. Everyone here is competitive and everyone here wants to play. But everyone will also have to make sacrifices. What's best for the team is for no one to complain about things like minutes. It's a constant battle in your head— you're competitive and want to play 40 minutes, but you can't let that enter your head during the game.

Game 2

#2/2 North Carolina 73
Winthrop 66
Nov. 15, 2006 • Charlotte Bobcats Arena, Charlotte, N.C.
Dick's Sporting Goods NIT Season Tip-Off

WU	FG	3FG	FT	REB	PF	TP	A	TO	B	S	Min
Martin*	9-20	7-16	0-0	3-4-7	1	25	0	3	0	0	37
Williams*	0-2	0-1	0-0	2-2-4	4	0	0	2	0	1	21
Bradshaw*	7-18	0-3	0-1	4-4-8	3	14	3	5	1	0	38
Gaynor*	2-7	2-6	0-0	1-3-4	3	6	7	4	0	1	35
Jenkins*	5-14	5-11	0-0	3-5-8	5	15	8	2	0	3	35
Moore	0-0	0-0	0-0	0-0-0	0	0	0	0	0	0	0+
Robinson	0-0	0-0	0-0	0-0-0	1	0	0	1	0	1	10
Adams	0-2	0-0	0-0	0-1-1	1	0	1	0	0	0	7
McCullough	3-6	0-1	0-0	2-1-3	4	6	0	0	0	0	17
McCullough				1-0-1				1			
Totals	26-69	14-38	0-1	16-20-36	22	66	19	18	1	6	200
Pct.	.377	.368	.000	DB: 1							

FG: (1st half: 15-33, .455; 2nd half: 11-36, .306)
3FG: (1st half: 8-15, .533; 2nd half: 6-23, .261)
FT: (1st half: 0-1, .000; 2nd half: 0-0, —)

UNC	FG	3FG	FT	REB	PF	TP	A	TO	B	S	Min
Terry*	1-6	1-3	0-0	0-3-3	4	3	1	2	2	0	24
Wright*	6-9	0-0	0-2	1-3-4	2	12	1	2	1	1	27
Hansbrough*	9-13	0-0	2-3	5-5-10	1	20	2	3	0	3	33
Ellington*	6-11	1-5	0-0	0-2-2	0	13	0	3	0	0	26
Frasor*	1-2	0-1	0-0	0-1-1	0	2	5	1	0	2	22
Ginyard	1-1	0-0	2-4	3-4-7	1	4	2	1	0	1	17
Lawson	2-5	1-3	4-6	2-2-4	1	9	4	5	0	0	18
Thomas	0-0	0-0	0-0	0-0-0	0	0	0	0	0	0	0+
Green	1-4	1-2	0-0	0-1-1	0	3	0	0	0	1	9
Thompson	2-3	0-0	0-0	0-1-1	0	4	0	0	0	0	7
Miller	0-2	0-2	3-4	0-1-1	1	3	0	0	0	0	13
Stephenson	0-0	0-0	0-0	0-0-0	0	0	0	0	0	0	4
TEAM				1-4-5							
Totals	29-56	4-16	11-19	12-27-39	10	73	15	17	3	8	200
Pct.	.518	.250	.579	DB: 3							

FG: (1st half: 13-26, .500; 2nd half: 16-30, .533)
3FG: (1st half: 2-7, .286; 2nd half: 2-9, .222)
FT: (1st half: 2-4, .500; 2nd half: 9-15, .600)

Officials: Mike Kitts, Tom Lopes, Bernard Clinton
Attendance: 7,362 • **Technical Fouls:** None

Score by Periods	1st	2nd	Total
Winthrop	38	28	66
North Carolina	30	43	73

A prime example is Quentin Thomas. He played four minutes against Sacred Heart. After that game, I told him I respected him more than anyone I've ever played with. I think he thought I was joking, and I had to tell him a couple times to make sure he knew I was serious. I've been telling my dad for two years what a good person Q is. He is a very talented basketball player—you can watch us play pickup in the summer, and there are a lot of days you'd leave the gym thinking Quentin is the best player on the team. He has been through a lot with injuries and playing time at Carolina. But somehow he stays so positive and is always the first person to support everyone else. It's remarkable.

In the Winthrop game, I didn't even hit the rim on my second 3-pointer. I came out of the game, and the first person who shook my hand was Quentin. He said, "Keep your head up. You'll hit the next one." I sat down on the bench, and while the game was going on I thought, "That's just typical Quentin." My dad was sitting right behind the bench, so he saw it. After the game he told me now he saw exactly what I had been talking about for the last couple of years.

So after the win over Sacred Heart, I told him to keep his head up and that his opportunity was going to come. He said, "I know, I'm fine." I have more respect for him than anyone I've ever played with.

LUCAS: THE CLOSER

Nov. 16, 2006

CHARLOTTE—Somebody get Marcus Ginyard an entrance song.

That's what the ace closers are supposed to have, right? The manager looks into the bullpen, taps his right arm, the stadium lights start to flash, and then the speakers are pumping with "Hell's Bells" or "Enter Sandman."

That's how Ginyard should enter a game, because he's turned into Carolina's closer.

For most of the first half Wednesday night, he sat on the Tar Heel bench and watched Winthrop's Torrell Martin pile up three-pointers. At first Martin simply had a nice little hot streak going, but by halftime, when he had already tied his career high with six three-pointers and notched 20 points, he was in danger of joining the Barry brothers, Geoff Brower, Harold Arceneaux, and every other hot-shooting guard who has ever downed the Tar Heels.

Some closers take naps early in the game. Some stretch.

Ginyard simply watched. Maybe took a couple of mental notes. He played just 4 first-half minutes, but he knew his time was coming.

Finally, after Martin began the second half with five quick points in the first 2:50 to raise his game total to 25, Roy Williams had seen enough. He walked down his bench. Forty seconds later, Ginyard entered the game for Reyshawn Terry.

At that point, Torrell Martin was 9-for-13 from the field and 7-for-9 from three-point range. And Ginyard couldn't have been happier.

Martin's tear was unacceptable. And Ginyard was prepared to stop it.

"We can't let a guy go off like that," he said. "That's something that gets our whole team down. So what I love to do is watch a guy get hot, and then I go in and change the game around."

You caught that, right? He loves it. That's why

he's so good at it. Jackie Manuel used to get significant attention for his spidery build and quick first step, a combination that made him a quality defender. But he also had a quiet confidence that no one could score on him—and that if they did somehow manage to put the ball into the basket, it was just a fluke.

Ginyard has that same air about him. He didn't exactly strut onto the court, but it was evident in his expression that he felt Martin's hot streak was over.

"He looked real comfortable out there," Ginyard said. "I tried to take him out of that comfort zone. I wanted to get a little closer to him and go after him aggressively when I was boxing him out to keep him off the boards. I could tell he was getting frustrated. Once I saw that, I knew I was doing something good and wanted to stay in his head."

There's that intangible that is part of Ginyard's defensive package. Physically, he's a good defender. But he also pays attention to subtle details that allow him a window into his opponent's mindset.

"In the first half, I noticed he was really going to the boards hard," Ginyard said. "In the second half, as his shots stopped falling, he was just watching other shots go up and wasn't going to the boards as hard. Then we could hear them talking to each other and yelling, so we knew they were frustrated."

Like all closers, Ginyard had the help of an underappreciated setup man. Danny Green won't get much attention for his performance against the

Eagles. He played just 9 minutes because of a sprained ankle, and the stat sheet says he was responsible for just 1 rebound and 1 steal.

But he also may have turned the game. Late in the first half, Winthrop stretched their lead to 38–26. Tywon Lawson went coast-to-coast and fed Tyler Hansbrough for a dunk, and then Green forced a Martin turnover. One possession later, he tied up Martin to force a jump ball; when Carolina regained possession, Bobby Frasor hit Brandan Wright with an alley-oop pass that Wright caught near the top of the square on the backboard and slammed through.

It had looked like the Eagles would enjoy—at minimum—a 10-point halftime lead. Green isn't the most technically sound defender, but his constant harassment of Martin during that one-minute stretch began the Carolina comeback.

"I was trying to make him do something he hadn't done all game, because he had just been catching and shooting," Green said. "I wanted to make him put the ball on the floor and he didn't look comfortable doing it. So I kept after him."

One day, the 73–66 victory could probably go in the Roy Williams and Dean Smith clinic tape as an illustration of why they believe in the power of the big man. Winthrop looked unbeatable when they were firing in 3-pointers at a 53.3% clip in the first half. But Carolina's gamble for the last 40 years has been that the opponent's outside shots will stop falling in time for the Tar Heels' more high-percentage shots—

usually taken by players like Hansbrough or Wright—to put the game away.

And that's exactly what happened. Effective field goal percentage is supposed to account for the value of a three-pointer by adding extra emphasis to made shots from beyond the stripe. Even using that formula, though, Carolina still outshot Winthrop, 55.4% to 47.8%.

Martin, by the way, missed his last seven shots and ended the night with those same 25 points he had when Ginyard entered the game.

Be honest, Marcus. When you saw him rack up 20 points, didn't at least a little piece of you want the challenge of stopping him? Just to see if you could close him out?

Ginyard laughs.

"Definitely."

WEEK SIX

WE CAME BACK HOME and got a win over Gardner-Webb, but everyone was talking about the upcoming trip to New York for the Preseason NIT. I definitely think I'm a New York City kind of guy—as long as it's only as a visitor. I've always enjoyed taking trips there, but I don't think I could live there. There's always so much going on. Being around the whole aura of New York City is a lot of fun, and our hotel was in Times Square, so we were in the middle of everything.

The guys were excited, because no one wants to be on campus over Thanksgiving. Everyone else is gone and it's basically a ghost town, and it can be lonely. The young guys were especially looking forward to being in the big city and playing in a tournament against great competition on national television. We needed some time to get away and bond as a team. On the road, you have to hang out together. You have to eat together. There's nothing else to do.

Game 3

#2/2 North Carolina 103
Gardner-Webb 50
Nov. 19, 2006 • Smith Center, Chapel Hill

GWU	FG	3FG	FT	REB	PF	TP	A	TO	B	S	Min
Gash*	6-13	2-6	0-0	0-2-2	1	14	2	2	0	1	31
MacMillan*	2-3	0-0	0-0	0-0-0	4	4	1	0	0	0	8
Sims*	2-9	1-5	3-3	3-2-5	2	8	1	2	0	3	26
McPhee*	1-12	1-9	0-1	1-1-2	2	3	3	6	0	0	36
Siddle*	4-10	2-8	0-0	1-1-2	2	10	1	2	0	1	29
Fall	0-5	0-0	0-0	1-3-4	2	0	0	2	0	1	22
Sanders	2-6	0-0	1-1	1-0-1	4	5	2	4	2	2	14
Graham	0-1	0-0	0-0	0-2-2	3	0	0	2	0	0	10
Mincey	1-2	1-2	0-0	0-1-1	4	3	0	1	0	1	12
Edwards	1-5	0-2	0-0	0-0-0	1	2	0	0	0	0	7
Flittner	0-0	0-0	1-2	0-0-0	0	1	0	0	0	0	3
Wheeler	0-1	0-1	0-0	0-0-0	1	0	0	0	0	0	1
French	0-0	0-0	0-0	0-0-0	0	0	0	0	0	0	1
Team				1-0-1							
Totals	**19-67**	**7-33**	**5-7**	**8-12-20**	**26**	**50**	**10**	**21**	**2**	**9**	**200**
Pct.	.284	.212	.714	DB: 2							

FG: (1st half: 7-26, .269; 2nd half: 12-41, .293)
3FG: (1st half: 2-14, .143; 2nd half: 5-19, .263)
FT: (1st half: 3-4, .750; 2nd half: 2-3, .667)

UNC	FG	3FG	FT	REB	PF	TP	A	TO	B	S	Min
Terry*	2-8	1-4	4-4	3-6-9	2	9	3	2	2	0	18
Wright*	8-12	0-0	5-7	5-4-9	1	21	1	2	1	2	24
Hansbrough*	4-10	0-1	10-11	3-4-7	1	18	1	1	0	0	25
Ellington*	8-10	2-4	1-1	1-3-4	2	19	0	2	0	2	24
Frasor*	2-4	1-2	0-0	0-1-1	0	5	3	1	0	0	16
Ginyard	3-6	0-0	1-2	1-2-3	2	7	4	1	0	3	21
Thompson	2-4	0-0	1-2	1-3-4	2	5	1	2	1	0	11
Lawson	4-5	1-1	0-0	0-1-1	0	9	2	4	0	2	17
Miller	1-2	1-2	0-0	0-1-1	1	3	1	1	0	1	15
Thomas	1-1	0-0	0-0	0-2-2	1	2	2	2	0	2	11
Stepheson	0-1	0-0	3-4	1-5-6	2	3	0	3	0	0	9
Burke	0-2	0-2	0-0	0-1-1	0	0	0	0	0	0	3
Wood	0-1	0-0	0-0	1-1-2	0	0	0	0	0	0	3
Copeland	0-0	0-0	2-2	2-1-3	0	2	1	0	0	0	3
TEAM				1-4-5							
Totals	**35-66**	**6-16**	**27-33**	**19-39-58**	**14**	**103**	**19**	**21**	**4**	**12**	**200**
Pct.	.530	.375	.818	DB: 7							

FG: (1st half: 21-36, .583; 2nd half: 14-30, .467)
3FG: (1st half: 4-9, .444; 2nd half: 2-7, .286)
FT: (1st half: 11-13, .846; 2nd half: 16-20, .800)

Officials: Les Jones, Jerry Heater, Mark Schnur
Attendance: 19,045 • **Technical Fouls:** None

Score by Periods	1st	2nd	Total
Gardner-Webb	19	31	50
North Carolina	57	46	103

Unless you have a lot of schoolwork to do, which I did. I

had a 10-page paper due that I needed to finish. I worked on it until about 3:30 a.m. Monday night, and on Tuesday afternoon we had some free time in New York. I spent my free time working on the paper. That's the glamorous life of a college athlete. The rest of the guys were hanging out in Times Square, and some of them walked down to Madison Square Garden. For a lot of them, it was their first time in New York City, so they wanted to get the full experience of all the bright lights.

Even though I'd been to New York several times, I had only been inside the Garden once and I'd never played there. You can feel the history and tradition when you walk in the building. It's an old building, but it's a lot of fun to look up in the rafters and see all the retired jerseys and think about all the classic games and famous players that have played there before you. To walk in those footsteps is very special.

I thought we would play well against Gonzaga. We knew we had some things to work on, but it was early in the season—every team feels that way. Individually, I hit 28 of 30 shots in warm-ups. We only had 20 minutes to warm up because Tennessee played Butler right before our game, so Dewey Burke was rebounding for me. He's the one who told me I had made 28 of 30 from the three-point line. Once he told me that, I felt about as good as I could possibly feel from an individual perspective.

Then I went out and shot 0-for-6 in the game and we lost 82–74.

As a team, we didn't play with much defensive intensity in the first half. We didn't play smart and we didn't take good shots. It was frustrating at halftime because everyone knew exactly what we had done wrong. For a game that big, we didn't have the attitude you have to have to play on that stage. But then in the second half we clawed back into it.

Every time we got close, Gonzaga would make a big play. That got very frustrating.

Game 4

#-/23 Gonzaga 82
#2/2 North Carolina 74
Nov. 22, 2006 • Madison Square Garden, New York, N.Y.
Dick's Sporting Goods NIT Season Tip-Off Semifinal

GU	FG	3FG	FT	REB	PF	TP	A	TO	B	S	Min
Altidor-Cespedes*	1-3	0-1	0-0	1-2-3	0	2	3	5	0	0	27
Mallon*	0-3	0-0	0-0	0-6-6	4	0	0	0	0	0	10
Heytvelt*	8-13	1-2	2-2	1-7-8	4	19	0	1	3	0	32
Pargo*	6-11	0-2	4-5	1-2-3	5	16	3	3	0	1	32
Raivio*	7-17	5-7	2-3	2-6-8	4	21	4	4	0	0	38
Pendergraft	1-1	0-0	0-0	0-1-1	3	2	1	0	0	0	19
Kuso	4-6	0-0	0-0	2-2-4	4	8	0	0	1	0	11
Bouldin	5-8	2-3	2-3	0-4-4	2	14	6	4	0	0	31
TEAM				0-6-6							
Totals	**32-62**	**8-15**	**10-13**	**7-36-43**	**26**	**82**	**17**	**17**	**4**	**1**	**200**
Pct.	.516	.533	.769	DB: 0							

FG: (1st half: 16-34, .471; 2nd half: 16-28, .571)
3FG: (1st half: 3-6, .500; 2nd half: 5-9, .556)
FT: (1st half: 5-6, .714; 2nd half: 5-7, .714)

UNC	FG	3FG	FT	REB	PF	TP	A	TO	B	S	Min
Hansbrough*	2-5	0-0	5-9	4-5-9	3	9	0	3	0	1	32
Terry*	2-6	0-1	0-1	2-1-3	3	4	2	2	0	2	17
Wright*	7-15	0-0	7-14	3-10-13	3	21	0	2	3	1	31
Ellington*	2-11	1-7	0-0	0-2-2	1	5	3	1	0	0	24
Frasor*	4-9	3-6	0-0	0-1-1	2	11	2	1	0	1	20
Miller	0-6	0-6	0-0	1-0-1	1	0	1	0	0	0	15
Green	1-4	1-4	2-2	1-1-2	1	5	1	0	1	0	11
Thompson	1-2	0-0	2-2	2-1-3	0	4	0	0	0	0	8
Stephenson	1-2	0-0	0-0	0-1-1	0	2	0	0	0	0	2
Lawson	4-5	1-2	2-2	1-2-3	3	11	1	2	0	1	23
Thomas	0-0	0-0	0-0	0-0-0	1	0	1	0	0	0	5
Ginyard	1-3	0-1	0-0	1-0-1	0	2	0	1	0	0	12
TEAM				1-2-3							
Totals	**25-68**	**6-27**	**18-30**	**16-26-42**	**18**	**74**	**11**	**12**	**4**	**6**	**200**
Pct.	.368	.222	.600	DB: 3							

FG: (1st half: 14-33, .424; 2nd half: 11-35, .314)
3FG: (1st half: 3-10, .300; 2nd half: 3-17, .176)
FT: (1st half: 6-11, .545; 2nd half: 12-19, .632)

Officials: Jim Burr, Ed Corbett, Mike Stephens
Attendance: 9,123 • Technical Fouls: None

Score by Periods	1st	2nd	Total
Gonzaga	40	42	82
North Carolina	37	37	74

We made a run and got within three points, so it felt like the comeback was happening. But then we had a big-time breakdown, and of course they capitalized on it. When we went back and looked at it on film, we didn't do a lot of the little things we've been working on in practice all year. We didn't run a certain play that had been called in our secondary break. We didn't run the right defensive call on a sideline out of bounds play. We didn't box out. Those seem like minor things, but they all led to baskets.

And of course my shooting didn't help. I try to have the mentality that the next one is always going in. One or two misses don't bother me. But when it gets up to four or five misses, you can't help but think about it. The thing was that all six of my shots felt good when they left my hand. I never felt like I lost confidence to take a shot.

As a shooter, in most cases all shots feel the same. You don't have time to think about whether it's a big shot. But I definitely realized I had missed a big one in the second half. We finally made our run and I got a good look from the left side. Ty penetrated and kicked it to me. When I caught it, you could feel the intensity in the arena and the crowd starting to get into it. It felt like they were about to erupt if I knocked it down. But I missed it, and in the next timeout, I thought, "Wow, that was a big one that I missed." Those thoughts usually don't occur to me, but I knew it could have been a momentum-changer and maybe a game-changer.

Coach was as frustrated as I have seen him after the game. He seemed very discouraged. It felt like a turning point with this team. He had been so patient with us, because he knew it was a new group of guys and everyone was learning at different speeds. As soon as the Gonzaga game was over he felt our learning curve was over. He said we'd had our time to get up to speed, and we didn't have time to wait for anyone who couldn't catch up. The point he got across was that we have to improve on the little things we're doing wrong, and he's not going to accept anything less than that. He made it very clear, as he's done with other teams, that this coaching staff knows what they are doing. Their way is the right way. They've proven that to be a fact. They are not going to accept the way anyone else wants to do it.

That's a very powerful statement. As soon as he said it, I knew he was right: his way *is* the right way. He's earned the right to say that. But I think it might have been an eye-opener for some of the younger guys who had never heard it before. It's a time when Coach Williams draws a distinct line: you're either going to do it his way, or you're not going to do it at all.

It was a small detail, but as he talked to us in the locker room, Coach told Deon and Ty to take off their headbands. I thought that was very symbolic, that the other stuff that he might have let slide wasn't working. Traditionally, Carolina players have never worn headbands. We don't believe in that kind of individualism. Now we were going back to his way.

It was a very quiet locker room. The freshmen hadn't experienced a loss in a North Carolina uniform, so they might have been feeling invincible. The first experience of losing is tough, and it hurts. When Coach left the room, everyone was reflecting on what had happened. Nobody talked to each other. The question you have to ask yourself is what you can do better that will help the team. I know that's what I was thinking.

Personally, the game really bothered me. I was already battling a cold, so couple the cold with the game and I didn't sleep well at all. I have a tendency to overthink things, and from an individual perspective I knew two or three of the shots I missed could have changed the outcome of the game. That's a hard thing to live with as a player. Missing shots is part of the game and it's always going to happen. But to know that two or three shots—good shots, shots I feel like should be automatic for me—could have changed the mood in that locker room was painful. In many ways, I felt I was responsible for the loss.

As a senior, I like to think I'm now mature enough to handle disappointment and not let it impact my confidence. That's the battle I was having with myself that night and the next morning. I was very frustrated. But at the same time, I've played enough college games to know you have to be ready to play the next time out.

✦

The next day was Thanksgiving. In some places, maybe that means turkey and football. For us, it meant practice.

We had a practice scheduled for Thursday anyway. But our itinerary had changed some, because now we had to play the early game on Friday rather than the late game. So we got up early, had breakfast, and went to practice at the Garden. After a game like Gonzaga, a good, hard practice is a great way to cure some of the frustration created by a loss. That's exactly the kind of practice we had. For a practice on the day between games, it was very tough. I was shocked at how hard we were going—well, I would have been shocked if you had told me before we got to New York that we'd practice that hard on Thursday. But after the way we played, it wasn't that surprising.

It was very competitive. Coach was very intense, and he continued the message that he's not going to accept little mistakes and those things aren't acceptable at North Carolina. It felt good to be back on the court. I made a couple of shots and felt I picked it up defensively, so it felt like the team was moving in the right direction.

When we got back to the hotel, we watched film of the Gonzaga game. That just emphasized what Coach Williams had told us all morning. Give Gonzaga credit for playing a great game and making shots. But we had a chance to make it a very different game with a few minor corrections.

Once film was finished, it was time to celebrate Thanksgiving. We ate in a big banquet room with the other three NIT teams. It was a big room, so we didn't have much contact with the other teams. There were three tables of team personnel, so it felt like we had our own little corner of the room. It felt just like a normal team meal.

One of the difficult things about transitioning from high school basketball to college basketball is the loss of family time. You don't have that normal time with your family, especially around the holidays because it's the middle of the season. I haven't had Thanksgiving dinner with my family in five or six years. But if I can't be with them, I want to be with my Carolina family.

When we sat down, it was obvious everyone else was feeling the same way. We joke around just like anyone else, but before we ate, Quentin said, "Let's go around and tell what we're thankful for." It started out as a joke, but it turned serious. Each person expressed how thankful they were for having the chance to be together at that moment. We all missed our families. But we were all grateful that we had this extended family to spend time with on Thanksgiving. It reinforced how much I enjoy being on this team and the bond we share.

The great thing about playing in an event like the NIT is this: if you have a bad game, you get to turn around and make up for it in 48 hours. All of us wanted to be in the championship game. But instead we were matched with Tennessee in the consolation game, and we saw it as a chance to redeem ourselves.

We did some nice things in the first half. We built a 56–35 lead at halftime, and we extended our pressure better than we did against Gonzaga. Coach had been frustrated with the lack of attention we had been paying to scouting reports, and that improved in the first half. Chris Lofton is Tennessee's best scorer and we held him to two points.

Game 5

#22/21 Tennessee 87
#2/2 North Carolina 101
Nov. 24, 2006 • Madison Square Garden, New York, N.Y.
Dick's Sporting Goods NIT Season Tip-Off Third-Place Game

UT	FG	3FG	FT	REB	PF	TP	A	TO	B	S	Min
Bradshaw*	4-6	1-1	1-3	2-1-3	3	10	7	3	1	4	29
Crews*	4-9	0-0	2-4	3-1-4	2	10	0	1	1	2	17
J. Smith*	5-12	4-7	4-5	0-1-1	2	18	2	2	0	1	22
Lofton*	6-13	5-8	1-3	2-2-4	4	18	2	2	0	0	27
R. Smith*	3-9	0-1	0-0	1-1-2	3	6	1	2	0	2	24
Chism	4-5	3-4	1-5	1-3-4	4	12	0	3	0	0	20
Passley	0-2	0-0	5-10	2-2-4	3	5	1	1	0	0	13
Howell	1-6	1-5	2-2	0-0-0	1	5	5	0	0	0	19
Tabb	1-3	1-2	0-0	0-0-0	3	3	0	0	0	1	15
Childress	0-3	0-0	0-0	0-3-3	1	0	0	0	0	0	14
TEAM				2-3-5							
Totals	28-68	15-28	16-32	13-17-30	26	87	18	14	2	10	200
Pct.	.412	.536	.500	DB: 8							

FG: (1st half: 11-32, .344; 2nd half: 17-36, .472)
3FG: (1st half: 4-7, .571; 2nd half: 11-21, .524)
FT: (1st half: 9-18, .500; 2nd half: 7-14, .500)

UNC	FG	3FG	FT	REB	PF	TP	A	TO	B	S	Min
Terry*	3-4	0-0	4-6	1-7-8	3	10	3	5	3	0	26
Wright*	9-10	0-0	1-1	2-6-8	2	19	1	2	0	1	29
Hansbrough*	8-17	0-0	11-15	4-5-9	3	27	6	1	0	1	29
Ellington*	5-9	2-3	2-3	1-3-4	3	14	1	2	0	1	22
Frasor*	1-5	1-3	0-0	1-4-5	2	3	1	1	0	0	19
Ginyard	1-3	0-0	0-0	4-0-4	4	2	1	5	0	1	17
Lawson	5-8	1-3	3-4	0-1-1	3	14	6	4	0	1	25
Green	1-1	1-1	2-2	0-4-4	2	5	1	2	0	0	10
Thompson	1-2	0-0	0-0	1-3-4	1	2	0	4	0	0	9
Miller	1-1	1-1	0-0	0-0-0	0	3	0	0	0	1	12
Stephenson	0-1	0-0	2-2	0-1-1	0	2	0	0	0	0	2
TEAM				1-1-2							
Totals	35-61	6-11	25-33	15-35-50	23	101	20	26	3	6	200
Pct.	.574	.545	.758	DB: 2							

FG: (1st half: 22-38, .579; 2nd half: 13-23, .565)
3FG: (1st half: 4-7, .571; 2nd half: 2-4, .500)
FT: (1st half: 8-9, .889; 2nd half: 17-24, .708)

Officials: Joe Lindsay, Jamie Luckie, Doug Shows
Attendance: 9,498 • **Technical Fouls:** None

Score by Periods	1st	2nd	Total
Tennessee	35	52	87
North Carolina	56	45	101

But the second half was different. We still won the game,

but Coach wasn't happy at all. Instead of going out and putting Tennessee away, we made bad decisions, and we let some of their shooters (like Lofton) get open looks. We gave them too many second chances on the offensive boards, and that's something Coach can't stand. You could see his frustration building. He'd told us at practice he was going to hold us to the standards he expects from a North Carolina team, and we weren't meeting those standards.

So with 3:30 left, we were up by 12 but we had a breakdown on awareness of time and score. That's something he preaches all the time. So he called a timeout, and it was obvious he was mad. It was one of the few times I've ever seen him walk out of the huddle. He just paced around the perimeter and fumed. His quote after the game was actually pretty funny: "I told them to go home and ask for some brains for Christmas." That's the thing with Coach—he can handle the physical errors much better than he handles the mental errors, because those are simple carelessness.

After the game, I went out to dinner with my girlfriend and her family. They're from New Jersey, so they were in town for the game. We went to a little Italian restaurant, and by the time we finished it was about 11 p.m. We had an early flight home the next morning, so I went back to the hotel.

Until we get to the NCAA Tournament, we switch roommates on the road for each trip. It's a good policy, because you get to spend extensive time with everyone on the team. In New York my roommate was Brandan Wright. Earlier in the semester, I started taking Brandan and Wayne Ellington to breakfast every week so I could get to know them better.

Brandan is a great kid and he's very mature for a freshman in college. One thing I've learned about him very quickly is how knowledgeable he is about sports. That makes us a good match, because I'm a sports fanatic. He knows as much about college football and NFL football as anyone I know. He's a big SEC football fan, so we watched a lot of games in the room this week.

But Friday night there weren't any games on. Brandan had been talking about wanting to watch the new Al Gore documentary. I'm a political science major, so I thought that was something that might be good for me. So he ordered *An Inconvenient Truth* and we watched it until about 1 in the morning. Sometimes being a college athlete isn't as glamorous as everyone thinks.

We had an incident on the way home when one of my teammates was late for the bus that was taking us to the airport. Coach Williams hates it when anyone is late. It's just something you don't do. And this individual was *very* late for the bus.

Coach Williams was at the front of the bus and it was obvious he was mad. It reminded me of watching him get frustrated with us the night before during the timeout. But this was on a much larger scale because no TV cameras were present.

My first year or two, I think I would have responded to that situation by worrying about what might happen to us as a team or to that individual. It was obvious there would be consequences. But as a senior, I was more mad or disappointed than scared. We were coming off two games when we didn't play very well. We weren't playing the right way. And we didn't need another distraction. We had plenty of other things to worry about—we didn't need to worry about whether people could be on time.

My other concern was that everyone had a roommate, and this guy's roommate was already on the bus. An expression we use a lot is, "Help a teammate." That can apply to anything, from on-court things to off-court situations. When you're someone's roommate, you're responsible for them. If one person is late, his roommate is late, too. That's an unwritten rule. And neither of those guys were looking after each other.

When we got back to the Smith Center, I told a couple guys that this was not a distraction we needed. And the individual's roommate also heard it from a couple of guys, and he knew he had made a mistake. Then the person who was late had to do some running, and the entire team had to watch him. It was a lot of running, and it was an example to the rest of the team that being late is not tolerated. Coach Williams did a good job of making it clear that the incident had happened, the punishment was going to happen, and when it was over, he considered the matter closed. Then we moved on. That's how he kept it from becoming a lingering issue.

At the time, it wasn't a fun situation. But I have the feeling it's the kind of thing we'll still be laughing about when we get together 50 years from now.

The last piece of our Thanksgiving celebration came Sunday night when Coach Williams had us over to his home for dinner. My first year at Carolina, that dinner was kind of weird. I didn't have the same kind of relationship with Coach that I have now. You're not just going to your coach's house, you're going to Roy Williams's house, and that's a big deal for anyone who knows anything about basketball.

But now it feels comfortable for me. We really are a family. That word is thrown around a lot in our society, but it applies to our program. I feel as comfortable talking to Coach Williams on the practice floor as I do walking into his house. That's how comfortable he makes everyone feel. We know he has our best interests at heart and he cares about us off the floor.

Of course, it helps that Mrs. Williams does an amazing job of cooking for everyone. You can cure a lot of nervousness in college kids by giving them good food. It was probably the best sweet potato casserole I've ever had in my life. I went back for thirds on that, and Deon was right behind me.

People don't know this about me, but for a little guy, I can eat. But Deon eats as much as anyone I've ever seen in my life. He was in double figures on rolls.

LUCAS: NOT NATURAL

Nov. 23, 2006

NEW YORK—One day, there will be a statistic to measure it.

Call it chemistry, call it cohesiveness, call it playing like a team. Whatever you call it, Gonzaga had more of it than North Carolina Wednesday night.

Carolina had Sports Illustrated covers and Sporting News covers and ESPN The Magazine covers and lofty national rankings and All-Americans.

Gonzaga had a team.

Guess which counted for more on the 94 feet of hardwood.

The `Zags played the kind of basketball that made you assume they must have plenty of experience. They knew where each other would be on the court, found open teammates, and defended like a group that has been together a long time. In truth, they haven't—three of the five players who played at least 27 minutes were freshmen or sophomores.

But they played and moved as a unit, and there was no better illustration than the 2–3 sagging defense they employed to limit Tyler Hansbrough to a scant five shots. It wasn't just one player who stopped Hansbrough. It was an entire team moving and sliding and jumping together.

"They were guarding Tyler perfectly where it wasn't easy to throw him the ball," Bobby Frasor said. "But you didn't want to go ahead and shoot it because they had five guys inside the paint, so it wasn't a great shot."

That's the definition of a Carolina conundrum and it's the basic explanation for why the Tar Heels occasionally run into trouble against zones. Wayne Ellington and Wes Miller, Carolina's two primary perimeter threats, were a combined 2-for-17 from the field. Reyshawn Terry, Carolina's primary slasher, was ineffective and played just 17 minutes.

That left a problematic choice on offense: either force-feed the ball into the post or take a low percentage outside shot. And as so often happens when the Tar Heels have a night like this, the outside shots weren't falling—Carolina made just 6-of-27 three-pointers. Even just one more of those shots finding the net could have loosened the Gonzaga defense; instead, a couple potentially big three-pointers rimmed out and snuffed Tar Heel runs.

It left Tyler Hansbrough the most frustrated he's been in his career.

"We didn't let him get very many open looks," said Gonzaga's Josh Heytvelt, who had a career game with 19 points and tremendous defense on Hansbrough. "He started shying away from posting up in the second half because he knew we had guarded him so well in the first half."

Shying away? Hansbrough? These are words that do not go together.

There will be so much attention paid to Carolina's offensive struggles that it may overshadow a disappointing defensive effort. The Tar Heels allowed Gonzaga to shoot a completely unacceptable 51.6% from the field, with many of those shots coming on what has been a bugaboo so far this year—dribble penetration.

There's been plenty of discussion about how this year's team is especially suited to play more full-court defense, to trap and terrorize the opposition into miscues. But Roy Williams isn't going to turn his team loose defensively until they prove—individually and collectively—they can stop the ball. It's one of the most fundamental parts of basketball, and it's something the Tar Heels haven't been very good at through four games.

Williams told his team in the locker room he

hasn't coached them well enough to put them in position to win the game. That's what you would expect him to say. But he's also treading water until that all-important month of December. That's when the Tar Heels have significant uninterrupted practice time once exams are finished, and that's when Williams will operate a basketball laboratory that will turn his collection of talent into a team—into something more like what Gonzaga showed Wednesday night.

Ellington stood at his locker and sighed. "It didn't feel natural at all," he said.

He was talking about his shot, about the way he was never able to get into a rhythm. He might as well have been talking about the entire team's performance. Just four games into the season, things don't come naturally for this team. There's a split second of hesitation, a pause to process the situation and examine the alternatives, that leads to herky-jerky performances.

It's the kind of problem that can only be ironed out by experience and comprehension of Williams's system. Until then, it won't feel natural, and by extension it won't look natural.

And the outcome, the 82–74 defeat?

Given the rest of the circumstances, it was only natural.

WEEK SEVEN

ON THE DAY BEFORE the Ohio State game, my body felt like we were back in the preseason. On Sunday and Monday, we got after it in practice just like we do in October. We went back and worked on fundamentals like moving your feet, closeouts, guarding the ball, defending, and ball screens. Those are some of the most basic defensive fundamentals in the game, but we hadn't been doing them well.

Usually, practices at this time of year are around an hour and 45 minutes, because Coach doesn't want to exhaust us during game week. He was straightforward with us. He said, "It's not about having an hour and 45-minute practice. It's about the fact that we have certain things we need to work on.

And if those things take over two hours, that's how long practice will last."

Coach also added a competitive element to practice. We did quick slides—a drill that emphasizes moving your feet and sliding from one side of the lane to the other—for 30 seconds. We did it in two groups, so everyone had 30 seconds on and 30 seconds off. We were going hard, and there was a lot of talking. Then Coach said, "We're going to make this count. I want to know who can touch the side of the lane the most times in 30 seconds."

I thought we were going hard before he said that. That was nothing compared to what we were doing once we knew he was counting. The intensity level doubled. It was amazing how much the intensity picked up when we knew we were being watched that closely and we were going to be accountable for our performance.

I did 32 touches in 30 seconds, which was the best on the team on Sunday. On Monday, Tyler tied me for the lead. Tyler is one of those guys who will try to win no matter what kind of competition it is. It doesn't matter if it's a basketball game, ping-pong, or a practice drill. He is not a good loser. He gets the most attention, but we have several ultra-competitive guys on this team. That's why Coach Williams holds us to such a high standard. He knows what kind of talent we have and what kind of team we should become. That's why he pushes us.

Once the drill was over, he had another message for us: "This is how you have to play every time you are on defense. Every single time you get in a defensive stance you have to go that hard. That's the only way to play defense and that's the only way we are going to accept."

Playing in Madison Square Garden is always a special feeling. But the first game when we could really feel that "big game" feeling in the air was against Ohio State in Chapel Hill.

Over the weekend, most of us had watched the Kansas-Florida game. It was one of the best regular season college basketball games I had seen in a long time. It was right up there with any game I'd seen in a long time.

And we all knew they were playing at a higher level than us. The way we played in New York and the way those two teams played can't even be compared. That helped add to the intensity in practice, because we knew we needed to play at a higher level if we were going to have any chance to compete with the teams we were mentioned with in the preseason.

That game had another impact on us: it moved Ohio State to number-one in the country. As an athlete, you want the opportunity to play against the best. When they moved up to the top, we knew we'd have a chance to measure our team against the team the pollsters thought was the best in the country. It didn't really matter which team was ranked number-one. The name on their jerseys could have said anything. The fact that we knew they were supposed to be the best was very important.

I felt the buzz around the Smith Center all day. Our first time out of the tunnel, there were more people in the stands than usual for that point in warmups. But when we came back out the second time, with about five minutes until tipoff, the place was jammed. We could hear the roar even before we came out of the tunnel. Making that run, you think, "I remember now. This is what a big game is like at the Smith Center. This means the preseason is over, and this is big."

But once the game starts, the crowd fades away. Several people have told me the Smith Center was as loud that night as they've ever heard it. One of the little things people don't appreciate about Coach Williams is that he's better than anyone I've ever seen at getting his team to focus solely on him. When I'm on the floor, the only thing I care about is Coach Williams. I'm not worried about the stands. So I don't hear the individual things from the stands. I'm too worried about what the bench is trying to communicate to me. It's tunnel vision.

It can be as loud as possible in the arena, but I can hear the coaches and my teammates clearly. There's something about Coach that makes you exclusively focused on playing as well as possible for him. There's no time to worry about the crowd. I'm too worried about doing the right thing for Coach, for our team, and ultimately for North Carolina. One day I'd like to be a coach. And one of the things I most want to emulate about Coach Williams is the way he's able to foster that feeling of absolute focus in his team. It's not something they teach in a coaching clinic.

One of Coach's favorite sayings is, "It's not about the name on the back of the jersey. It's about the name on the front." That's his way of telling us not to play for ourselves, but for the team. It's one of the first things he told us when we went to his house for ice cream this fall.

Since the Tennessee game, he's really started emphasizing it again. When we watched film, we saw ourselves catching the ball and trying to make a play alone. We were called for eight charging fouls. That's unacceptable. When have you ever seen that from a North Carolina team? There were plays where someone caught the ball and drove recklessly into the lane, trying to do everything by themselves. That was hurting our team. You could see it in the way we played—we'd have a couple bad possessions, people would start hunting their shot, and the offense would turn into a bunch of individuals.

Since then, Coach has gone back to talking about the name on the front of the jersey. That will ultimately be the key to any team, and especially a team with as much individual talent as this one. At some point, everyone has to commit to the idea that what they do as an individual doesn't matter. It's pretty simple: if North Carolina is doing well, then I'm doing well. That's very powerful, and that's what put our 2005 championship team over the top. We had all kinds of talent, maybe even more than this team. But at some point during the season, everyone stopped caring about how they were doing individually.

That's why I felt even worse about what happened to Danny Green in the first half. I've already apologized to him. Ohio State had the ball, and I helped up the lane, which is one of our don't-do's on defense. My man caught it, Danny came over to help—exactly like he should have—and he got dunked on hard. It was all over *SportsCenter* this morning. Anybody watching the show would think it was Danny's fault. But everyone in our locker room knows it was on me. It was a big mistake.

But we didn't have many defensive mistakes like that. We played our most complete game of the year, and that's because we played solid defense. It wasn't just one person. It was all five players on the floor working together and playing our principles. We denied the pass on the perimeter and we played the screen on the ball properly. It's fun to watch, because when one guy moves, another guy moves. That changes the game. Ohio State had to take bad shots because they couldn't get a good look at the basket. When they missed those shots, we got rebounds and turned those into transition baskets. That changed the momentum in the second half and that's what won us the game.

Sometimes being a solid fundamental team sounds boring to fans. Not when your fundamentals are getting in the passing lanes and creating havoc. When we're playing with solid fundamentals, you see guys flying around. It looks hectic out there, but there's a technique to it.

There was a neat moment near the end of the game. I've always felt like our practices are unique because everything we do has a point. Every drill can be applied to a game situation. In fast break drill number-one, we're learning to catch the ball at the free throw line and don't get too deep and pick up a charging foul. For us, it's a warmup drill, but it also has a game application.

For four years, one of our most frequent end-of-practice drills has been for Coach to ask the managers to put the scoreboard at 86–80 in our favor with three minutes to play. For those three minutes, we work on time and score situations—sometimes the white team is ahead and sometimes the blue team is ahead. I've never given much thought to it, but it's always 86–80.

I'm sitting on the bench near the end of the Ohio State game and I look up, and it's 86–80 with 2:50 left. I chuckled to myself, and it reminded me how amazing Coach Williams is. We all understand he knows what he's doing. But to have something down to that fine a point is remarkable. He never pointed it out, but I'm sure he noticed it. And you couldn't help but feel like it was familiar when you looked at the clock, because we do that almost every single day.

The locker room after the win was completely different from how the room felt after Gonzaga. I walked in the room, and everyone was already standing up and smiling. As soon as Coach Williams comes in the room, we start jumping around in our mosh pit. Everybody was laughing and having a good time. At that moment, it doesn't matter how you played as an individual. The only thing you can think about is how happy you are to be part of the team, to be in that situation where you've all achieved a common goal together.

It's not just pure joy, though. Once the mosh pit is over and you have a chance to take stock of how you feel, you realize how tired you are. For a game like Ohio State, it's very intense on the court. So we all put everything we have into it, and when it was over, I was spent.

I went home and watched a little bit of SportsCenter, because I wanted to make sure the ACC won the ACC-Big Ten Challenge. I really take pride in the ACC. I knew we took care of business, and since the ACC has never lost, I wanted to make sure our conference came through with another win—and we did, 8 games to 3. When I was in the locker room, I was ecstatic with the win. Once I got home, though, I started thinking about how I had played. Some of the plays I made were just inexcusable. I thought they were very uncharacteristic of me. The second half was the worst defensive stretch I've had since I've been a Carolina basketball player. That bothered me. But the flip side is that it's much easier to reconcile when the team wins.

I don't know if fans really understand how we have to balance the way we feel about our individual performances with the way we feel about the team. Our team is doing well, which is great. But I don't want to pretend that I'm OK with the way I'm playing. The trick is making sure that doesn't come through in the locker room as being too concerned with my individual play. I don't want anyone to know that I'm upset with the way I'm playing.

I find that I don't really talk to many people about the way I'm playing. I have a couple close friends at other schools who

I can call, and I'll lean on them. Within the team, though, I really buy into what Coach preaches: it's not about me. It's not about Wes Miller. It's about North Carolina.

Game 6											

#3/1 Ohio State 89
#7/6 North Carolina 98
Nov. 29, 2006 • Smith Center, Chapel Hill
ACC/Big Ten Challenge

OSU	FG	3FG	FT	REB	PF	TP	A	TO	B	S	Min
Hunter*	3-6	0-0	0-0	1-1-2	3	6	0	1	1	0	18
Lighty*	3-6	2-3	0-0	1-2-3	3	8	1	2	0	1	18
Butler*	2-4	2-2	0-0	0-0-0	0	6	5	0	0	1	29
Lewis*	11-16	2-4	6-8	1-1-2	3	39	3	4	0	1	36
Conley Jr.*	3-9	0-3	2-2	0-2-2	4	8	8	3	0	0	27
Harris	6-10	5-8	0-0	0-1-1	3	17	0	1	0	0	18
Terwilliger	0-1	0-1	0-2	2-4-6	3	0	0	1	2	1	21
Cook	6-13	2-5	0-1	2-7-9	4	14	1	2	0	0	28
TEAM				2-0-2				1			
Totals	34-65	13-26	8-13	9-18-27	23	89	18	15	3	5	200
Pct.	.523	.500	.615	DB: 2							

FG: (1st half: 18-33, .545; 2nd half: 16-32, .500)
3FG: (1st half: 8-13, .615; 2nd half: 5-13, .385)
FT: (1st half: 4-8, .500; 2nd half: 4-5, .800)

UNC	FG	3FG	FT	REB	PF	TP	A	TO	B	S	Min
Terry*	2-5	1-2	1-2	1-3-4	1	6	2	2	2	0	22
Wright*	4-5	0-0	3-4	1-4-5	2	11	1	3	0	0	22
Hansbrough*	8-16	0-0	5-7	5-9-14	0	21	2	0	0	2	31
Ellington*	7-13	3-8	2-3	0-1-1	1	19	1	2	0	2	28
Lawson*	3-6	1-1	6-12	1-1-2	3	13	5	0	0	1	22
Green	1-1	0-0	1-2	0-2-2	1	3	2	0	1	1	11
Ginyard	3-6	0-0	2-2	5-3-8	2	8	1	2	1	3	25
Thompson	3-4	0-0	0-0	1-1-2	1	6	0	1	1	0	9
Miller	1-3	1-3	0-0	0-0-0	1	3	2	1	0	1	11
Frasor	2-4	2-4	0-0	0-0-0	1	6	3	0	0	1	18
Stepheson	0-1	0-0	2-2	0-0-0	0	2	0	0	0	0	1
TEAM				2-1-3							
Totals	34-64	8-18	22-34	16-25-41	13	98	19	11	7	10	200
Pct.	.531	.444	.647	DB: 8							

FG: (1st half: 15-35, .429; 2nd half: 19-29, .655)
3FG: (1st half: 4-10, .400; 2nd half: 4-8, .500)
FT: (1st half: 10-14, .714; 2nd half: 12-20, .600)

Officials: Bryan Kersey, Tony Greene, Les Jones
Attendance: 21,750 • **Technical Fouls:** None

Score by Periods	1st	2nd	Total
Ohio State	48	41	89
North Carolina	44	54	98

The reason I try to be very careful about letting anyone know how I'm feeling is that I think it's only natural that people would assume it's about playing time. I'm not saying that I don't want to play more. Every college basketball player in the country wants to play more. What I'm really concerned with right now is playing better in the minutes I get, and playing better in practice every day. I'm missing shots I don't usually miss. That's frustrating, but we're 5–1. So I have to keep leading while at the same time figuring out a way to contribute more when I'm on the court.

The only way I know how to improve my individual performance is to work even harder. We had the day off after Ohio State, but I still went to the Smith Center and took around 250 makes. I'd shot 1–3 against OSU, but I felt like I missed some easy ones. But it's not a situation where I'm going in to take extra shots because I don't feel confident. I do the same thing every off day, whether I'm shooting well or shooting poorly.

Right now, I feel good about the mechanics of my shot. I'm disappointed that it hasn't been going in more. That's frustrating for me. I talked to one of my friends from high school on the phone and told him that I'm not happy with the way I'm shooting the ball. That's not the first time that's ever happened. The difference now is that I'm mature enough and strong enough mentally to avoid letting it impact my confidence. A couple of years ago, I might have really let it get to me. I'm not happy and I'm not satisfied. But I'm strong enough that I'm going to keep shooting.

LUCAS: LOSE YOURSELF

Nov. 29, 2006

What were you thinking? How did you do it? What was the plan?

These are the questions you ask a Carolina basketball team that exactly one week ago looked like they had just been introduced to each other and then turned into the Showtime Lakers in a 98–89 win over Ohio State.

So, what were you thinking? You had to be thinking something, right?

Nope. And that's why it worked.

"Everybody stopped thinking so much and started playing and lost themselves in the game," Danny Green said. "When you lose yourself in the game, that's when you have fun."

Come to think of it, it did look like fun out there, didn't it? For the first time all year, it looked like Carolina's 2006–07 Tar Heels enjoyed each other's company and enjoyed the game of basketball.

Leading by 8 points with just under 6 minutes to play, Wayne Ellington had a breakaway layup. No one was within a Brandan Wright wingspan of him. He had plans for something grand—"I was going to get up in the air, and whatever happened, happened," he said—but they dissolved about the time his plant foot hit a wet spot on the Smith Center floor. His legs buckled awkwardly and he was forced to drop the ball into the hoop with all the grace of a tap-dancing grizzly bear. It was perhaps the first time in his freshman season that the normally perfectly balanced Ellington has looked askew.

Steve Robinson thought it was hilarious.

As the Tar Heels got back on defense, they held a 10-point lead. The game was not over; this team has already seen similar leads dissolve this season. But as Ellington ran back on defense, he glanced over at the Carolina bench and saw Robinson with an enormous grin on his face.

"Oh man, we had a timeout right after that and

my teammates got all over me," Ellington said. "You know what? It was fun, though."

Consider a play. It's later in the game and Carolina holds an 86–80 advantage. Under three minutes remain, and after a hectic possession, Marcus Ginyard gets the offensive rebound.

Of course he does. That's what he does.

So Ginyard gets the offensive rebound and gives Carolina another possession. This is a point in the game when every possession is crucial, every basket seems like a potential back-breaker.

When play restarts, the Tar Heels allow 15 seconds to melt away. They are methodical, almost casual.

And then they strike. Lawson catches a pass from Hansbrough 23 feet from the basket. Actually, he does not catch it. The ball is barely in his hands long enough to qualify as a catch. He just controls it, just for a second, and then he redirects it on a flat angle straight down the length of the court. It arches perfectly into the waiting arms of Brandan Wright, who catches it—really catches it—and then slams home a dunk to provide an 8-point margin.

It is the kind of play only teammates can make, the kind that is triggered by an imperceptible nod from one player to another.

"When we reversed the ball, I saw him push his man up the lane," Lawson said. "I knew there was nobody back and I could throw the ball over the top."

"The whole night they were fronting me really hard," Wright said. "They were trying not to give up any easy post entries. So I turned and rolled my man up the lane. I looked at Ty, put my hand up, and he made the perfect pass."

It took them longer to describe it than it did to execute it. Ohio State spent the evening writing almost every offensive play on a white dry-erase board held in the air by one of their assistants. Players checked the board and ran to their spots.

At a time when Carolina badly needed a basket, though, they didn't need a scripted play or a side-line diagram. They just needed the eye, big man to point guard.

Sure, sometimes they need a little refresher. With 32.3 seconds left, Lawson went to the free throw line. His team was lollygagging down the court in anticipation of the freshman's free throws, so Roy Williams stomped his foot. "Come here!" he said.

What he told his starters was simple: when Lawson made the second free throw, apply pressure in the backcourt.

The second free throw went in the basket, Car-olina applied the defense, and Ohio State—taken aback by the sudden pressure—had to burn their last timeout of the game.

That was only one of numerous subtle contribu-tions by Williams on a night when everyone on the roster played a significant role. Green was enor-mous in the first half, drawing charges and creating deflections that turned the momentum after the Buckeyes built a 10-point lead. Deon Thompson and Alex Stepheson provided 6 first-half points in relief of Wright, who had foul trouble. Ginyard was, well, he was just Ginyard. And for the second time this year, Bobby Frasor tapped the ball ahead from the seat of his pants to create a dunk.

"I just wanted to get on the floor before the Ohio State guy did," Frasor said.

No time to think. Just dive.

The logical question now is how this happened. A whole team can't simply click like that, can they? How do you go from losing in New York City to simply losing yourself?

"Defense," Ellington said. "We had to dig deep on defense. In that second half, we were selfless representing that name on the front of the jersey. We lost ourselves in the game."

Basketball is funny that way. Sometimes it takes getting lost to find what's been missing.

It's hard to imagine that a Carolina-Kentucky game could be a letdown, but it did feel that way after Ohio State. I don't know if the crowd wasn't excited because it wasn't a great game or if we didn't play a great game because the crowd wasn't excited. I've never been one who believes a quiet crowd is a good excuse for bad play. It probably wasn't the most exciting game this year, but it was still Carolina-Kentucky and we still won the game, so we were a little surprised it wasn't louder in the Smith Center. In the locker room after the game, some of the guys who have been around for other big games said, "That atmosphere didn't feel like a Carolina-Kentucky game."

But we're basketball players. Every day when we go

through practice, there's no one in the stands. You have to create your own energy off your own motivation, so it should be easy to do it in a game.

Some people have said Carolina fans take basketball for granted. I've never felt that way. As players, we all know there are certain expectations for North Carolina basketball players. Those expectations are simple: you're going to be competitive, you're going to challenge for an ACC championship, and you're going to challenge for a Final Four and national championship. Some people might see that as pressure, but I think the type of person who wants to come to Carolina is attracted to that pressure.

The Kentucky game gave Coach Williams 499 wins. That's an amazing mark. And do you know how many times he has mentioned it to us? Zero. The only way I know he has 499 is because after the game, several reporters asked me about it. I knew he would hit the 500 mark at some point this year, but I wasn't sure where he was right now.

Since I've been here, Coach has made a real effort to help guys get individual accolades. We all know—because he tells us constantly—that it's more important for our team to get a win than for Rashad McCants to break a scoring record. But if Coach is ever in a situation that he can help a player get a record, and it doesn't hurt the team, he'll always do it. In my redshirt year we played Clemson at home, and Rashad was close to the record for most 3-pointers made at the Smith Center. Coach left Rashad in and ran two plays for him so he could try to break the record. And that same year, Raymond Felton had a chance to break the school single-game assist record against George Mason. The game was a blowout but Coach left Raymond in and ran a couple plays he knew would result in assists.

I think Coach gets joy out of helping in situations like that. Now we've got a chance to do the same thing for him. That's a pretty cool thing, that he's been a part of so many other individual achievements and now we can get him his 500th win. I don't know if he'll even act excited about it. But I'll know that we were a part of the team that helped him reach the milestone.

It's a very unique relationship between team and individual when you play at North Carolina. At some point last week, Danny Green said in a press conference that he was unsure of his role. Then ESPN reporter Doris Burke mentioned something about that comment to Coach Williams. I understand what Danny meant. It's natural to want to go out there and compete. I wanted to play every minute of the national championship game in 2005. That was the first time I realized how much bigger a team's accomplishment can be than an individual's. That helped me a lot, and I think I'm less selfish now than I was even two years ago. People may not appreciate what a learning experience that was for the entire 2005 team. There came a point that we realized it was a better situation to play 10 minutes per game on the 2005 team, when we were winning, than it was to play 35 minutes on the 2004 team, when we were so inconsistent. Everyone talked about "buying in" in 2004. When we bought in, we realized the path to get the individual accolades everyone wanted was by winning as a team. That sounds so simple, but it really was a profound realization.

And even though I've learned that, I still understand what Danny meant. I'm still a basketball player, and so is he. There's nothing wrong with wanting to play a lot and wanting to play well. But Coach Williams wants everyone to be so invested in the team that your feelings about the team's success supersede what you want for yourself. That's why I think it's important that after a big win, even if I didn't play well individually, that you shouldn't show any disappointment. At that moment, it's all about the team. I can get in the gym tomorrow and try to correct what went wrong for me personally. That will come later.

So I knew Coach wasn't going to like Danny's comment. And in practice later, he asked him directly about it. He said, "Danny, I'll let you explain, because I know sometimes people misconstrue things that are said." We were in the locker room, and Coach actually went around to a couple people talking about roles. He said, "It's simple. Your role is to go out there and play hard, play smart, and play together. That's your role."

Then he looked at me. "Wes, have I ever gotten mad at you for not getting 10 rebounds in a game?"

"No sir," I said.

Then he pointed at Tyler. "Have I ever gotten mad at you for not hitting 10 3-pointers in a game?"

And of course the answer was no. We knew what he was saying. He shouldn't have to explain roles to us. Our role is to go out and do what we're capable of doing to the best of our ability.

To his credit, Danny explained that he did a poor job of expressing what he was trying to say. He meant that early in the season a team is still coming together and sometimes it's uncertain who will fall into which role. That makes sense, and I think we all feel that way. It's early December, and right now we're still not sure which guys are going to play which minutes. But it was still a good lesson about roles.

Danny wouldn't be on this team if he thought his individual stats or achievements were more important than the team's achievements. Coach Williams does as good a job of finding guys like that as anyone I've ever seen. When you play for him, the first thing you have to accept is that it's not about you, it's not about the team's superstar, it's not even about Coach Williams. It's about winning games, period. And on this team, it's my job as a senior to make sure everyone feels the same way. It's not something we deal with on a daily basis, because the players in this program are good people. But it's human nature to occasionally feel like you should be playing more, and that's when these lessons are valuable.

Game 7

Kentucky 63
#7/6 North Carolina 75
Dec. 2, 2006 • Smith Center, Chapel Hill

UK	FG	3FG	FT	REB	PF	TP	A	TO	B	S	Min
Perry*	5-8	2-3	0-0	2-4-6	2	12	1	2	0	0	25
Thomas*	1-4	0-1	0-0	1-3-4	2	2	3	3	0	1	23
Morris*	10-11	0-0	1-3	2-5-7	3	21	0	3	3	0	31
Crawford*	6-13	0-5	4-5	3-5-8	4	16	2	7	0	0	35
Bradley*	1-7	1-4	4-5	0-2-2	3	7	3	2	0	2	35
Stevenson	0-1	0-0	0-0	3-4-7	0	0	0	0	1	0	12
Jasper	0-1	0-1	1-4	0-2-2	3	1	4	3	0	2	17
Meeks	1-6	0-1	0-0	0-2-2	0	2	0	2	0	0	10
Obrzut	0-1	0-0	0-0	0-0-0	0	0	0	0	0	0	3
Porter	1-1	0-0	0-0	0-1-1	1	2	0	0	0	0	6
Carter	0-1	0-0	0-0	0-0-0	1	0	0	0	0	0	3
TEAM				1-2-3							
Totals	**25-54**	**3-15**	**10-17**	**12-30-42**	**19**	**63**	**13**	**22**	**4**	**5**	**200**
Pct.	.463	.200	.588	DB: 2							

FG: (1st half: 11-28, .393; 2nd half: 14-26, .538)
3FG: (1st half: 0-9, .000; 2nd half: 3-6, .500)
FT: (1st half: 2-4, .500; 2nd half: 8-13, .615)

UNC	FG	3FG	FT	REB	PF	TP	A	TO	B	S	Min
Terry*	5-12	4-6	2-2	3-6-9	1	16	3	1	1	2	27
Wright*	7-12	0-0	2-2	2-3-5	0	16	1	0	1	1	27
Hansbrough*	2-10	0-0	3-6	1-2-3	3	7	1	1	0	2	30
Ellington*	6-14	3-8	2-2	1-0-1	3	17	2	2	0	2	24
Lawson*	1-2	1-2	2-2	0-0-0	5	5	7	2	0	2	27
Green	0-3	0-2	0-0	0-2-2	2	0	0	0	0	0	9
Thompson	2-5	0-0	0-0	2-2-4	1	4	0	0	0	0	11
Frasor	0-1	0-1	0-0	0-0-0	2	0	3	1	0	0	12
Miller	1-2	1-2	3-4	0-1-1	0	6	1	0	0	0	8
Ginyard	0-2	0-0	2-4	1-2-3	3	2	1	2	1	1	17
Stepheson	1-4	0-0	0-0	2-2-4	0	2	1	0	1	0	8
TEAM				3-1-4							
Totals	**25-67**	**9-21**	**16-22**	**15-21-36**	**20**	**75**	**20**	**9**	**4**	**10**	**200**
Pct.	.373	.429	.727	DB: 4							

FG: (1st half: 12-34, .353; 2nd half: 13-33, .394)
3FG: (1st half: 3-10, .300; 2nd half: 6-11, .545)
FT: (1st half: 4-8, .500; 2nd half: 12-14, .857)

Officials: Karl Hess, Ted Valentine, Tom Lopes
Attendance: 21,147 • **Technical Fouls:** None

Score by Periods	1st	2nd	Total
Kentucky	24	39	63
North Carolina	31	44	75

WEEK EIGHT

THIS IS MY LAST big period of exams as a college student. Next semester I'll have a much lighter course load, so this is the last time I'll be doing significant studying for exams. I have three exams and one big paper due. My toughest exam will come Saturday, the same day as the High Point game. It's in my global issues class, which is an international studies class about globalization. It will be two essay questions and a lot of identification, so there's a lot of writing involved.

Before I came to college, I wanted to be a business major or maybe an economics major. It took me one semester to realize that I could major in those things, but it would be a four- or five-year battle and I might be better served to take courses in subjects that interest me. Politics and world conflict, especially current events, really interest me. I've found some really interesting classes in political science. For the most part, I've really enjoyed it as my major.

I know people have the perception that athletes at Division I schools get a break on classwork. If that's the case, then why do I have an exam at 8 a.m. Saturday morning and then we have a game that night? That's what being a college athlete is all about. This is the first time I've had an exam on a game day, but there have been plenty of times I've had a paper due on the day after a game or a quiz a few hours before a game. It's not like a professional sport where the game is your job. Here, if you don't balance the academics, you won't play the game.

But I also don't think it's true to say that between academics and basketball, a college basketball player doesn't have time to have a life. Having a social life definitely requires a new approach to time management. You learn how to structure everything according to three main groups: academics, basketball, and time with your friends. If you spend too much on the last one, the other two will suffer.

When I'm doing something outside basketball, it's usually with my roommates, Eric Hoots and Preston Puckett. Hoots is our video assistant and he used to be a manager, and Preston is the head manager on this year's team. The guys on the team hang out a good bit off the floor also. We're essentially our own little fraternity. Now that I'm a little older—the guys would say I'm a lot older—I also spend quite a bit of time with my girlfriend, Ashley.

We met in the summer at the beach. She's from Wilmington and went to UNC-W, so she really didn't know much of anything about Carolina basketball. It wasn't a big deal to her that I was on the team, and that can be both good and bad. It's good because she doesn't want to break down every single play of every game. But it's bad because I don't think she really knew what to expect. She didn't understand the type of commitment that was involved and how important it is to me.

There's no question that sometimes she has a hard time being with someone who gets some attention from strangers. Ashley knows that when I go out, someone may recognize me and want to talk to me. The part of that that is hard for her to deal with is other girls. In her head, every girl wants to talk to me just because I play basketball at Carolina. Trust me, that's not the case. But she does enjoy coming to games. She enjoys the guys on the team and being a part of that group. That part of being with a Carolina basketball player is a positive. But some of the other off-court aspects can be a challenge.

On the court, the month of December is important because it's a chance to improve every facet of our game. Now that we're past Ohio State and Kentucky, the rest of the schedule this month isn't full of big-name teams. But it's still the chance to play a game. It's a chance to showcase the skills we've learned in practice in front of a crowd. I don't know any other way to say it—games are just fun. Whether it's an exhibition against Mt. Olive or an ESPN game against Ohio State, it's a really unique experience. So I'm not worried about letdowns or getting rusty against teams that aren't as gifted and talented—as Coach Williams always says—as we are.

I think he would tell you that the more important part of this month will come on the practice floor. We've had shorter practices this week, but they've been very intense. Since we got back from New York, the intensity has been consistent.

We'll spend some time on parts of our game that haven't been used as much to this point. For example, the scramble defense. By the time conference play starts we should be able to take other teams out of their offense and find a defensive identity. Recently, Coach has been saying he is tired of watching other teams run their offense against us. He doesn't just want us to stand around and watch them run their plays. He wants us to disrupt everything they're trying to do. The easy way to do that is to sit down in our base 22— or man-to-man—defense and deny every pass. It also means throwing in an occasional scramble, and we haven't been good at that at all this year.

Part of the problem with the scramble is the number of young players we have. When I got to Carolina, I didn't understand it at all. I had played the basic full-court zone press or full-court man-to-man, but I'd never played on a team that jumped and scrambled. The scramble is simple: if two people do it right and three people do it wrong, you're going to give up a layup. If four people do it right and just one person does it wrong, there's still a pretty good chance you're giving up a layup. So it's a matter of all five people on the court working together and also reacting to each other. Everyone has to rotate at the same time and knowing where to be is very important. Moving as a unit is something we don't do well yet.

When outsiders look at our traps, all they see is the trap. It looks simple: if you get a good trap, the defense works. But it's much more complicated than that. While two guys are trapping, the other three have designated spots. It's difficult to figure out where your spot might be, and it can only be learned through time and communication. The next month will give us that time we need. Coach has said he wants to trap a little more this year, but he's not going to use it if we can't play it well. He can't walk out on the court during a game and point to a spot and say, "This is where you're supposed to be." That defense requires a real feel for the game, because you have to feel where the trap is forming and then react to that. It's not set in stone. Coach always uses the word "savvy." You have to have a certain feel about when to break on the ball and where to be at the right moment.

Individually, I always like to use the exam period to get up more shots. When you're in class and you're also practicing every day, it's hard to find time or energy to get in the gym and work on your individual game. But right now, and especially after exams are over, all we're doing is playing basketball. It's the one time of year we can pretend to be a professional, and that means a chance to work on some things I otherwise might not be able to because my body is too tired.

Somehow I became known as the guy who does the Roy Williams impression at Late Night. I don't mind doing it, but I thought it had been retired forever after this year's Late Night. But as Ken Cleary and our video guys were preparing for Coach Williams's 500th victory, they asked me to bring it out of retirement. They're putting together a video to play after the game, and they thought it would be funny to have me—as Coach Williams—introduce it. I couldn't turn down a chance to be part of history, so I filmed a little spot wearing my Coach Williams suit and this gray wig someone found.

				Game 8							

High Point 69
#3/3 North Carolina 94
Dec. 9, 2006 • Smith Center, Chapel Hill

HPU	FG	3FG	FT	REB	PF	TP	A	TO	B	S	Min
Minnis*	3-3	0-0	0-1	1-2-3	3	6	0	1	0	0	25
Reid*	13-23	0-1	0-0	3-5-8	2	26	3	2	0	2	32
Bowen*	0-3	0-3	0-0	1-0-1	3	0	1	0	0	1	20
Quick*	3-11	1-3	0-0	2-1-3	3	7	0	2	0	1	33
Jefferson*	5-13	2-7	2-4	0-0-0	4	14	7	2	0	4	31
Harris	2-7	2-6	0-0	0-2-2	2	6	2	2	0	0	27
Daniels	2-2	0-0	1-1	2-0-2	4	5	0	0	0	0	11
Burns	1-2	1-1	0-0	0-0-0	0	3	0	0	0	0	8
Crowder	0-1	0-0	0-0	0-1-1	3	0	2	0	1	0	8
Flowers	0-1	0-1	0-0	1-0-1	1	0	0	1	0	0	1
Witek	0-0	0-0	0-0	0-0-0	0	0	0	0	0	0	1
Boswell	1-1	0-0	0-0	0-0-0	0	2	0	0	0	0	1
Davidson	0-2	0-2	0-0	0-0-0	0	0	1	0	0	0	1
Taylor	0-0	0-0	0-0	0-0-0	0	0	0	0	0	0	1
TEAM				4-0-4							
Totals	**30-69**	**6-24**	**3-6**	**14-11-25**	**25**	**69**	**16**	**10**	**1**	**8**	**200**
Pct.	.435	.250	.500	DB: 1							

FG: (1st half: 13-35, .371; 2nd half: 17-34, .500)
3FG: (1st half: 2-13, .154; 2nd half: 4-11, .364)
FT: (1st half: 0-0, .000; 2nd half: 3-6, .500)

UNC	FG	3FG	FT	REB	PF	TP	A	TO	B	S	Min
Terry*	4-8	1-3	2-2	3-5-8	1	11	2	1	0	0	24
Wright*	5-7	0-0	1-5	2-2-4	0	11	3	3	2	1	23
Hansbrough*	9-11	1-1	5-5	2-3-5	1	24	2	3	1	1	27
Ellington*	3-5	1-1	0-0	0-7-7	3	7	3	2	0	1	21
Lawson*	3-6	0-2	5-6	0-2-2	2	11	6	2	0	1	27
Thompson	2-2	0-0	5-6	0-2-2	1	9	0	1	0	0	16
Ginyard	5-6	0-0	0-0	2-1-3	1	10	2	0	0	1	19
Green	3-5	1-3	0-0	2-1-3	2	7	3	1	0	1	16
Miller	0-3	0-3	0-0	1-0-1	2	0	4	1	0	0	12
Stephenson	1-2	0-0	1-5	3-1-4	0	3	0	0	0	0	12
Burke	0-0	0-0	1-2	0-0-0	0	1	0	0	0	0	1
Wood	0-0	0-0	0-0	0-0-0	0	0	0	0	0	0	1
Copeland	0-0	0-0	0-0	0-1-1	0	0	0	0	1	0	1
TEAM				1-2-3							
Totals	**35-55**	**4-13**	**20-31**	**16-27-43**	**13**	**94**	**25**	**14**	**4**	**6**	**200**
Pct.	.636	.308	.645	DB: 4							

FG: (1st half: 19-29, .655; 2nd half: 16-26, .615)
3FG: (1st half: 3-8, .375; 2nd half: 1-5, .200)
FT: (1st half: 4-8, .500; 2nd half: 16-23, .696)

Officials: Manny Upton, Jerry Heater, Roger Ayers
Attendance: 19,955 • **Technical Fouls:** None

Score by Periods	1st	2nd	Total
High Point	28	41	69
North Carolina	45	49	94

Before we could play the game, though, I had to finish my exam. I think I underestimated the kind of intense focus that's required to get through a tough exam. It had two essays and five short-answer questions. We had two and a half hours to finish it, and I used every minute of the time that was allowed. To be honest, I was exhausted when I finished. It's nowhere close to the kind of physical exertion we do on a daily basis in practice, but it was very mentally draining.

Pregame meal started 30 minutes after my exam finished. And when I walked in, Coach Robinson said immediately, "You must have just finished an exam." I must have looked spent, because that's how I felt. By game time, I was ready to play, but it turned out to be a longer day than I had anticipated.

The game itself wasn't that memorable. We're a better team than High Point, and we won 94–69. I'll remember the postgame longer than any specific play during the game. All the players put on special t-shirts commemorating Coach Williams's 500th win, and we watched the video—that included my Coach Williams impression—on the Smith Center video boards. Coach does so many things for us, and every player on the court would tell you it was special to be a part of a team that was able to do something for him. In some small way, we're all part of that milestone.

LUCAS: 500 WORDS

DEC. 9, 2006

These are the rules: use one or two words to describe Roy Williams. He has just won his 500th game as a head coach, and he did it faster than anyone in history. We will do this in 500 words, one for each win, all the way from Alaska-Anchorage (#1) to High Point University (#500).

Talk fast. We have already used 65 words.

Jerod Haase: "Genuine."

Williams is in the locker room after the 94–69 win. He has been given a cake. Actually, "cake" does not do this monstrosity justice. This cake laughs at other cakes.

He is sharing it, passing it out to some assembled friends. He hands out plates stacked with cake, then walks away. Then he reappears. He looks concerned.

"Hey, did you get a fork?" he asks.

"The guy just won his 500th game and he's passing out forks," says one bystander, shaking his head.

Probably, at other places after 500 wins, someone else passes out the forks.

Marcus Ginyard: "Passionate."

Williams made it through exactly 31 seconds of the tribute video played on the Smith Center video boards after the game before getting misty. The photo that pushed him over the edge: a posed shot with Dean Smith in the Smith Center stands.

How many pictures make you cry? There aren't many. That tells you how he feels about that picture—and that person.

Woody Durham: "Competitive."

Steve Robinson: "Competitive."

Wes Miller: "Competitive and tenacious."

Bob Frederick: "Intensely competitive."

This is a man who for a year has dealt with a

painful back injury. And yet, ball up a piece of paper and throw it at him in the basketball office—imagine for just a moment that you would actually be willing to commit such a transgression—and he will dive on the floor to pick it up before you can recover it.

Really. He does.

Tyler Hansbrough: "Honest."

Eric Montross: "Mentor."

Jennifer Holbrook: "Integrity."

Quentin Thomas: "Devoted."

This one requires more explanation. Devoted to what, Quentin?

"To his family, first," Thomas says. "To his team and to his players."

Dick Baddour: "Focused. Caring."

They tell stories about him. Golfing with him and working with him and listening to his constant claims of being *this*close to being a "fine physical specimen." What they all do—every single one of them—is smile when they talk about him.

Notice what is not here? No one says "Winner."

He is, of course. The record book proves it. But to the people closest to him, he is so much more than that.

He waves to the crowd, makes a quick speech, and closes with these words: "Thank you for letting me be your coach."

Later, he uses these two words to explain his success: "Extremely lucky."

Consider this: we've already had Dean Smith. Now we have Roy Williams.

So maybe he was right. Maybe "extremely lucky" are the most appropriate words of the evening. But he can't have them.

They don't apply to him.

They apply to us.

WEEK NINE

ON TUESDAY NIGHT we made our annual team Christmas shopping trip to Target. It's a project Coach Williams brought with him from Kansas. Each player gets a wish list from a local family in need, and we use basketball office funds to pick out items we think they would like. We always have fun with it, and it can get pretty competitive because we all want to be the one who comes closest to the $50-per-family member limit. Eric Hoots and I won in 2005, but sales tax got us this year. Ty Lawson finished at $99.52 for his two people, which was the closest of the night. I have no idea how he won. Maybe between watching cartoons he watched a lot of The Price is Right.

Coach has done a good job of getting us involved in the community. We're in a position that we have a big impact on a lot of people. It means something for a Carolina basketball player to make a gesture like the shopping trip. Sometimes we don't realize, as kids ourselves, how much people pay attention to what we do. We get caught up in our own lives and the season and everything else going on, and it always shocks me when I remember the weight that goes with playing for Carolina. Especially at Christmas time, we're lucky to be able to be involved this way.

When Coach was talking to us in the locker room about the Target trip, he made the point that everyone in the room comes from different backgrounds and different economic levels. Financially, some of us were very lucky growing up. Others weren't. But the people we're helping with the shopping trip were worse off than any of us. They're struggling just to survive, and that makes all of us realize how lucky we are.

Basketball is fun and I play the game because I love it. But I also value it because it has always helped me keep a sense of perspective. When I was applying to Mercersburg Academy in 10th grade, they required an essay. At the time, that was a big deal, because it was almost like a college application. I wrote my essay on the way basketball opened my eyes to the different types of people in the world. It started with AAU basketball. I went to a private school in Charlotte and grew up in a nice neighborhood. Everyone around me was pretty much the same. That's not necessarily bad—most of us grow up around people who are similar to us in socioeconomic status or race or interests.

When I started playing AAU basketball, practice was 25 minutes across town. All of a sudden I was around people I had never been exposed to before. Our team traveled a good bit, so

I was going on trips and staying in hotels with a new bunch of people. We would have practices and only five or six people would show up out of a 12-player team. It would frustrate me, too, because I wanted to practice. My teammates would show up late, and I'd say, "Man, where have you been?"

"I didn't have a ride," they'd say.

That was confusing to me. "What do you mean you don't have a ride?"

I remember one guy told me he had to wait for his uncle to come pick him up. And I didn't know any better, so I asked why his parents didn't bring him. They were both at work and they only had one car.

That was shocking to me. I had never really considered that. I knew if I needed to be at practice or get a haircut or get anywhere in town, my mom or dad—even though they were divorced—would be there to do it. I was just 12 or 13 years old, but there was no way I'd ever thought about taking a bus across town to practice.

Another funny thing about practice: we practiced at this gym on the west side of Charlotte. When I go by there now, I wouldn't think twice about walking around there. But at the time, because it was so different from where I grew up, I would be very nervous if I had to wait outside because my parents weren't there when we finished practice. I wasn't comfortable in that environment. And now when I drive through that part of town it seems perfectly natural. AAU basketball changed me tremendously as a person. And I still count a lot of those guys I played with as my very good friends. Basketball facilitated many of the relationships I still have today.

There was a time, though, when I was nervous about meeting different people. When I first started playing, I would try to hide the fact that my family had things that other families didn't. As a kid, you never want to be different. I didn't want to be the rich white kid. I just wanted to be a basketball player, and I wanted my teammates to accept me because I was good enough to earn their respect. I consciously made an effort to avoid revealing things like what kind of cars we had or even how many cars we had.

In high school, I was always in prep school or on the road with my AAU team, so my friends wouldn't necessarily see where I lived. But my thinking also changed. I decided I didn't have to hide it. I felt comfortable enough with my friends that it was OK for them to know that I was fortunate—as long as they realized that I knew I was fortunate. It wasn't something I took for granted then, and I don't take it for granted now. Part of the change came when I realized my dad works very hard. He'll come right out and tell you he's been very lucky. He grew up in a Maryland housing project right outside of DC, and he went to a really rough high school. He made it out of there, and I'm proud of that. I realized that it was OK to be proud of him and what he has accomplished as long as I wasn't gloating about it.

It might have been easier not to play basketball because I didn't really fit in. But my mom has pictures of me at two years old shooting baskets on my Nerf goal. When I was four or five, I spent all my time outside shooting. It's something I have always loved. Around seventh grade I started really working on it, but up to that point it was what I loved to do the most. If I wasn't playing, I was watching a game on TV.

Then, in seventh grade I got the opportunity to play AAU. That's when I saw how competitive basketball was, and I discovered I enjoyed being challenged and competing with other players who were as good or better than me. The competitiveness fueled me. It got started with one goal: I wanted to make the AAU team after seventh grade. In eighth grade, I wanted to make the varsity. In ninth grade, I wanted to start on the varsity. It was one goal after another, until finally it became earning a Division I scholarship. The more involved I got in reaching those goals, the more basketball became a part of my life.

Some people think it was a strange choice, because I could have spent that time doing lots of other things. I could have gone to summer camps all summer. A lot of the kids from my neighborhood went on trips to Europe, and I never did that. I was as happy as possible when I was in the gym with a ball in my hands. There's something about the game I love, and I gravitate to it.

Sometimes I'd have second thoughts. I missed a lot of family trips. Every year at Christmas, my dad would take my brothers and sister down to the Caribbean on a boat trip, and I never went because it was basketball season. My mom would take everybody somewhere for spring break each year, and I wouldn't go because it was basketball season. But I never looked at it as missing something. I felt the opposite way: if I had gone on the trips, then I would have been missing something, because I would have missed practice or games. And no one should feel sorry for me. I still found time to do plenty of fun things. I just never wanted to do anything that conflicted with basketball. And that's a big part of why I'm a North Carolina basketball player today.

WEEK TEN

Sometimes I wonder how my life might be different if I had gone to Davidson. I was very involved with them during my recruiting process, although they never offered me. After my postgraduate season at New Hampton, I started seriously looking at my offers. I didn't have any high-major offers. I had a handful of low-major and mid-major scholarship offers, but there just weren't very many schools I felt comfortable with. I visited Wofford and Furman, and I was recruited by several schools in the northeast. But when I went to visit, I never felt like I could see myself living at that place.

That's when I started thinking about walking on at a high-major. Wake Forest and Carolina were both pursuing me as a recruited walk-on. I visited Carolina and sat down with Matt Doherty, the head coach at the time. We looked at the depth chart and my father and I decided there was very little chance for playing time in Chapel Hill. I knew playing at Carolina's level would be hard and there would always be talent there. But with six or seven guys bunched up at the same positions, it looked impossible. At the time, I didn't know some transfers were going to leave UNC.

When I looked at the Wake Forest depth chart, it was only about half as crowded. I actually told my dad I was going to Wake. But before I made a commitment, I had agreed to take a visit to James Madison. Dad said, "Are you sure you don't want to call Wake?" And I told him I wanted to make sure by going on the visit to JMU so I wouldn't have any regrets.

The visit to James Madison was great. I enjoyed the other guys on the team. I liked the school. I had a lot of fun on my visit. We played a pickup game during the visit and I played well, so I felt good about my chances of playing time. That's when I decided to go to James Madison. I told everyone it was because I had felt so comfortable there, and I really had.

Truthfully, I also think a lot of my decision was because of the scholarship offer. I liked that they were offering me a scholarship. My whole life, my goal had been to get a Division I basketball scholarship. To achieve that goal, I made several sacrifices—I went away to school and I did a year of prep school. I couldn't reconcile the idea of walking on at Wake Forest with those sacrifices.

My dad felt like the decision to attend James Madison was impulsive. I hadn't been very serious about them before the visit, and now all of a sudden I was going to spend my college career there. Everyone was shocked—including me. My father played baseball at Wake Forest and is very involved with their athletic department as a donor. He never pressured me to go there, even though I'm sure that like any father he would have enjoyed watching me play for his school. But my parents have always supported me, even when they're not sure if I'm doing the right thing.

They didn't gloat when I decided to transfer after my first year. When I got my release, the coaches at Wake Forest called and asked if they could do anything to help. They said they'd love to have me at Wake if I was interested, but they also offered to call other schools. I'm still grateful to them for that.

This was all taking place approximately a month after Coach Williams got the job at Carolina. I had basically decided I'd use basketball to get a great education, so I took a visit to Penn and a visit to Columbia. I was ready to make a decision between those two schools. But just like when I made my first college choice, another option came up—and this time it was North Carolina. A couple friends had made calls to Joe Holladay, Coach Williams's assistant. I got in touch with him and asked if I could visit Chapel Hill with my dad.

The visit blew me away. I had no idea Coach Williams was going to say, "We'd love for you to be part of this program," and that's exactly what he told me. We talked for a couple of hours, and he told me he couldn't make any promises about playing time. I told him I had an interest in coaching, and he told me there was no better place to come to school if I wanted to pursue that dream.

That conversation with Coach is the reason I came to Carolina. I knew playing time was going to be difficult, and I wasn't sure I would ever play. But it made an enormous impact for Roy Williams to look me in the eye and tell me he'd do whatever he could to help me pursue my dreams after college. I didn't know him at all. Until that day, I'd just watched him on television. Before we left, he told me one other thing that really hit home:

"It's your job to come here and work hard every single day to improve as a basketball player, and it's my job to help you improve."

I'd never had a coach say that to me. My dad and I both felt he was so genuine, and that he was really committed to making me a better player. He wasn't just saying what he thought I wanted to hear. I knew right then I wanted to come to Carolina. But I was worried about making the same impulsive decision I had made about James Madison, so I asked him if I could go home and think about it.

I gave it a couple days, and I still felt great about Carolina. I never seriously thought about Wake. At that time, I thought of myself as a point guard, and Wake had Chris Paul. Everybody knew how good he was and I thought he would be there a long time. Raymond Felton had been at Carolina a year and people were already talking about him going to the NBA. I saw an opportunity, and the meeting with Coach Williams sealed the decision.

I might have thought of myself as a point guard when I came to Carolina, but I've had the most success as a shooting guard. That's where I played as a junior, and that's where I spent the first part of this season. But both Bobby Frasor and Quentin Thomas are battling injuries, which means Ty Lawson is our only point guard right now. When those guys went down, Coach pulled me aside in practice and said, "I want you to get more reps at point guard." Three days later, my name was in the point guard slot on the practice plan and that's where it has been ever since. We didn't sit down and have a big conversation about it, and in some ways it goes back to that conversation about roles: my role is to do whatever the team needs. Right now, the team needs a point guard.

I'm not fully up-to-date on what's happening with Bobby and Q, because I try not to ask them about it. I know everyone in the world is talking about their injuries with them, and they don't need another person saying, "How's your foot?" every time they see them. When I'm hurt, it's not something I like to talk about. And it's tough, because in many ways what happens with them also has an impact on me.

It just goes to show that you can't predict what's going to happen. When I was looking at our roster this summer, I never thought there was any chance I'd see any minutes at point guard. We had Bobby, who is last year's returning starter, Quentin, who could start at most places in the country, and a freshman in Ty who was a high school All-American. You don't need four point guards. In this offense, you never know when you'll be the one bringing the ball up, so I never stopped working on those skills, but I never thought I'd see game minutes there. It's kind of ironic—when I came to Carolina, I'd been a point guard all my life. Then I moved to the two-guard and have success, and now I'm back at point guard. I like it, though. I feel like I'm being useful and filling a need for the team.

Ty has picked up the slack perfectly, but he can't do it all by himself. I've been able to focus on distributing a little more, which might be beneficial because I'm shooting below 30 percent from the floor. I've gotten some good looks and they haven't gone in. I've passed up some shots because my confidence was down a little. Coach always says, "You don't have to shoot it, but at least look at it. Make the defense think you're shooting and make them play you."

At one point, Coach Williams pulled me aside and said, "Keep shooting and stay confident. I have confidence in you. It's difficult because we're asking you to play so much point guard. You're worrying about your jump shot and about playing point guard, and we need you to stay with it." It meant a lot for him to say he had confidence in me. I haven't shot the ball well and he could have given up on me.

The other day they showed me on tape that I was catching the ball on the wing and moving it immediately without looking at the basket. Coach Haase brought me in his office and said, "You're playing point guard, but that doesn't mean you have to change the way you play. Get the ball up the court and get it into someone else's hands, but once you get into the halfcourt offense, play the way you always have."

That clicked with me, and that's the way I've tried to play lately. My game in the halfcourt is not necessarily setting people up and creating. I'm a guy who can spread the defense by knocking down shots. Over the last week, I've shot the ball better in practice. I'm feeling more confident all over the floor, and it's showing in my form and also the way I'm playing in other areas. My assist/error right now is almost 3:1, and I'm very happy with that.

My mindset until that conversation with Coach Haase had been, "I'm a point guard, I must distribute the ball." Now I'm playing point guard . . . but also trying to do what I do best, which is provide perimeter scoring. It's so valuable to have two coaches on the staff—Jerod and C.B. McGrath—who played for Coach Williams. Coach Haase is the one I've relied on the most. He knows the system really well because he played in it recently, but he also understands what it's like to be a player on a day-to-day basis. He knows what it's like to have a tough day in practice. He does a great job bridging the gap between the players and coaches. He looks at everything as a coach—but with a player's unique perspective.

He's been so valuable to me that I know it has been tough for him not being on the bench this year. Jerod and C.B. rotate each year, with one serving as the operations man and one serving as the third assistant coach. Some teams fudge that rule a little, but we follow it strictly by the rulebook. Jerod doesn't sit on our bench with us and he doesn't come on the practice court. But even when he's not technically a coach, it's still nice to meet him in his office to talk about anything that's happening.

Another benefit of this stretch where we've been hurt by injuries: Ty is maturing. Sometimes I look at him and it's amazing how far he has come in such a short amount of time. Earlier in the year, there were some guys worried about him. Sometimes he seemed a little aloof, like he wasn't really into it. He showed up late for some things, and that never happens at North Carolina. Some of the coaches were frustrated.

But when we got into practice, his attitude improved significantly. Part of it is that he's used to college and used to being a college basketball player. Like a lot of college freshmen, he had struggled some with having the choice to do certain things rather than having it mandated to him. And like a lot of freshmen, he had to learn the hard way.

But at the same time I've seen him mature as a person, his game has also gotten so much better. If you go back and watch the first couple of games, he looks like a freshman. Now he looks like he belongs in the Carolina system. He makes me think of Raymond in the way he can make a play whenever he wants and control the tempo of the game. He plays so fast, but just like Raymond, he can play fast and under control. That's what separates him.

Game 9

UNC Asheville 62
#3/3 North Carolina 93
Dec. 16, 2006 • Smith Center, Chapel Hill

UNCA	FG	3FG	FT	REB	PF	TP	A	TO	B	S	Min
James*	4-12	1-5	2-4	2-2-4	3	11	1	2	1	1	30
Harrell*	3-8	1-3	2-4	1-5-6	2	9	1	4	0	1	33
Walker*	1-3	0-0	0-0	1-1-2	4	2	0	2	3	0	15
Garland*	2-9	1-4	6-6	0-3-3	1	11	2	1	0	1	35
Smithson*	6-13	1-3	7-8	0-4-4	4	20	2	2	0	4	28
Warner	1-4	1-2	0-0	2-4-6	2	3	1	4	0	0	15
Jones	0-2	0-0	2-4	1-2-3	1	2	1	1	0	1	15
Augst	0-2	0-1	0-0	0-1-1	1	0	2	0	1	0	13
George	2-2	0-0	0-0	0-1-1	1	4	0	0	1	0	7
Moles	0-0	0-0	0-0	0-0-0	1	0	0	1	0	0	6
Smith	0-0	0-0	0-0	0-0-0	0	0	0	0	0	0	2
Ridenhour	0-1	0-0	0-0	0-0-0	0	0	0	0	0	0	1
TEAM				3-1-4			1				
Totals	**19-56**	**5-18**	**19-26**	**10-24-34**	**20**	**62**	**10**	**18**	**6**	**8**	**200**
Pct.	**.339**	**.278**	**.731**	**DB: 3**							

FG: (1st half: 12-26, .462; 2nd half: 7-30, .233)
3FG: (1st half: 4-10, .400; 2nd half: 1-8, .125)
FT: (1st half: 11-13, .846; 2nd half: 8-13, .615)

UNC	FG	3FG	FT	REB	PF	TP	A	TO	B	S	Min
Terry*	5-6	3-3	0-0	1-5-6	1	13	3	0	1	0	23
Wright*	7-9	0-0	7-9	5-4-9	1	21	0	2	1	1	23
Hansbrough*	5-12	0-0	5-6	4-3-7	3	15	2	3	0	2	27
Ellington*	6-14	2-4	1-1	2-3-5	1	15	4	0	0	0	24
Lawson*	3-7	0-2	0-1	0-3-3	2	6	8	1	0	2	26
Thompson	2-5	0-0	0-0	2-1-3	2	4	1	0	0	0	15
Green	1-4	1-2	2-2	1-1-2	2	5	1	1	2	1	17
Miller	0-4	0-3	0-1	0-0-0	2	0	3	1	0	0	14
Ginyard	3-5	0-0	0-0	0-4-4	3	6	1	3	0	3	14
Stepheson	4-6	0-0	0-2	3-3-6	0	8	0	0	1	0	8
Copeland	0-1	0-0	0-0	0-1-1	1	0	1	0	0	0	5
Burke	0-1	0-1	0-0	0-1-1	1	0	0	1	0	0	2
Wood	0-1	0-0	0-0	0-1-1	0	0	0	0	0	1	2
TEAM				1-1-2							
Totals	**36-75**	**6-15**	**15-22**	**19-31-50**	**19**	**93**	**24**	**12**	**5**	**10**	**200**
Pct.	**.480**	**.400**	**.682**	**DB: 3**							

FG: (1st half: 20-38, .526; 2nd half: 16-37, .432)
3FG: (1st half: 5-10, .500; 2nd half: 1-5, .200)
FT: (1st half: 11-12, .917; 2nd half: 4-10, .400)

Officials: Mike Wood, Dan Stryffeler, Raymond Styons
Attendance: 18,923 • **Technical Fouls:** None

Score by Periods	1st	2nd	Total
UNC Asheville	39	23	62
North Carolina	56	37	93

Game 10

Florida Atlantic 52
#2/2 North Carolina 105
Dec. 19, 2006 • Smith Center, Chapel Hill

FAU	FG	3FG	FT	REB	PF	TP	A	TO	B	S	Min
Simmons*	1-6	0-1	1-2	1-4-5	5	3	0	4	0	1	31
Parmer*	4-10	1-3	2-4	4-1-5	3	11	0	5	1	1	31
Alarcon*	2-5	1-3	0-0	0-2-2	3	5	4	1	1	2	32
Crews*	4-8	1-3	0-0	0-1-1	4	9	4	4	0	1	29
Holley*	0-1	0-1	0-0	0-0-0	0	0	1	1	0	0	7
Rice	4-15	2-8	3-4	0-1-1	1	13	3	6	0	2	35
Cuka	1-4	1-3	0-1	1-0-1	1	3	0	2	0	0	13
Kone	3-5	0-0	0-0	0-3-3	1	6	0	1	1	1	18
Anderson	1-2	0-0	0-0	1-1-2	1	2	0	0	1	0	4
TEAM				2-2-4			0				
Totals	20-56	6-22	6-11	9-15-24	19	52	12	24	4	8	200
Pct.	.357	.273	.545	DB: 2							

FG: (1st half: 6-25, .240; 2nd half: 14-31, .452)
3FG: (1st half: 2-8, .250; 2nd half: 4-14, .286)
FT: (1st half: 4-6, .667; 2nd half: 2-5, .400)

UNC	FG	3FG	FT	REB	PF	TP	A	TO	B	S	Min
Terry*	5-6	3-4	1-1	0-7-7	1	14	1	0	0	2	17
Wright*	5-7	0-0	5-6	0-8-8	1	15	0	1	3	0	17
Hansbrough*	6-7	0-0	8-9	1-2-3	0	20	0	1	0	1	19
Ellington*	5-9	3-3	1-2	2-3-5	1	14	2	2	0	0	22
Lawson*	5-6	0-0	1-2	0-0-0	0	11	8	3	0	4	19
Green	4-8	0-3	0-0	1-1-2	3	8	1	1	1	3	23
Miller	1-3	1-3	0-0	0-0-0	0	3	5	2	0	1	18
Ginyard	1-1	0-0	4-4	0-3-3	0	6	3	0	0	0	14
Thompson	3-4	0-0	2-2	0-2-2	3	8	3	3	0	1	21
Stephenson	2-2	0-0	2-4	2-3-5	2	6	0	2	0	0	16
Copeland	0-0	0-0	0-0	0-0-0	1	0	0	0	0	0	7
Burke	0-2	0-2	0-0	0-0-0	0	0	0	0	0	0	4
Wood	0-1	0-0	0-0	0-0-0	0	0	0	0	0	0	3
TEAM				2-1-3							
Totals	37-56	7-15	24-30	8-30-38	12	105	23	15	4	12	200
Pct.	.661	.467	.800	DB: 2							

FG: (1st half: 20-27, .741; 2nd half: 17-29, .586)
3FG: (1st half: 3-4, .750; 2nd half: 4-11, .364)
FT: (1st half: 22-24, .917; 2nd half: 2-6, .333)

Officials: Les Jones, Tim Nestor, Sean Hull
Attendance: 18,162 • **Technical Fouls:** None

Score by Periods	1st	2nd	Total
Florida Atlantic	18	34	52
North Carolina	65	40	105

WEEK ELEVEN

I'VE ALWAYS LOVED PLAYING on the road. Our first real chance to do that came this week at Saint Louis. Running out of the tunnel at the Smith Center is amazing and it gives me goose bumps every time. But I love putting on the blue jerseys and going into a hostile environment with everyone against us. We have a young team, so no one was certain how they would react on the road, but I wasn't concerned. Other than my redshirt year, when everyone was getting adjusted to the new program, we've always played well on the road.

It was a typical road game for us: Saint Louis had their biggest crowd in a decade and the biggest crowd in the history of their building. That's what's fun about playing for Carolina.

It's a big deal when we come to town. It was an even bigger deal for Tyler, because the game was a chance for him to return home to Missouri. He talks about Poplar Bluff with us all the time, except he just calls it, "The Bluff." He's not exactly the best storyteller around, so we didn't know how much of it to believe.

For the last couple of years, Coach Holladay has told me how crazy the people in Poplar Bluff are about Tyler. He told me when he was recruiting Tyler, everyone knew you had to get to the gym a couple of hours early or you wouldn't get a seat for his high school games. They had to play a lot of their games in a separate convention center because of the hysteria over Tyler. After seeing it in person, he was absolutely right. When we got off the bus in St. Louis, a bunch of Poplar Bluff people were there to meet us. Usually, we don't get a big crowd in the lobby sending us off until the NCAA Tournament. But on game day as we walked to our bus there were 150 people standing there to cheer for us.

I was Tyler's roommate for the trip, so I got a first-hand look at how excited he was. He was really fired up the night before the game. I didn't notice him being nervous. Before the game, his older brother Greg called him in the room. Greg was on his way to the game, and Tyler put him on speaker. They were so excited that they just started yelling at each other. Tyler calls Greg "Snake Diesel," so Tyler would shout, "Snake Diesel!" and then Greg would shout back, "T-Bone!"

Literally, they did that for about a minute, just shouting at each other. Then they hung up and that was it. It showed how fired up Tyler was for the game.

It was great to see all the fans from his hometown with their Poplar Bluff Mules shirts. After the game, all the players split up because we all go our separate ways for a quick

Christmas break. I ended up on the concourse with my dad, and there were at least 250 people from Poplar Bluff waiting in line for Tyler's autograph. They knew me, because they follow the team so closely. They'd ask for a picture or an autograph, and the very next words out of their mouth would be, "When is Tyler coming out?" Tyler is big in Chapel Hill. But he's legendary in Poplar Bluff.

We were able to have fun with him and the way everyone loves him because we won the game. We were terrible offensively in the first half—we shot 29.4% from the field. But we had a 1-point halftime lead because we really got down and defended well. Saint Louis really tried to slow down the tempo, which we have to take as a compliment. We pride ourselves on running, and if an opponent doesn't feel like they can run, that says we're pretty good at it. But I think we can get a lot better. We want to get to the point that when a team tries to slow the tempo, we just run over them.

That's what we did in the second half, and that's how we got a 69–48 win. There's nothing more satisfying than watching people leave early because you're blowing their team out. The gym can be extremely loud in the first half, and it's that much more satisfying to listen to it get quiet in the second half. That's why road wins are so special.

Getting more of them will start with our defense. Around the UNC-Asheville game, we started playing much better defensively. Coach Williams stressed that this is the time of year when we can make a lot of progress. There's a big correlation between the way we play defensively and Coach's attitude in practice. When we defend better and move together better, he seems much happier. Practice gets easier, because we don't have to do defensive stations.

Game 11

#2/2 North Carolina 69
Saint Louis 48
Dec. 22, 2006 • Scottrade Center, St. Louis, Mo.

UNC	FG	3FG	FT	REB	PF	TP	A	TO	B	S	Min
Terry*	2-5	0-2	2-2	1-2-3	2	6	1	0	0	1	19
Wright*	4-7	0-0	4-6	0-3-3	1	12	1	0	4	1	30
Hansbrough*	6-13	0-0	3-6	4-9-13	3	15	1	1	1	2	35
Ellington*	1-7	0-4	1-2	0-0-0	1	3	2	3	0	1	18
Lawson*	4-11	2-3	2-2	1-7-8	1	12	8	2	1	1	33
Ginyard	1-4	1-1	0-0	2-1-3	0	3	4	0	0	0	21
Green	5-8	4-5	0-0	2-4-6	1	14	1	1	1	0	20
Burke	0-0	0-0	0-0	0-0-0	0	0	0	0	0	0	1
Thompson	2-3	0-0	0-0	0-0-0	4	4	0	1	0	0	7
Miller	0-0	0-0	0-0	0-0-0	0	0	0	0	0	0	9
Wood	0-0	0-0	0-0	0-0-0	0	0	0	0	0	0	1
Stepheson	0-1	0-0	0-0	0-0-0	1	0	0	0	0	1	5
Copeland	0-0	0-0	0-0	0-0-0	0	0	0	0	0	0	1
TEAM				4-1-5							
Totals	**25-59**	**7-15**	**12-18**	**14-27-41**	**14**	**69**	**18**	**8**	**7**	**7**	**200**
Pct.	.424	.467	.667	DB: 2							

FG: (1st half: 10-34, .294; 2nd half: 15-25, .600)
3FG: (1st half: 2-6, .333; 2nd half: 5-9, .556)
FT: (1st half: 5-7, .714; 2nd half: 7-11, .636)

SLU	FG	3FG	FT	REB	PF	TP	A	TO	B	S	Min
Meyer*	3-7	0-0	0-0	0-4-4	4	6	1	1	0	2	34
Vouyoukas*	6-12	0-1	2-3	3-10-13	4	14	0	3	2	0	32
Polk*	1-6	1-5	2-2	0-0-0	3	5	0	2	0	0	33
Lisch*	3-13	0-3	0-0	0-2-2	2	6	1	1	1	1	36
Liddell*	4-10	0-2	5-6	0-4-4	2	13	1	2	0	1	31
Brown	2-2	0-0	0-0	0-0-0	2	4	2	0	0	0	18
Bennett	0-0	0-0	0-0	0-0-0	0	0	0	0	0	0	1
Maguire	0-0	0-0	0-0	0-0-0	0	0	0	0	0	0	1
Johnson	0-1	0-0	0-0	0-4-4	2	0	1	1	0	0	12
Knollmeyer	0-0	0-0	0-0	0-0-0	0	0	0	1	0	0	1
Husak	0-1	0-0	0-0	2-0-2	0	0	0	1	0	0	1
TEAM				2-0-2							
Totals	**19-52**	**1-11**	**9-11**	**7-24-31**	**19**	**48**	**6**	**12**	**3**	**4**	**200**
Pct.	.365	.091	.818	DB: 1							

FG: (1st half: 9-27, .333; 2nd half: 10-25, .400)
3FG: (1st half: 1-8, .125; 2nd half: 0-3, .000)
FT: (1st half: 7-8, .875; 2nd half: 2-3, .667)

Officials: Bob Donato, Jim Burr, Ray Perone
Attendance: 22,539 • **Technical Fouls:** None

Score by Periods	1st	2nd	Total
North Carolina	27	42	69
Saint Louis	26	22	48

For a couple of weeks at the beginning of December, our practices were brutal defensively. We weren't moving as a unit and we were having a lot of mental breakdowns. So practice was full of defensive slides, deny-help-deny drills, and every defensive station. It always takes a while for a defensive mentality to click with a young team, and that may be happening right now. They've learned if we pressure the way we want to pressure, we're going to get turnovers and we're going to get easy baskets, which makes it a lot more fun to play. There's a payoff to really getting down and grinding somebody defensively for 35 seconds.

We have so much depth and so many guys that can hurt you in so many ways. If we play defense the way we should play, we can be as good as any team I've been on at Carolina. We have to keep improving all the way through March. If we do that, a lot of special things could happen with this team.

LUCAS: SEEING IS BELIEVING

DEC. 22, 2006

ST. LOUIS—This was nothing to smile about.

This was ugly basketball. This was Carolina scoring just 27 points in the first half at Saint Louis. They shot 29.4%. Here is a snapshot of the first two minutes:

Ty Lawson pulls up for an ill-advised 17-footer. Wayne Ellington throws a bad entry pass that is intercepted. Reyshawn Terry picks up two quick fouls and is yanked. Saint Louis builds a quick 5–0 lead.

That's how the entire first half went offensively. No rhythm, no flow.

The Carolina custom is for the coaches to meet as a group before Roy Williams addresses the players. It's a way for everyone to decompress and make sure any comments aren't influenced by the emotion of the game.

The Tar Heel coaches looked at the grimy, pock-marked stat sheet. It was replete with missed shots and missed opportunities.

And they smiled. Just a little bit.

Sometimes, games aren't a reflection of what they see in practice. This time, it was. They'd seen a team that was making progress on defense.

With about 5 minutes left in the first half, that team arrived at the Scottrade Center. Through the first 15 minutes of the half, the Billikens had just one turnover. But then the Tar Heels started tossing in an occasional halfcourt trap. First one . . . and Saint Louis seemed bothered by it. In general, Williams prefers to trap more frequently at home, but he saw an opening. So here came another trap, and another. Saint Louis picked up 5 turnovers in the last 5 minutes and Carolina stole the lead for just the second time in the half.

"It helped speed up the game," said Ty Lawson, who merely turned in another 8-assist, 2-turnover performance. "They were taking the whole shot clock to shoot and that was slowing us down. So we threw in the traps and that sped up the tempo."

Suddenly there were loose balls. Suddenly there were passing lanes and fast break opportunities. Suddenly there was Carolina basketball dashing up and down the court, blitzing through the second half and causing Saint Louis coach Brad Soderberg to use two timeouts in the first 6 minutes and burn through all of his allotted stoppages by the 4:40 mark.

This is the kind of game that makes players believe. They hear Williams harp on defense, hear him say that a good defensive game will beat a good offensive game. But these are 18- and 19-year-olds and they want to *see* it, not hear it.

This was seeing it. Sure, the defense led to easy scoring chances, and the offense eventually started rolling on the way to a 60-percent effort in the final 20 minutes. But Saint Louis probably could have stopped the Carolina offense.

They had no answer, none, for the UNC defense.

The Tar Heels helped. The Tar Heels denied. They defended off the ball and on the ball. On one possession late in the second half, burly Ian Vouyoukas was trying to post up Tyler Hansbrough. He banged, he pushed, and he pulled.

Then he just stopped. He stepped back, gazed at official Bob Donato and threw up his hands. His teammates continued to operate around him, but he was totally out of the play. Sometimes a team is able to metaphorically take an opponent out of their offense. Now Carolina had succeeded in literally removing one Billiken from the offense.

That's frustrating, sticky defense. And winning defense.

"We changed up a little bit and started pressuring them a little more," said Danny Green, the evening's offensive star. "We trapped them and made them play to our tempo. That changed their offense. We started making shots and playing our game and our tempo."

"Let's be honest," Williams told the media. "In the second half, we got it going pretty good."

And then he smiled. Just a little, but it was there. Remember, it was just a month ago that he stayed consistently frustrated with this team on a daily basis. Now, he sees something. Just a simple win doesn't necessarily spark that smile.

It almost seems like a bad time for a three-day break.

"It kind of does," Lawson said. "We're making good strides."

Now listen to this and try to guess the speaker:

"The first half we shoot 29 percent, but we play great defense and stay in the game . . . Defense is the thing that wins games. We can have off nights offensively like tonight and still win if we play defense like this."

Who might that be? Not Williams. Not a veteran like Reyshawn Terry or an all-around wizard like Marcus Ginyard.

It's Lawson, a freshman.

Christmas is here. And he believes.

WEEK TWELVE

CHRISTMAS IS ESSENTIALLY the only break you get during the season. From October to April, at least part of every day is devoted to basketball. Spending time with his family during the holidays is important to Coach Williams, and he's been great about making sure we all get that time. It's good to get away for a couple days and recharge your batteries, and it's always nice to get to see your family. We have our family here in Chapel Hill, and we're with each other all the time. There isn't any time for your family at home during the season. You might get to see them for a couple minutes after a game, and you talk to them on the phone, but it's not like other college students where you go home for a weekend to do laundry. So getting some home cooking, opening presents, and just getting to hang out with your family allows you to recharge your batteries. Just having two or three days serves as a chance to catch your breath.

My dad lives in Greensboro and my mom and her whole family is in Charlotte. That means there's a good bit of driving involved in the holidays. When I got back from St. Louis, I spent the night in Greensboro. I woke up on the 23rd and drove to Charlotte. I spent the 23rd, 24th, and Christmas morning in Charlotte. Then my brother, sister, and I drove to Greensboro on Christmas Day and spent the rest of the day and all day on the 26th until practice started with my dad. That's how we do it every Christmas. It's a lot of driving, but it's the best way to get to see everyone.

I've had people ask me if it's bad to not have my whole family together at Christmas. I don't look at it that way. I get to see both of my families each Christmas and celebrate Christmas twice. At this point, that's just routine. My parents separated when I was seven, so this is the way I've known it for the vast majority of my life. To be honest, it would seem kind of odd to have everyone together. My parents have been really understanding about the whole thing, and we've each established our own traditions.

The most special gift I received this year was a 12-gauge Browning shotgun from my dad. It's hand-engraved and it's a beautiful gun. I went hunting with my grandfather when I was young, but haven't had time to do it hardly at all the last 10 years because of basketball. The gun is something I'll cherish for the rest of my life, and hopefully down the road I'll have the opportunity to get back into some hunting or clay shooting.

My favorite gift that I gave: I got Ashley a portable DVD

player-type thing for her iPod. It plays the movies from her iPod on a bigger screen, so you can take it on the road. She had been talking about how much she wanted it, so it felt good to be able to get it for her.

When you're so accustomed to playing basketball, it's hard to totally get away from it. So I shot at my dad's house on the 23rd before I left for Charlotte. On Christmas Eve, Coach Witman, the head football coach at Charlotte Country Day, came up to the school and unlocked the gym for me so I could shoot. He's always done that for me when I'm at home, and it's become a little tradition that my brother rebounds for me on Christmas Eve. Then we finish up with some one-on-one, which always gets my confidence up. And then on Christmas Day I shot at my dad's house again. So even though we were on a break, I still got my shots up.

It's amazing how much a short break can reenergize you. We came back and practiced on the night of the 26th, and I was really looking forward to it. Talking to the other guys, they all said the same thing—it's good to get home and see your family, but it's also good to get back because we felt like we had our legs back and we were ready to make a big push in January.

The very first night of practice, I hit four or five 3-pointers during a drill. Coach Holladay came over and said, "Hey, did you work on your shot over the break?"

"Yeah, I worked on it every day," I told him.

His response—"I can tell."—made me feel good.

For three days, I didn't worry about anything other than my shot. I didn't play defense. I didn't distribute the ball. I just shot, and when you combine that with getting my legs back under me and being a little more relaxed, I'm much more confident.

That led to what I think was my best effort at point guard since I've been at Carolina against Rutgers. It started when I came to the scorer's table to check into the game. I usually get so involved in the game that I don't hear any special cheers for me. A lot of people told me last year that the crowd picked up when I checked in or out of the game. I never really noticed that. But against Rutgers I heard a little buzz when I went to the table and heard them again when I came out. It wasn't because I've been playing great. I think it showed how great Carolina fans are. They realize I've been struggling and wanted to pick me up. As a player, that means a lot, because it helps you know no one has forgotten about me and they still think I'm important to the team. I've gotten the same kind of reinforcement from my coaches and teammates. No one has said I should hesitate to shoot, and they've all continued to express confidence in me. When you have your team and your crowd behind you that way, it's impossible to get down. It's meant so much to me.

We won the game 87–48 and I made one of my three 3-pointers. But I was most happy with the way I got the ball to my teammates in position to make some shots. I finished with five assists and zero turnovers. Of course, it helped that Wayne was on fire. He hit five of six 3-pointers and a couple of my assists came to him. It's easy to get an assist when you can pass it to a guy 20 feet from the basket and he tosses it in. But what made me so comfortable was that I wasn't thinking about what I was doing. I was just playing the game and really got in the flow.

I get asked about Bobby's situation a lot by the media, but

I don't really know what is going on with his injury. I'm not in the meetings with the doctors, so I leave that to them. Until I hear differently, I'm going to play point guard. It's one game at a time. Until I see my name back at the two-guard position on the practice plan, I'm going to play with a point guard's mentality.

The shot I hit felt great. There have been times this year that I've shot the ball and as soon as it leaves my hand, I'm hoping that it goes in rather than knowing it's in. On that one, I knew it. That's how it's supposed to feel and it's one of the best feelings in the world. It reassured me that I haven't lost my jump shot. I just need to step up and shoot it with confidence.

There's a fine line between being confident and being over-confident. We've won six games in a row by double figures, and we've won the last five by at least 21 points. We have two winnable home games—Dayton and Penn—coming up before we start Atlantic Coast Conference play against Florida State. It's nice to have a swagger that you know you're going to bury teams. But you can't be cocky.

Coach Williams usually takes care of that. He's not going to let us overestimate how good we are. His leadership shows us we're not close to being as good as we can be. We're feeling pretty good right now, but we haven't played a single ACC game and it was just a month ago that we lost to Gonzaga and everyone was feeling terrible. Being ranked number-one or number-two in the country doesn't mean anything in December. It's nice for the fans, but what matters to us is being at the top at the end of the season.

Any time we start feeling too good, all we have to do is look around the country. There are a lot of good teams out there this year. Right before Christmas Ohio State—which we felt like was a good team when we played them, and now they've got Greg Oden back—went into Florida and got whipped, 86–60. Right now, Florida is the team to beat. To beat a team like Ohio State that way shows you how tough they're going to be. I was recording the game, and as I was watching it I'd pause it or rewind it to watch certain players or certain plays each team runs.

Game 12

Rutgers 48
#2/2 North Carolina 87
Dec. 28, 2006 • Smith Center, Chapel Hill

RU	FG	3FG	FT	REB	PF	TP	A	TO	B	S	Min
Hill*	6-11	0-0	1-3	4-4-8	3	13	1	1	0	0	32
Griffin*	4-17	0-7	2-2	2-3-5	2	10	0	2	0	0	37
N'diaye*	2-3	0-0	0-0	3-3-6	3	4	0	1	3	1	26
Webb*	2-8	1-3	0-0	0-2-2	0	5	3	4	0	2	35
Nelson*	0-8	0-3	0-2	0-0-0	2	0	2	8	0	1	30
Russell	2-2	0-0	0-0	1-1-2	4	4	0	0	1	0	14
Bailey	3-5	0-0	2-2	1-1-2	0	8	0	0	0	0	16
Keating	1-2	0-0	0-0-0	1	2	0	2	0	0	7	
Mimmo	1-1	0-0	0-1	0-0-0	0	2	0	0	0	1	1
Cherry	0-1	0-1	0-0	0-0-0	0	0	0	0	0	0	1
Colon	0-0	0-0	0-0	0-0-0	0	0	0	0	0	0	1
TEAM				3-2-5			0				
Totals	21-58	1-14	5-10	14-16-30	15	48	6	18	4	5	200
Pct.	.362	.071	.500	DB: 3							

FG: (1st half: 8-28, .286; 2nd half: 13-30, .433)
3FG: (1st half: 1-6, .167; 2nd half: 0-8, .000)
FT: (1st half: 2-2, 1.000; 2nd half: 3-8, .375)

UNC	FG	3FG	FT	REB	PF	TP	A	TO	B	S	Min
Terry*	2-3	1-2	1-2	0-2-2	3	6	2	5	0	0	21
Wright*	8-10	0-0	3-4	3-4-7	0	19	1	2	3	0	24
Hansbrough*	5-13	0-0	3-3	3-4-7	2	13	1	1	0	1	29
Ellington*	5-7	5-6	2-2	0-2-2	0	17	2	2	0	1	27
Lawson*	2-6	0-2	2-3	0-4-4	0	6	9	0	1	2	25
Green	2-4	1-2	0-0	1-2-3	1	5	3	0	1	1	18
Thompson	3-6	0-0	1-2	1-2-3	3	7	1	0	1	1	14
Ginyard	0-1	0-0	1-2	0-0-0	0	1	3	1	0	2	13
Stepheson	3-4	0-0	0-0	2-2-4	0	6	0	0	0	0	11
Miller	1-3	1-3	0-0	1-0-1	1	3	5	0	0	0	14
Copeland	2-2	0-0	0-0	0-1-1	1	4	0	0	0	0	2
Burke	0-0	0-0	0-0	0-0-0	1	0	0	0	0	0	1
Wood	0-1	0-0	0-0	0-0-0	0	0	0	0	0	0	1
TEAM				2-3-5							
Totals	33-60	8-15	13-18	13-26-39	12	87	27	11	6	8	200
Pct.	.550	.533	.722	DB: 2							

FG: (1st half: 13-29, .448; 2nd half: 20-31, .645)
3FG: (1st half: 1-5, .200; 2nd half: 7-10, .700)
FT: (1st half: 6-9, .667; 2nd half: 7-9, .778)

Officials: Karl Hess, Bernard Clinton, Michael Stephens
Attendance: 20,997 • **Technical Fouls:** None

Score by Periods	1st	2nd	Total
Rutgers	19	29	48
North Carolina	33	54	87

It's impossible to watch a game like that and not think about how we match up with those teams. It gets me excited, because our whole goal is to be one of those elite teams at the end of the season and have an opportunity to play in a championship-level game. Some teams are separating themselves from the pack. Florida is certainly one of them. Ohio State and Kansas are very talented. I've watched UCLA quite a few times this year, and I'm impressed with how they grind it out defensively. Are we one of those teams yet? I don't think so. But we have a chance to be, and that's why it's important to keep playing our best during this stretch when the opposition isn't as tough as it will be in conference play. The best teams in the country play that way even on nights when the spotlight isn't quite as bright.

LUCAS: THE SIDELINE STORY

DEC. 28, 2006

Reyshawn Terry does not have a particularly flat three-point stroke.

The importance of this seemingly miniscule fact will soon become evident.

Carolina was in the process of polishing off Rutgers in the second half Thursday night. Four minutes remained, and reserves were waiting at the scorer's table to relieve the Tar Heel starters. As a media timeout approached, Ty Lawson went to the floor to recover a loose ball. The ball eventually found Terry, who was standing all alone at the top of the key.

Terry had time to ponderously load up his shot. Roy Williams, meanwhile, had time to load up the springs in his shoes. He started near the scorer's table, took a hop, and then leaped just as his senior released the ball. He soared . . . OK, hovered . . . er, maybe hopped through the air in tandem with the basketball. Just as the ball dropped through the net, the head coach came back to earth, touching down in front of the Carolina bench with a triumphant pump of his fist.

"Atta boy!" he shouted, as though this was a game-changing moment.

That play came just 9 minutes after he'd skipped down the sideline giddily clapping his hands after Marcus Ginyard dropped to the ground to recover a loose ball, fed Ty Lawson, and the Tar Heels eventually ended up with a Danny Green 3-pointer.

"Atta boy, Marcus!" Williams shouted with a smile.

There are several ways to tell how much better Carolina has played recently. The most vivid illustration can be found on the Tar Heel sideline.

A couple weeks ago, Williams spent most of Carolina's games stomping his feet or massaging his temples. He looked like he was enduring rather than enjoying.

Now, he looks like a fan with a ticket at the front of section 109. He claps. He points to thank the passer, as he did when he stood to point to Ginyard after a late Mike Copeland dunk. He smiles (just a little).

Ginyard has become the go-to guy for postgame quotes. Surely he will have some sage insight into his head coach's personality change over the past month. After all, the two are practically blood brothers.

This is what the sophomore said:

"He's not screaming as much, I know that," Ginyard said.

That doesn't exactly qualify as groundbreaking. But it's true.

"He just looks less stressed," Lawson said. "In practice, he laughs and giggles a little. Before, he wasn't in a playful mood. Now he'll laugh with us, tell us jokes."

Even a freshman knows why the head coach has changed.

"We're playing more the way he wants us to play," Lawson said. "We get up and defend. Everybody is putting pressure on the ball and everybody is getting in the passing lanes. When we turn the pressure up, it makes it easier to play defense because we don't have to play defense for as long and it gets the tempo going."

For about 18 minutes, it looked like Thursday's game would be played at a tempo chosen by Rutgers—glacial. The Scarlet Knights walked, strolled, and sauntered through the first half. Rutgers head coach Fred Hill spent most of the half with his left arm straight out in front of him, palm outstretched, asking his guards to slow down. The game turned into such a grinder that the Knights were zapped with a 10-second violation with three minutes remaining. Not because the Tar Heels were applying much pressure, but because Rutgers simply wasn't in a hurry.

But then Lawson decided he was tired of waiting.

"I hate games where the other team slows it down and grinds it out," he said. "We all like to run. It wasn't fun for anyone on our team. So I got everybody together and said, 'We're going to push the ball.'"

Anybody can push the ball. Williams requires that his point guards push the ball *under control*, which is exactly what Lawson did. He zipped down the court on a 3-on-2 fast break and drew a foul. On the next possession, he pulled up for a jumper.

Rutgers couldn't help it. They were drawn in by the little point guard, and suddenly all of Hill's pleading couldn't stop them. With a chance to take the last shot of the first half, the Scarlet Knights instead flung up a shot with 18 seconds remaining. That gave Carolina plenty of time for Hansbrough to rebound Green's missed 3-pointer and stick it back for a 33–19 halftime lead.

From there, the Carolina second half was comparatively a blitzkrieg. It was well-played, it was solid defensively, and it was fun to watch.

Even for the head coach.

I got my grades back this week—two A's, two B+'s, and one C. I was more pleased with that C than any other C I've gotten in college. It was in statistics, and I've never done well in math or science class. I needed a second-level math class to graduate, and my academic advisor suggested statistics. It was nothing like shooting statistics or scoring statistics.

Those are easy for me to understand. This class was a monster. I met with a tutor two or three times each week, and I think I had a low C going into the exam. I met with my tutor two days in a row for four hours each, stayed up until 4 a.m. the night before studying, and then got up the day of the exam and studied some more. I did well enough on the final to bring my grade up to a solid C and I was really fired up about that.

With this essentially being my last semester of true college work, I was excited to go out that way. I only have two classes in the spring. Since I arrived at Carolina, one of my goals has been to be able to focus even more on basketball in the last semester of my senior year. This is when that redshirt year is completely worth it, because I had an extra year to boost my credits.

WEEK THIRTEEN

THE FIRST THING ANYONE DOES when they walk into the Smith Center is look up in the rafters at the jerseys. I see opposing teams doing it sometimes. I even still do it pretty regularly. They represent some of the greatest players in history—not just in Carolina history, but in college basketball history. So it's nice to be able to look up there and see everyone who came before me.

But I have to admit that it feels a little strange to have three guys up there I played with. Rashad McCants, Raymond Felton, and Sean May all had their jerseys honored during the Dayton game. It seems like yesterday that I was practicing with them and they were beating me up while I was on the Blue Team.

It makes me feel old. That's no surprise, because everyone on the team gets on me about my age—Bobby is on me the most with his "old man" jokes. I think of the rafters as a place for guys who were way before my time, and now I look up there and see three guys who I consider friends. I felt great for them, because all three of them deserve it. It was a little bit special for me, too, to know that I was a part of some big things that happened at North Carolina.

I've known Rashad since he was 13 years old. When he was at Carolina, I was the go-to guy for writers when they were writing their "understanding Rashad" stories. It was a little bit of a shock when he left, because suddenly writers wanted to talk to me but they didn't want to ask about Rashad. I had to learn a new set of answers. For two years, most every interview I did had something to do with him. It didn't get old, but I certainly became very familiar with the questions they needed to ask. When he was here, he received a good bit of negative publicity. I felt I had the opportunity to get him some positive press and shed some light on a different side of him. It's just not in his personality to show the more positive side of himself to outsiders.

I got to know him when we were on a 15-and-under Charlotte Royals AAU team. We were just drawn to each other as friends. At that time, his family had to drive him from Asheville to Charlotte every day we practiced. We started talking about making that drive, and we just became closer. He talked to me about how he wanted to leave Asheville not just to play AAU but for high school—he thought that would be good for him. He was considering Oak Hill Academy and a few other places. I was at New Hampton at the time and mentioned the kind of program we had, the players who had come through, and convinced him to consider it. I put his parents in touch with my coach and things progressed from there. We were great friends in high school and we won a championship at New Hampton.

A lot of people think Rashad is complicated. I think that's because most people don't get the chance to know him. He likes to seal himself off. He keeps a very tight-knit group of friends, and if you're not in that group, you're probably not going to get to know him. That's just Rashad.

I'm not sure how I got inside that group at first. Everyone asks me, "What made you and Rashad such good friends?" On the first day I met him in practice, I threw him a couple good passes, he threw me a couple of good passes, and we both hit some shots. I was impressed with the way he played and we had good chemistry on the court. It reached the point that we lived together in high school and we could essentially talk about anything. When we got to college, we went our separate ways to a certain point, but we always had that bond.

It was a thrill for me to see him go into the rafters, and I think he would admit it was a thrill for him, too. He's always been a guy who has had a good appreciation for Carolina basketball history. Some guys just know those jerseys represent good players. For the most part, he knows who they are and what they accomplished here.

I'll tell anyone who listens that Raymond is one of the toughest players to guard I've ever faced, and Sean May is one of my best friends in the world. He was here all summer last year and I'm sure he'll be here in future summers. We'll start playing pickup, and those games can get pretty talkative. Sean can talk with the best of them, and I can already picture him pointing straight up to the rafters at his jersey if any of the young guys start talking too much. He's got bragging rights now. There's not much even the most chatty guys could say to trump an honored jersey and a national championship banner.

Being talkative on the court doesn't make him unique among the guys we've had here. There was a time a couple years ago when it was hard to get a game in because Raymond and Rashad were always disagreeing about the score or whose ball it was or whether a foul should be called. Now they're the veterans and there's a whole new group of young guys who want to impress them. It's cyclical—the old guys are trying to make sure they get the respect they've earned, and the young guys want to earn respect from the old guys. Sean does quite a bit of talking, and so does Rashad. Melvin Scott never stops running his mouth. That's how it is in the summertime. We had a joke this summer that Reyshawn was trying to talk junk to every single former player who played in a pickup game. It seemed to me that he was trying to establish himself. He was entering his senior year and he wanted to show everyone that this was his team now. He got in some good battles. There was one day he and Raymond were going at it, and it takes a good bit to get Raymond outwardly frustrated.

Other than the jersey ceremony and the game, it wasn't exactly a wild and crazy New Year's. I went to the Melting Pot with my girlfriend and that was about it. In the past, I've always celebrated New Year's by being in the gym to shoot when the clock hits midnight. Unfortunately, this year the streak was broken because I had to be back at the Smith Center at 8:15 on January 1.

Game 13

Dayton 51
#2/2 North Carolina 81
Dec. 31, 2006 • Smith Center, Chapel Hill

UD	FG	3FG	FT	REB	PF	TP	A	TO	B	S	Min
Scott*	3-7	3-6	2-2	1-3-4	5	11	1	4	0	0	26
Little*	0-2	0-0	0-0	2-1-3	5	0	2	3	0	1	10
Huelsman*	2-5	0-0	0-0	0-4-4	1	4	0	1	1	0	26
Johnson*	6-13	1-2	1-2	0-4-4	1	14	1	2	0	4	29
Roberts*	5-17	2-7	2-3	0-2-2	3	14	1	4	0	2	32
Sandoval	0-4	0-1	2-2	0-1-1	1	2	3	1	0	2	18
Plummer	2-7	0-0	2-4	3-2-5	1	6	2	0	1	2	21
Binnie	0-3	0-1	0-0	0-1-1	3	0	0	3	0	1	19
Warren	0-1	0-0	0-1	0-0-0	1	0	4	3	0	1	14
Stafford	0-0	0-0	0-0	0-0-0	0	0	0	0	0	0	2
Adedeji	0-0	0-0	0-0	0-0-0	0	0	0	0	0	0	2
Hogan	0-0	0-0	0-0	0-0-0	0	0	0	0	0	0	1
TEAM				5-2-7							
Totals	18-59	6-17	9-14	11-20-31	21	51	14	21	2	13	200
Pct.	.305	.353	.643	DB: 2							

FG: (1st half: 7-32, .219; 2nd half: 11-27, .407)
3FG: (1st half: 2-8, .250; 2nd half: 4-9, .444)
FT: (1st half: 2-4, .500; 2nd half: 7-10, .700)

UNC	FG	3FG	FT	REB	PF	TP	A	TO	B	S	Min
Terry*	2-7	1-4	1-2	0-7-7	1	6	3	3	0	0	21
Wright*	8-9	0-0	0-0	2-4-6	1	16	1	3	1	1	26
Hansbrough*	7-11	0-1	3-5	3-0-3	1	17	0	2	0	0	26
Ellington*	6-11	3-5	0-0	0-2-2	1	15	1	2	0	0	24
Lawson*	2-4	0-1	1-3	1-2-3	1	5	7	1	0	3	19
Green	1-5	1-3	2-2	1-7-8	1	5	7	1	2	0	20
Thompson	0-2	0-0	2-2	0-2-2	4	2	1	4	2	2	14
Stepheson	2-4	0-0	1-2	2-4-6	3	5	0	1	2	0	12
Ginyard	1-1	0-0	0-0	0-1-1	3	2	0	2	1	1	14
Miller	1-2	1-1	2-2	0-1-1	1	5	2	1	0	3	18
Burke	1-1	1-1	0-0	0-0-0	0	3	0	1	0	0	2
Wood	0-1	0-1	0-0	0-0-0	0	0	1	0	0	0	2
Copeland	0-0	0-0	0-0	0-0-0	0	0	0	0	0	0	2
TEAM				2-3-5							
Totals	31-58	7-17	12-18	11-33-44	17	81	23	21	8	10	200
Pct.	.534	.412	.667	DB: 2							

FG: (1st half: 14-28, .500; 2nd half: 17-30, .567)
3FG: (1st half: 3-9, .333; 2nd half: 4-8, .500)
FT: (1st half: 3-5, .600; 2nd half: 9-13, .692)

Officials: Karl Hess, Mike Eades, Brian Dorsey
Attendance: 19,967 • Technical Fouls: None

Score by Periods	1st	2nd	Total
Dayton	18	33	51
North Carolina	34	47	81

The biggest change in January hasn't been the new calendar. It's been the fact that Bobby and Quentin are back from their injuries. Instead of just Ty and me getting repetitions at point guard, we've got four players trying to squeeze into that rotation. For that reason, I'm starting to also see some action at two-guard. That changes my role, but I'm a senior—I should be able to handle it. The main goal is to win basketball games.

I try not to spend too much time worrying about the rotation or minutes. If I don't have confidence in Coach Williams and his ability to handle those types of things, then I shouldn't be here. One thing I've learned about him during my time here: he is always going to make the best decision he can make to win a basketball game. Whether that's playing time, running a certain play, or any other coaching decision, he is making the choices he feels are best to help the team win. Because of that mindset, if you're on the bench it's hard to be upset because he's the leader, we trust him, and even those of us on the bench know he's doing the right thing to help us win.

That doesn't mean you never think about yourself. I didn't feel like I played very well when we beat Penn 102–64. I passed up a good shot during the game, which was something I've done less recently. When I went home after Penn, I thought to myself, 'If I'm not taking open shots or shots I should take, I'm hurting the team.' I'm a shooter. My role on offense is to spread the floor and open things up for everyone else. If I don't take those shots, then I'm just a 5-foot-10 guy playing defense.

I had been frustrated about my play after the game, and I tried to get out of the locker room pretty quickly after the game because we won by 38 points and I didn't want to drag anyone down. But you should never underestimate Coach Williams. While we were shooting free throws at practice the next day, he came up and said, "After the game yesterday, you had a look on your face I've never seen before. What was wrong?" I told him I was down on myself because I made a careless turnover. He said, "You have to be careful. You can't get too down on yourself. You have to understand the other guys look up to you. Be careful what you show on your face, because someone might interpret it the wrong way."

That hit home with me. I really was happy that we won the game. But even if I'm thinking about something that I could have done better individually, I can't let someone else interpret it as me having a bad attitude. That can lead to negative chemistry on our team. I'm in a position of leadership this year, and I have to constantly be aware of that position. I don't want anyone on our team to think it's OK to be upset about playing time. It all goes back to that name on the front of the jersey.

Our senior leader last year, David Noel, went through something similar. There was a stretch when he was really struggling and we weren't playing well at all. It's pretty easy to read his emotions, and Coach mentioned to David that other players were taking their cues from him—whether positive or negative. Being a senior comes with so much responsibility. Even the most talented guys will look to the older players to see how they handle certain situations. There is a time to reflect on your individual play. What I've learned is that it's not time to do that when you're in the locker room after a game. That time belongs to the team.

At the same time I was coming to the realization about leadership, I also made a new commitment to playing more effectively. It's pretty simple: I have to start shooting the ball. I have the confidence and my shot feels good, but I've been passing up shots. That has to stop. It paid off immediately, because the day after the Penn game in practice during live practice, I hit about 7 out of 10 of my three-pointers. It was the best shooting day I've had in practice by far this year. I hit open ones, I hit them with guys in my face, I hit them off the dribble, and I hit them on the move. It felt good, and I really felt a change in my mentality.

Game 14

Pennsylvania 64
#2/2 North Carolina 102
Jan. 3, 2007 • Smith Center, Chapel Hill

UP	FG	3FG	FT	REB	PF	TP	A	TO	B	S	Min
McMahon*	2-2	1-1	0-0	0-1-1	2	5	1	5	0	0	15
Zoller*	4-9	0-2	0-0	4-6-10	4	8	0	6	0	2	36
Danley*	1-5	0-1	4-7	0-2-2	3	6	2	1	0	0	20
Grandieri*	1-4	0-3	1-2	0-1-1	1	3	3	1	0	0	27
Jaaber*	8-12	2-4	3-4	2-2-4	2	21	8	2	2	3	35
Votel	2-5	0-1	0-0	2-1-3	3	4	3	0	0	0	10
Egee	3-12	2-6	0-0	1-1-2	2	8	0	3	1	0	22
Lewis	0-0	0-0	0-0	0-0-0	1	0	0	1	1	0	4
Kach	2-4	0-1	0-0	0-0-0	0	4	0	1	0	0	14
Reilly	1-2	0-0	0-0	0-0-0	1	2	0	0	0	0	4
Smith	0-1	0-1	1-2	0-1-1	0	1	0	0	0	0	7
Schreiber	1-3	0-0	0-0	1-0-1	3	2	1	0	0	0	6
TEAM				2-4-6				1			
Totals	**25-59**	**5-20**	**9-15**	**12-19-31**	**22**	**64**	**18**	**21**	**4**	**5**	**200**
Pct.	.424	.250	.600	DB: 8							

FG: (1st half: 13-23, .565; 2nd half: 12-36, .333)
3FG: (1st half: 3-8, .375; 2nd half: 2-12, .167)
FT: (1st half: 1-2, .500; 2nd half: 8-13, .615)

UNC	FG	3FG	FT	REB	PF	TP	A	TO	B	S	Min
Terry*	7-10	1-2	4-4	2-7-9	3	19	3	3	0	1	16
Wright*	5-7	0-0	2-3	1-6-7	0	12	2	1	1	0	25
Hansbrough*	6-13	0-0	7-10	3-2-5	1	19	3	0	1	4	28
Ellington*	6-13	4-8	1-2	1-2-3	2	17	1	0	0	1	25
Lawson*	2-4	0-1	0-0	0-1-1	1	4	2	1	0	2	22
Thompson	2-3	0-0	2-3	1-1-2	3	6	0	1	0	0	12
Green	1-3	0-1	2-2	1-0-1	3	4	1	1	1	0	14
Ginyard	1-3	0-0	0-0	0-2-2	1	2	1	0	0	2	13
Frasor	2-2	1-1	0-0	0-0-0	0	5	2	0	0	0	7
Miller	0-2	0-2	0-0	0-0-0	1	0	2	1	0	0	13
Stephenson	3-4	0-0	2-2	1-0-1	1	8	0	1	2	0	9
Copeland	0-2	0-0	0-0	1-2-3	0	0	2	1	0	1	6
Thomas	0-0	0-0	0-0	0-0-0	1	0	4	0	0	0	6
Burke	2-2	2-2	0-0	0-0-0	0	6	0	0	0	0	2
Wood	0-0	0-0	0-0	1-0-1	0	0	0	0	0	0	2
TEAM				1-0-1							
Totals	**37-68**	**8-17**	**20-26**	**13-23-36**	**17**	**102**	**23**	**10**	**5**	**11**	**200**
Pct.	.544	.471	.769	DB: 2							

FG: (1st half: 15-32, .469; 2nd half: 22-36, .611)
3FG: (1st half: 3-6, .500; 2nd half: 5-11, .455)
FT: (1st half: 6-7, .857; 2nd half: 14-19, .737)

Officials: Jamie Luckie, Roger Ayers, Earl Walton
Attendance: 19,378 • **Technical Fouls:** None

Score by Periods	1st	2nd	Total
Pennsylvania	30	34	64
North Carolina	39	63	102

It really fired me up to play that way in practice. I remember thinking, This is what I'm supposed to do. The only difference is that I decided I was actually going to do it today. I wasn't thinking twice about whether it was a bad shot. I just took it. That sounds like such a small change, but it made a huge difference. Now I want to carry those same thoughts over into games so I can avoid thinking too much.

Percentage-wise, my shot doesn't look great right now. As I've worked on my shot over the last month, I haven't found any major flaws. There were a couple little adjustments to my technique, but I think the biggest problem was with the shots I wasn't taking. It wasn't a physical flaw. It was a mentality issue. I'm very excited looking ahead to ACC play because I feel like now I'm ready to make big contributions to our team.

LUCAS: GOING ON INSTINCT

JAN. 3, 2007

Quentin Thomas had no good explanation for his most exciting play of the night.

Forget for just a moment that it was exciting merely to have him on the court. If you're scoring at home, Carolina has gone from three point guards to one point guard to one potentially injured point guard back to three point guards . . . all in the span of about one month.

Neither Thomas nor Bobby Frasor was content to make a quiet return to the lineup. That's how these things are supposed to happen. Work them in, steal a few quiet minutes, get the feel of the game again, and maybe look fully operational in a couple of weeks.

Neither player followed that script. Most of the suspense regarding Frasor's status was removed when he trotted out for warm-ups wearing the ankle braces he hadn't been wearing when he was dressing out with no thought of playing. He still received a thunderous round of applause when he checked into the game for the first time with 14:35 left in the first half.

Maybe that was when he was truly back. Or maybe it was when he gunned in a 3-pointer two minutes later. Or maybe, as his buddy Tyler Hansbrough said, it was one possession later.

"I knew he was back when he hit that high arching shot off the dribble," Hansbrough said. "That put an exclamation point on him being back."

Frasor last played on Dec. 2. Wednesday night, he somehow appeared to have missed over a month of action without missing a step. Everything was how it was supposed to be in Carolina's 102–64 romp over Penn—from his jumper to his no-look pass to Hansbrough for a dunk to his lob pass to the big man earlier in the second half.

The lob pass wasn't perfect. But that's typical for Frasor.

"I've never been the best lob passer," the Illinois native said with a smile.

The pass, which gave Frasor his first assist of the game, almost sailed out of bounds before Hansbrough reeled it in and deposited it for a basket. By that point, Carolina had built a 62–43 lead, so there was time for a little bit of fun.

"Hey, I'm not Brandan (Wright)," Hansbrough told Frasor on his way back up the court.

Frasor just tapped his chest, acknowledging his error with a big smile.

In many ways, Frasor was the ringleader of last year's freshman class and was assuming that role with the entire 2007 team when the injury dropped him in December. So maybe it wasn't a jumper or a pass, but a moment on the sidelines when he truly returned. With Carolina sitting on 98 points and needing another pair for the magical 100 mark, Frasor was in the middle of a delighted Tar Heel bench as the reserves searched for the century mark.

Dewey Burke had already made one 3-pointer. When he passed up another on the next possession, Frasor crashed his foot against the hardwood, expressing mock frustration at Burke's hesitation. There was no apparent concern for his foot, but there was an apparent release of a significant buildup of emotion.

"These last few weeks have been really tough on him," Marcus Ginyard said. "He's done a great job of putting a smile on and looking at it as positively as possible. If he could do something in practice, he was doing it. He did everything he could possibly do even though he wasn't playing in games."

In most cases, Frasor joined Thomas on the sideline during practice, the duo pedaling a stationary bike while their teammates sprinted.

The California junior, as seems to be his habit, snuck into the game without many fans noticing with 7:15 left in the first half. He quickly proved to have been studying the team intently from the sideline, as his first two passes found the red-hot Wayne Ellington for a pair of assists.

"My main issue was getting back out there and

feeling comfortable," Thomas said. "After an injury a lot of people are very timid, and I can honestly say when I first stepped out there I was kind of timid because I was hoping there was no pain."

By the second half, when the Tar Heels were turning deflections into points fast enough to earn cheap biscuits, the timidity was gone. And with two minutes left, Thomas added a bit of dazzle, dribbling between his legs at the top of the key, drawing a pair of Penn defenders, and then whipping a pass to Ginyard for an easy dunk.

"Had you been standing there a long time?" Thomas asked Ginyard during the next timeout.

"Nah, I just got there," the sophomore said.

Thomas smiled when recalling the play.

"I couldn't tell you how I saw him," he said. "I really don't know. Instinct, I guess. My guys know I love to pass.

"Instincts stay with you. I don't think you lose that instinct even when you miss some time."

Playing at North Carolina means everything we do will be scrutinized. People know who we are on campus, we have a big media group that comes to all our games, and we're on television almost every game.

I try not to pay attention to any of it.

My mom collects every single thing written about our team. She made a scrapbook of my junior season and it's got articles from websites and newspapers across the country. When I went back to look at it after the season, most of it was new to me.

During the season, I make it a point not to read about our team. That's a philosophy I started when I came to school here. No matter what you do at Carolina, because of the volume of people paying attention, there are always going to be those who like it and those who don't. Even when we're undefeated people will find flaws. My decision when I came to Carolina was that in order to be mentally tough enough to play here, I had to ignore it. I don't look at the papers and I don't read the internet.

That means it amazes me after the season when I go back and read and see the detail people get caught up in with our team. We're in a bubble within our team. We're so caught up with what's going on in the locker room or on the court that we don't think about what a big deal it is on a national level. People spend a phenomenal amount of time and money keeping up with us, and we kind of take the interest for granted. We're only interested in pleasing the coach and our teammates. It's a little strange to think that there are thousands of people out there who are living and dying with what we do every day.

Of course, it's human nature to care what other people say about you. That's why I don't want to know. If I don't know, then I don't care. The other big factor is that Coach Williams does such a great job of making us feel like the only thing that matters is what he and his staff think about us. They do that very simply: by evaluating every single thing we do. They grade every game and they chart every practice. It's such an organized system that there's no gray area. We're aware of the categories being judged and the standards for each one of them. We know what makes the coaches happy, and we know when we need to improve. That's why I don't worry so much if I hear about a story that says I'm playing poorly. If that's true, I already know it. If it's not true, I have the feedback from the coaching staff to show it's not true. More than any other team I've played on, Carolina basketball is all about pleasing the people in the locker room.

That doesn't mean other people don't tell us what to think. You can be playing terribly in Coach's eyes or on paper, and you'll still have people come up to you and say, "Wes, you're playing great. Coach isn't playing you as much as he should. You need more minutes." My mom is famous for doing that. She'll say, "I wish you played more." I usually say, "I'm not playing more because my defensive grades aren't good."

In my experience, people outside the program are always surprised when there's a definitive reason for why a certain player is starting or why someone is playing more than another guy. I guess they think Coach Williams is just doing things on feel or something. I can't think of one time since I've been here that I've felt someone was being treated wrongly or not played when they deserved to play.

Everything is in black-and-white if we have a question. All I have to do is look at my defensive grades or my assist-to-turnover ratio or my shooting percentages in games and practice. Coach spends a lot of time on little things—things like sprinting back to offense or sprinting back to defense. But Coach doesn't just talk about them, he shows us on video tape. When I'm not doing one of those little things, Coach doesn't just say, "Wes, you're not playing well." He says, "You're not defending the screen on the ball properly. I am going to show it to you on film. We work on this every day in Coach Holladay's guarding the ball station in defensive stations, and you do it right every day in practice but you're not carrying it through to games."

That has the effect of really diluting what we hear from outsiders. There's so much to back up what the coaches say. Even if you want to doubt them as a player because there's a natural tendency to believe you're always right, you can't keep doubting them when they have all this evidence. Nobody here denies that Coach Williams is the best person in the country at his job. So if it comes down to him telling you something against someone from your neighborhood telling you something, it's not productive to ignore what he's saying.

Defensive grades are a method the staff uses to quantify something—defensive production—that can be hard to put down on paper. They chart every single play after breaking down the film and we get the results at our next practice. Last year, I was often surprised because the grade I expected was lower than the actual grade I received. Now that I'm a senior and I've been around for so long, I have a much better feel for what those grades will be.

ACC games start next week. As a veteran, I'll try to explain to our team that there's nothing easy about what's coming up. We've had several blowouts in a row, and they need to understand it won't be that way in conference play. In Coach Williams's first year, we couldn't win a game on the road. Even the national championship season, we had some very tough battles. From the way practice has gone lately, I think we have the right mentality. In an ACC game, any win brings you that much closer to the regular season championship. That's how we want to play.

Maybe we haven't played the absolute toughest nonconference schedule. But we've still played some tough nonconference games. We went to New York and played a good Gonzaga team. We've played Tennessee, Kentucky, and Ohio State. We've been in some big games and we've responded well for the most part.

The one time we didn't respond well was against Gonzaga, which still hurts a little bit. I'd like to think we've improved so much since then. I'd hate to think we ever need a loss to jolt us, but the Gonzaga game had that effect on us. If you watch that game on tape and then watch any of our recent games, it's two different teams—not just defensively, but also offensively. We're moving the ball so much better now and we have a much better rhythm.

A big part of that offensive rhythm is Wayne Ellington. He has one of the best jump shots I've ever seen in my life. I'm a guy who has taken pride in my shot all my life, so I can really appreciate watching someone come in and perform the way he has. He shoots as well as anyone I've ever been on the court with.

Technically, he's fun to watch. I like the way he uses his legs and I like the way he really extends on his release and holds his follow-through. There are some mechanics there that might look funny to some people, but the rhythm and release are flawless.

Defensively, it's amazing how far he has come this year. The first couple games he looked a little lost, and he just picked up the defensive award in our last game. That's an impressive thing for a freshman to do.

You would think that a player with all those skills would be a little bit cocky. But I don't get that sense from him at all. He's plenty confident, but he doesn't carry it too far. I don't know one person on the team who has anything negative to say about him. Sometimes a freshman comes in and thinks he's the man and it has a ripple effect on the team. The combination of his attitude and his performance is the best possible situation for this team.

OUR FIRST CONFERENCE GAME was against Florida State, and it was the perfect illustration of how tough conference play will be. We've been blowing everyone out lately, and it was beneficial for our team to see a talented, athletic team like FSU. In the first half, we didn't play poorly, but we were still only ahead by six points. It was a nice reminder of what ACC play means. Then we came out in the second half and blitzed them defensively.

I don't think of a very athletic team like Florida State as one that gets tired easily. But when I looked out on the court in the second half, I saw an exhausted team. Al Thornton scored 29 points, but several of those were after the game was decided and I thought he was visibly tired in the second half. I give him a lot of credit, because he plays very hard, especially on the offensive end. That's much tougher to do when we're constantly running players in and out of the game and playing at our tempo.

Game 15

Florida State 58
#2/2 North Carolina 84
Jan. 7, 2007 • Smith Center, Chapel Hill

FSU	FG	3FG	FT	REB	PF	TP	A	TO	B	S	Min
Thornton*	11-19	3-4	4-5	4-8-12	3	29	0	3	0	1	33
Echefu	0-4	0-3	1-2	3-3-6	3	1	1	1	1	1	22
Rich*	4-8	1-1	1-2	0-5-5	0	10	1	1	1	0	29
Swann*	2-11	0-4	2-2	0-0-0	2	6	3	1	0	1	26
Douglas*	2-9	0-1	2-4	2-1-3	0	6	4	1	0	2	29
Mims	1-4	0-1	0-0	1-1-2	0	2	4	2	0	0	17
Allen	1-5	0-1	0-0	0-0-0	2	2	1	0	1	1	19
Reid	1-2	0-0	0-0	1-2-3	2	2	0	2	2	0	17
Breeden	0-2	0-0	0-0	0-2-2	4	0	0	0	0	0	8
TEAM				2-0-2							
Totals	**22-64**	**4-15**	**10-15**	**13-22-35**	**16**	**58**	**14**	**11**	**5**	**6**	**200**
Pct.	**.344**	**.267**	**.667**	**DB: 2**							

FG: (1st half: 12-30, .400; 2nd half: 10-34, .294)
3FG: (1st half: 2-5, .400; 2nd half: 2-10, .200)
FT: (1st half: 4-5, .800; 2nd half: 6-10, .600)

UNC	FG	3FG	FT	REB	PF	TP	A	TO	B	S	Min
Terry*	0-5	0-2	0-0	1-6-7	1	0	3	1	2	0	21
Wright*	9-13	0-0	2-2	3-2-5	0	20	1	1	0	0	26
Hansbrough*	8-12	0-0	9-10	4-9-13	3	25	1	1	1	0	28
Ellington*	3-12	1-7	0-0	1-3-4	2	7	5	1	0	0	20
Lawson*	2-6	0-0	0-0	0-3-3	3	4	4	2	0	4	26
Green	3-8	2-4	0-0	3-4-7	0	8	2	2	0	0	17
Thompson	1-1	0-0	2-2	0-0-0	2	4	0	1	0	1	16
Stephenson	1-2	0-0	0-0	1-1-2	1	2	0	0	0	0	4
Ginyard	3-4	0-0	1-2	2-1-3	0	7	2	0	0	0	19
Frasor	1-2	0-1	0-0	0-0-0	0	2	0	1	0	1	6
Thomas	0-0	0-0	0-0	1-1-2	2	0	3	0	0	1	7
Miller	1-4	1-3	0-0	0-0-0	0	3	0	0	0	0	7
Burke	0-0	0-0	0-0	0-0-0	0	0	0	0	0	0	1
Wood	1-1	0-0	0-0	0-0-0	0	2	0	0	0	0	1
Copeland	0-0	0-0	0-0	0-0-0	0	0	1	0	0	0	1
TEAM				0-1-1							
Totals	**33-70**	**4-17**	**14-16**	**16-31-47**	**14**	**84**	**22**	**10**	**3**	**7**	**200**
Pct.	**.471**	**.235**	**.875**	**DB: 2**							

FG: (1st half: 14-34, .412; 2nd half: 19-36, .528)
3FG: (1st half: 2-9, .222; 2nd half: 2-8, .250)
FT: (1st half: 6-8, .750; 2nd half: 8-8, 1.000)

Officials: Ted Valentine, Mike Eades, Gary Maxwell
Attendance: 21,010 • **Technical Fouls:** None

Score by Periods	1st	2nd	Total
Florida State	30	28	58
North Carolina	36	48	84

LUCAS: LOVING GOLIATH

JAN. 7, 2007

Frank Deford was looking exactly like you would expect Frank Deford to look.

This was last winter and he was sitting in his New York City apartment with an expansive view of the city to his right and books from floor to ceiling on his left. He looked every bit the part of the Manhattan fixture that he has become over his decades of standout sportswriting—he was even wearing an ascot. Seriously, an ascot.

He sat in a leather chair, hunched his 6-foot-4 frame while he was crossing his legs, and rubbed his chin as he pondered the question. All that was really needed to complete the scene was a smoldering pipe in one of his hands and Joe DiMaggio to walk into the room and start telling Marilyn Monroe stories.

There are some places in New York where you don't feel like you're in New York. In Frank Deford's living room, you are absolutely, positively, in New York City.

Deford was pondering this question: in sports, is there ever a completely loveable giant?

He answered it this way: "I don't think so. I don't think it can be loved. It's hard for me to imagine that in basketball at any level."

He was talking in the more specific sense about big players, about Wilt Chamberlain and Bill Russell. But he might also have been talking, in the bigger sense, about giant teams. Every year, in every sport, there exist a handful of teams that bludgeon their opponents into submission. They are the teams that cause other fans to storm the floor after an upset victory. They are the teams that some people hate.

Basketball is a fragile thing. Being number-one in January means absolutely nothing. But right now—right this minute, in the wake of the 84–58 win over what is an NCAA Tournament-quality Florida State team—Carolina is one of those teams.

And with all apologies to Frank Deford, it's delightful to watch.

Last year was fun. Really, it was. It was enjoyable to sneak up on everyone and scrap for every loose ball and play defense and be heartened by close losses to good teams.

But you know what else is fun? Dunking on people. Like when Tyler Hansbrough got the ball at the foul line early in the game, surveyed the defense, and decided his best option was to career towards the basket and finish the play with a vicious two-handed slam, causing his brother Greg to bounce out of his front-row seat and unleash a yell of "T-Booooonnnneeee" that could be heard all the way across the court.

Communicating on defense and contesting every pass is fun. Like when Florida State caught Carolina in a defensive switch in the first half and, for a brief moment, had superstar Al Thornton guarded by Wes Miller. Miller is a lot of things, but he is not the guy you want defending the rangy Thornton. But before FSU could take advantage of it, Danny Green had recognized the mismatch, and he and Miller shouted to each other to make the switch, and suddenly it was Green on Thornton, and that didn't seem like such a bad matchup. The possession ended in a missed Florida State jumper.

Missing shots is fun. Sometimes it is, and you know exactly what I mean. Like Vince Carter's off-the-backboard dunk attempt against Duke. Brandan Wright's first half one-hand alley-oop dunk attempt wasn't quite in that league, but it had the same quality that made everyone in the Smith Center rise out of their seats and start yelling, "Oooohhhhh!" as they saw the play develop. Then just as quickly the "Oooohhh!" turned to "Awwwww . . ." as the ball slammed off the back rim. They knew they had just missed, by the width of the iron, seeing an all-timer.

But they couldn't wait to see if it might happen again.

Maturity is fun. Like when Thornton dropped a three-pointer in Deon Thompson's face to make it 53–41 and then proceeded to tell him about it all the way down the court. What did Thompson do? He posted up, sealed off Thornton, and forced him to foul to prevent a basket. The foul was Thornton's third and he had to leave the game with 14:30 remaining.

Advantage: freshman.

So all those things are fun. Put them together and you get that moment in the game Roy Williams constantly preaches to his team about, the one they all wait to see: the moment when one team gives in.

Sunday night, it was as visible as perhaps you will ever see in an Atlantic Coast Conference basketball game.

"Oh yeah," said Brandan Wright, who played deceptively good defense on Thornton despite the Seminole's 29 points. "I started to see it at the end of the first half. They were really sucking wind. They were like eight deep and playing hard, but they were just outnumbered. Fatigue really set in."

Consider this: with seven minutes left Hansbrough took the ball from the wing to the basket and slammed through another two-hand dunk to make it 70–49. Four Seminoles were standing close by.

Not a single one even bothered to jump.

Thornton is a great player and will make All-ACC. But Sunday he couldn't keep up with a parade of Tar Heels.

"Al Thornton was really tired," Ty Lawson said. "He was really slowing down on defense."

"You could tell he was dead tired," Bobby Frasor said. "And when I saw that at that point in the game, I thought they probably didn't have anything left in the tank."

On Florida State's last possession, they melted 20 seconds off the clock and appeared content to run out the clock. Finally, Leonard Hamilton gave a half-hearted wave toward the basket, signaling for his team to somehow try to penetrate the pesky Carolina defense.

But they couldn't, and the 26-point margin of victory was preserved. This team hasn't won by less than double digits since November, and they haven't won by less than 21 points in 36 days.

After the usual exchange of handshakes, the two teams left the Smith Center court. Florida State players trudged toward the visiting locker room.

The Tar Heels, meanwhile, sprinted off the court. Hansbrough was the last player to leave. As he did, a fan leaned over the tunnel—11 rows above the court—and tried to slap Hansbrough's hand. The big man from Missouri jumped, extended his towel, and tried to connect.

He almost made it.

The Tar Heels continued down the tunnel, still bouncing. For the most part, they looked ready to play another half if needed. No one had any doubt what the outcome would be if 20 more minutes were placed on the clock.

"This may be the year we're glad we're not playing them but one time," Hamilton said.

That's a Goliath.

Don't you just love it?

Bobby and Quentin are back, and that's going to change my role. It's not something that has been specifically addressed, but it's obvious to me that with them back, my role shifts back to two-guard. I feel most comfortable at that position and had success there last year. The other issue, though, is playing time. You don't have to be a math major to figure out that with two very good players back in the rotation, minutes are going to become scarce. It's not just me—it's a lot of guys. With Bobby and Q back in the mix, Coach has reiterated that we're at the point of the season where the individual doesn't matter anymore. It's about our team.

I only played seven minutes against Florida State, and that's the fewest minutes I've played in a year and a half. After the game, the first thing Coach Williams said in the locker room in front of the whole team was how proud he was of the way I dealt with the situation. He liked that I played hard in the minutes I was on the floor. He made a good point, that he doesn't feel sorry for me because he doesn't feel sorry for anyone who plays college basketball. But to go from playing 20-plus minutes last year to this year's situation has been challenging. It meant a lot to me to have him recognize that. Lately I've been very conscious of making sure that if things aren't going well on the court, I can't let it get me down. If I get an opportunity to get in the game, that's great and I will do my best. If I don't, then I'm going to do the best job I can do to support my teammates. I'll find a way to be supportive on the bench and give them advice.

It's very evident right now that a lot of guys aren't going to play as many minutes as they played last year. So if one of them can look at me and say, "Wes played over 20 minutes per game last year and now he's playing single-digit minutes, but look at the way he's handling it. His main emphasis is helping North Carolina win basketball games." My hope is that if they're feeling a little down about their minutes, the way a senior handles a similar situation will be important to them. In some ways, that's my new role on this team. It's not an on-court role, but it's still something that can help us win. It's a great way for me to set an example, because a lot of people on this team are in the situation where they want to play more minutes.

I don't think there's been a point this year when I've had a bad attitude about minutes. But I still wanted to make a conscious effort to have a new attitude in the Florida State game. It was pretty simple: if I play, great, and I'm going to play hard. If I don't, great, and I'm going to cheer hard and support my teammates. What's so amazing is that in the first game with me trying hard to show that attitude, Coach Williams picked up on it. That's why he is going to be a Hall of Famer.

I gave some serious thought to the way I've handled the past month. I didn't realize that any frustrations were showing, but in hindsight I think they were. The Penn game was probably the low point. It's not that I was expecting more minutes, but based on the way the last few games had gone, I assumed that would probably be the case. When things didn't go the way I thought they would, I let that affect my play.

No other team I've played on could handle the playing time issue as well as this team has so far. We really have a group of great guys this year. I've been on enough teams to know that situation can cause major problems. But we don't have any issues at all in our locker room that I am aware of.

The Virginia game was a good one for all of us. We had been blowing teams out—the last time we won by less than 20 was over a month ago. We knew not to take Virginia for granted, because J.R. Reynolds and Sean Singletary are one of the best backcourts in the country. They're not just talented, they're also experienced, and that is significant in the Atlantic Coast Conference. Sometimes younger guys don't understand that. They see an opponent that's not one of our one or two biggest rivals and see that we're playing at home, and they take it for granted. The veterans tried to get across that when you're playing an ACC team, none of that matters. All these teams are good. All these teams want to beat us.

The first half was a big wake-up call for us. Coach Robinson had the scouting report for the game, and it included the fact that if you don't pick up Singletary early, he will come down and shoot it or he will penetrate and create easy shots. As a team, we didn't do a good job picking him up, and he was picking us apart. In our defense, that's not just the point guard's fault. It's the responsibility of the entire team.

I only played five minutes, but Coach did put me in the game at the end of the first half. The score was tied and we ran "Go," which is one of our favorite late-clock plays. I don't think it's a secret or anything: we go 1–4 and the point guard goes one-on-one, giving him a variety of choices. He can drop it down low, he can kick it to the wing, or he can take his own penetration and shot. It made me feel good that in a situation where I know the play calls for two good shooters on the wing, Coach wanted me to be one of those shooters.

As Ty was running down the clock, Reynolds was yelling at the man guarding me, "Don't leave him! He is a shooter!" As a shooter, that's good reinforcement for me. It also reminded me that even if I don't get the shot, I still have a role. People in the league remember the season I had last year and I still get a certain respect as a shooter. When they have to pay attention to me, that opens up other areas of the floor for my teammates. That's what happened on this play, because Ty kicked it to Reyshawn, and then Reyshawn made a good entry pass to Brandan Wright. The entry pass isn't necessarily a part of that play, but Coach always tells us that "playing basketball" is always part of the play. That's what

Reyshawn did, and it led to us scoring at the buzzer, which gave us a 39–37 lead.

Virginia shot over 44 percent in the first half, which is too high. In the second half, we adjusted. We did the things we'd gone over in practice the previous day, and we made the extra play on defense. We didn't shoot the ball that well, but we turned the game around with our defense. The game was nowhere near as pretty as some of our recent blowouts. But in the ACC, you have to be able to win a game when the shots aren't falling. I'd much rather see this team develop a defensive identity than an offensive identity. You can get through any situation with your defense. Offense isn't that simple. No matter how good you are on offense, there are still going to be nights when the shots don't fall. Every team has them. Even Michael Jordan had them. If you're completely reliant on your offense, you're opening yourself up for that one bad night, and in an NCAA Tournament situation one bad night can send you home. The way we run, developing that defensive identity will create our offense. We'll force turnovers, and that will lead to fast breaks, and that will lead to easy baskets.

Of course, that doesn't mean I don't want to knock down shots. I had a three-pointer in the second half that I felt might have been a back-breaker for Virginia. I was open on the wing, and I feel so comfortable in my shot right now that I knew it was going in. When it missed, it really pissed me off. I knew immediately it was a big shot, and I also knew it was my turn to be substituted for, which meant I wouldn't get another chance to make the big shot. But I thought the reaction of our team was amazing. Even before I got to the bench, Quentin and several other guys were meeting me, telling me to keep my head up, keep shooting, and keep playing good defense.

```
                          Game 16
Virginia 69
#1/1 North Carolina 79
Jan. 10, 2007 • Smith Center, Chapel Hill

UVa           FG    3FG   FT     REB    PF TP  A TO B  S  Min
Mikalauskas*  4-5   0-0   2-3    1-1-2   3 10  0  0 0  0   29
Cain*         4-7   0-0   0-0    1-7-8   5  8  1  2 1  1   28
Diane*        5-13  3-8   1-2    2-3-5   5 14  1  2 0  0   30
Reynolds*     5-14  1-5   4-5    1-2-3   4 15  7  2 0  1   35
Singletary*   5-11  3-8   1-1    0-1-1   4 14  7  8 0  1   32
Soroye        0-0   0-0   0-0    2-1-3   2  0  0  1 0  0   11
Josepth       1-2   1-2   0-0    0-3-3   1  3  0  1 0  0   12
Tucker        1-2   1-1   0-0    0-0-0   2  3  0  0 0  0    6
Harris        0-2   0-0   0-0    0-2-2   0  0  0  0 0  1    9
Tat           1-3   0-1   0-0    0-2-2   1  2  0  1 0  0    8
TEAM                             1-4-5            1
Totals        26-59 9-25  8-11   8-26-34 27 69 16 18 1  4  200
Pct.          .441  .360  .727   DB: 4
```

FG: (1st half: 15-34, .441; 2nd half: 11-25, .440)
3FG: (1st half: 5-13, .385; 2nd half: 4-12, .333)
FT: (1st half: 2-3, .667; 2nd half: 6-8, .750)

```
UNC           FG    3FG   FT     REB    PF TP  A TO B  S  Min
Terry*        0-1   0-1   4-4    3-2-5   3  4  1  1 1  1   21
Wright*       5-16  0-0   6-13   5-4-9   1 16  1  0 1  3   30
Hansbrough*   6-13  0-0   6-11   1-6-7   1 18  1  3 0  0   33
Ellington*    2-7   1-3   2-2    1-0-1   0  7  4  0 0  1   21
Lawson*       2-3   1-2   5-7    0-2-2   4 10  3  2 0  2   20
Thompson      4-8   0-0   0-0    3-1-4   0  8  0  1 2  2   13
Green         2-6   1-3   2-2    0-2-2   1  7  1  1 0  2   17
Ginyard       2-5   0-0   0-0    4-2-6   1  4  0  0 0  0   17
Frasor        0-3   0-2   0-0    0-1-1   2  0  2  0 0  0    9
Stepheson     0-0   0-0   0-0    1-0-1   0  0  0  1 0  0    4
Miller        0-2   0-2   0-0    0-0-0   1  0  1  0 0  0    5
Thomas        2-2   0-0   1-2    0-5-5   1  5  2  2 0  1   10
TEAM                             3-1-4
Totals        25-66 3-13  26-41  21-26-47 15 79 16 10 6 12 200
Pct.          .379  .231  .634   DB: 7
```

FG: (1st half: 14-37, .378; 2nd half: 11-29, .379)
3FG: (1st half: 2-9, .222; 2nd half: 1-4, .250)
FT: (1st half: 9-14, .643; 2nd half: 17-27, .630)

Officials: Mike Kitts, Curtis Shaw, Earl Walton
Attendance: 21,569 • Technical Fouls: None

```
Score by Periods  1st   2nd    Total
Virginia          37    32      69
North Carolina    39    40      79
```

Coming from Quentin, that didn't surprise me. He has come back from his injury and played some of the best games of his career. When he comes into the game, you feel a charge in the arena. He deserves to have so much success at Carolina. When I've felt like things aren't going the way I would like, he's the person who has inspired me about how to deal with those issues. Anyone who has seen our summer pickup games knows there are times you walk out of the gym thinking, "Quentin was the best player on the floor." Now he's showing it at a big time of year, and that makes our team that much better.

Reyshawn only took one shot against Virginia, and he missed it. He did get five rebounds, though, and he also had a steal and a block. As a senior, I have pressure. But Reyshawn has even more, because he's not just playing his last year of basketball at Carolina—he's trying to set himself up to make a living playing professionally. I haven't talked to him about it, but I'm sure that is weighing on him. If it is, he's done a good job of not bringing it into the locker room. Everyone knows that when he gets it going offensively, he's unstoppable. His place on the team is not in question.

LUCAS: ROLE PLAYING

JAN. 10, 2007

The mere mention of his comments from earlier this season caused Danny Green to wince.

Way back in late November, Green met with the media and dropped the following gem in a press conference:

"It's been a little confusing for some guys. Some guys are confused about what kind of roles they have on the team. We don't have a real set rotation, everybody doesn't have a set time that they're going to play."

The assembled media pounced on this quote like free Dove bars at the ACC Tournament. It was picked up by sideline reporters, dissected by fans, and eventually trickled back to Roy Williams.

Predictably, he was not pleased.

Despite running one of the nation's best college basketball programs, Williams believes in an extremely simple approach. Playing for him is easy: do what he asks, your minutes increase.

He is not big on defining roles. He does not have hour-long meetings throughout the week to discuss how players can contribute in upcoming games. He prefers just three assistant coaches sitting next to him, not six.

Before a practice soon after Green's comments, Williams faced his team with a perplexed look on his face. "Tyler, have I ever told you what your role is?" he asked Tyler Hansbrough.

The big sophomore answered in the negative. The question was repeated for several other players, with the consensus response that no one had ever had a specific responsibility outlined by the coaching staff. The role description for everyone was the same: be a basketball player. A smart, heady basketball player.

Green got the message. And for the record, he says he misspoke.

"I didn't mean that guys didn't know their roles," he said after Carolina's halting 79–69 win over Virginia. "I meant guys had to adjust to their roles. A lot of guys weren't used to playing the way they were playing. But that was early in the season. Now everyone has adjusted very well."

Carolina basketball observers devoted significant preseason time to figuring out who was going to start. Two months later, that talk seems silly— the real question is who's going to finish.

Wednesday, in one of the first late-game tests this team has had, Williams substituted 12 times in the final 2:25. In came Marcus Ginyard for defense. Out went Wayne Ellington. In came Green for free throw shooting. Out went Brandan Wright. With Ty Lawson in foul trouble, in came Wes Miller.

Williams made all his moves with a detached cool that suggested he already knew how things would work out. And, maybe, he did. Television cameras usually catch him when he's at his most volatile, like when he removed his jacket after a dubious charging call on Reyshawn Terry. But in the closing minutes, he has the best qualities of his mentor, Dean Smith. Remember Smith settling everyone on the sidelines in the closing seconds against Georgetown in 1982? Williams was one of those who had to be settled.

Those days are over. None of the 12 substitutions were made with any stomping. There was no screaming. Williams was at his most demonstrative when Virginia countered with a substitution and the Tar Heel head coach made the "Talk" motion with his right hand to make sure everyone knew which man they were guarding.

"He's at his most calm when the game is crazy," Bobby Frasor said. "I always think back to the game at Duke last year and how calm he was. When the other team is making runs, we look at our bench and see a leader who has faith in us and faith in the guys on the court.

"He's always thinking. Always. No matter

what's going on he is thinking, and to have him is a huge advantage for us."

It's an advantage because Williams knows how to use his pieces. He has three point guards. He deployed new fan favorite Quentin Thomas late in the first half. The stat sheet said Thomas had two turnovers and zero assists during that stretch, but he also earned a longer stint by playing solid defense on previously hot Sean Singletary.

Then, with 34 seconds left and the game tied at 37, Williams called timeout. He inserted Miller.

This is obvious, right? The Tar Heels were going to run the play that has worked so many times just before the half, with the point guard penetrating and kicking to Miller for a 3-pointer.

That's what Virginia thought. After all, they had seen it on film. They stuck to Miller on the wing. But when Lawson penetrated, he instead passed to Terry, who flicked it to Wright, who dropped in a 3-footer for a two-point halftime lead.

So maybe they don't have rigid roles. But with a 15–1 overall mark and 2–0 in the league, most of the Tar Heels have identified their own best qualities. No one had to meet with Ginyard to tell him he's a quality defender and offensive rebounding igniter. No one needed to inform Hansbrough he should pound away inside. And no, no one needed to tell Green he's the designated offensive sparkplug off the bench.

Everyone looks at the talent on the roster and thinks Carolina is a team of stars. In wins like Wednesday's, though, they look like a team of— sorry, Coach Williams—role players.

And what about those roles, Danny? Did you and your teammates ever figure them out?

"Right now, we don't really have any roles," he said. "We're just playing basketball. Just go out there and be a basketball player."

And what happens when everyone does exactly that?

The same expressive face that was wincing just minutes earlier now showed a wide smile.

"We get some wins."

Off the court, it's time to start my last semester at Carolina. I feel like I'm on permanent Christmas break. I have class on Monday and class on Wednesday and that's it. It's a beautiful thing. It's not like I'm cheating the system, because I've put in my time academically. I've taken all my classes, I've finished my major, and I've done pretty well academically.

My only class is naval weapons. It's absolutely fascinating. Our teacher is an active Navy pilot who is probably in his late 20s. I'm in that class Monday and Wednesday mornings, and then I'm also taking golf. So after learning about all these technologically advanced weapons, then I go out to the range and hit some golf balls—and that's for a class! It's a great way to finish out my academic career, to say the least.

I'm honestly not sure what I'm going to do with all my free time this semester. I'm not the kind of person who can sit around the house and watch TV. Who knows, maybe I'll really perfect my golf game this semester.

I'm still in my relationship with Ashley. It's difficult for her to date a guy who plays basketball for North Carolina. She didn't go to college here and doesn't live in Chapel Hill, so that makes it even more difficult. We get a lot of attention as players. Sometimes we don't even realize how much attention we get, because we're used to it. But people outside the team—like Ashley—realize every bit of it, and that can be tough for them. It's something we're working through.

In general, I think I'm pretty good about keeping off-the-court problems from impacting my on-court performance. It's much more difficult the opposite way—I have a hard time keeping my on-court problems from impacting me off the court. Ever since I was little, playing basketball has been an outlet for me. It's the one thing I can do where everything else is blocked out. When something is bothering me, the first thing I do is go to the gym to shoot. The flip side is that when something is bothering me on the court, it follows me everywhere I go. I've gotten better about restricting on-court problems to the court as I've gotten older, but it still sneaks in there sometimes. That's another reason why it can be hard to have a relationship when you're at this point of the season and everything is magnified.

WEEK FIFTEEN

As a veteran, I have learned something very important about this time of year. This is when we take a lot of one-night road trips for road Atlantic Coast Conference games, which means one thing: this is when you catch up on a lot of TV.

Not necessarily shows that are on television right now. But with so many shows coming out on DVD, you can buy a season of a show you might have missed and knock out several episodes on one trip. Last year during the season I got hooked on 24. During the course of the 2005–06 season, I watched all four seasons of 24. That's a lot of television. I can never watch that show when it comes on TV, because I get so hooked on it that I can't wait from week to week to see what will happen. I like watching it on DVD because there's no waiting.

But I've already exhausted all the *24* DVD's. So right now I've really gotten into a show called *The Wire*. When we're on the road, we don't have a rental car or a tour guide or anything like that. We have the team bus and we might have a shootaround at the gym and that's about it. So when I was stuck at the hotel during the Virginia Tech trip and there weren't any good basketball games on TV, I fired up a couple episodes of *The Wire* on my laptop. That probably makes me a pretty boring roommate—Wayne Ellington was my roommate in Blacksburg.

Unfortunately, my show selection was the only highlight of that trip. Before the game, everyone seemed loose. We were happy with how we had played recently. It wasn't one of those games where you get to the gym and it seems like everything goes wrong from the moment the team bus arrives. We jumped out to a lead and everyone thought it would be like so many of our other games this year—get an early lead and then sustain it throughout the game. But on the road in the ACC, it doesn't work that way.

The road environment shocked some of our guys. It was loud and their crowd was into it. You can't explain what it's like to play an ACC road game to someone who hasn't done it. We tried to tell some of the freshmen, but you can't appreciate it until fans are hanging over the rail yelling at you and they've looked in the media guide to find out the names of your parents and all that stuff. You could look at our freshmen and see they were taken aback by the way things went after we got that early lead, because we got down big quickly.

In addition to the problems on the scoreboard, Bobby Frasor hurt his foot again in the first half. I didn't see him do it, but when he came to the bench I heard people talking about it. I said, "Are you OK?" and he just shook his head. My initial reaction was one of disgust. I felt awful for him. To lose him when we were in a tight game really hurt our team. As a player, though, you have to put aside that initial reaction. I had to start thinking about how we were going to win the game and how Bobby's loss changed the way I needed to help us win.

Even with the deficit, the locker room was calm at halftime. Among the guys, we tried to come up with some constructive advice: "Do a better job taking care of the ball. Make the easy play. We're in the game, play better." We had the attitude that we had made some mistakes, but despite not playing well we were still in the game.

After halftime, when we were warming up, I told Bobby, "You might not be playing but we still need you in this game. We need you to be into it and we need you to pick guys up." In a lot of ways, Bobby is a natural leader. Part of it comes from being the point guard, but he also has a lot of natural leadership qualities. He understands the game and he understands where people need to be on the floor. I wanted to remind him that he could still provide some of the same leadership from the bench that he provides on the court.

I didn't feel like the first half was a major problem. We've come back from plenty of those deficits before. The big problem was continuing to play the same way for the first five or ten minutes of the second half. That's what put us in a bind. As the Virginia Tech lead kept growing, Coach Williams never totally lost it in the huddle. I've never seen him totally lose it. But it was obvious he was displeased with the way we were playing.

The amazing thing about Coach is that he can be very disappointed in us and still not call a timeout to let us know about it. He had confidence that we could work our way out of the hole and he wanted us to play through it. No matter what the situation was, he always seemed to believe we were going to win the game. I can't remember many games in my career when we were down by 23 points, but even in that situation, where a lot of coaches go through the motions, Coach Williams believes we're going to find a way to win the game.

Eventually, that carries over to the players. Coach tells us he's not going to be excited when we don't give up. Teams coached by Roy Williams never give up. Every one of his teams in every game in which they've trailed always makes a run. It's just an expectation at North Carolina when you play for Coach Williams. We're too good and too well-coached to get run out of any gym in the country.

That's why we kept battling against Virginia Tech. We still felt there was an opportunity to win the game. Tyler Hansbrough is not a big talker, but at one point he looked at me with his crazy voice and said, "Wes, we're winning this game." He said that three or four times over the course of the final six minutes. I said it right back to him, because everyone in our huddle had that same feeling. I've played basketball for a long time and I know how a blowout feels. You don't quit, but at a certain point some doubt comes into your mind and you realize winning the game might not happen.

I never felt that way in Blacksburg.

It's amazing how things snowball in the game of basketball. We were down 72–49 with 10:18 left and down 81–61 with 3:45 left. We got a couple baskets and a couple turnovers, and momentum started to shift. Of course, Coach had saved all his timeouts, so he was able to use them effectively and make all the right calls. We trapped more defensively.

Those late-game comebacks usually look frantic, but there's a method to our madness. It's a sign of how brilliant Coach Williams and his staff are with their game-planning. We're not just running around waving our arms, trying to get turnovers, and fouling. We wanted to trap the first pass after the in-bounds play. Then we wanted to sprint off and get another trap around halfcourt. And finally, after that we wanted to foul. When the comeback started, with over 3:30 left, we could afford to be selective. We wanted to foul anyone other than Zabian Dowdell because he is such a good free-throw shooter.

Inside the last 90 seconds, they were still up 85–77. At that point we didn't have time to wait for a second trap. Our strategy changed: if we didn't get a steal off the first trap, we fouled immediately on anyone other than Dowdell.

Ty Lawson made a layup and free throw with 16 seconds left to cut it to 91–88. We had taken it from a 20-point deficit to a one-possession game in a little over three minutes. At that point, though, we didn't have a choice of avoiding Dowdell anymore. We fouled him with 14 seconds left and he went to the line for a two-shot foul. At that moment, it actually went through my head that we were truly going to win the game. Until that point everything had been about getting close enough to make it interesting. Now I honestly felt we were going to win.

Earlier in the week, Coach Williams had told us that for his television show they did a segment on great Carolina comebacks, and they highlighted a 1983 game against Virginia. That team came back from ten points down in 4 minutes. We watched the entire finish to that game. That was in my mind when Dowdell was walking to the free throw line. I remember thinking, "This is so ironic. We just watched this on tape and now we're about to do it ourselves."

I'm not much of a talker on the court. But I was standing right behind him when he went to the free throw line and I said, "Just miss this for me, Zabian. Just miss this one." It just came out of me. He did miss the first shot, and I almost got chills. I could see what was going to happen in my head: he was going to miss the second one, we were going to come down the court and hit a three-pointer. It might even be me who hit the three-pointer. I thought, "If I get a good look at a three, I'm knocking it down."

But he made his second shot. We got a good look on our next possession, but it didn't go down. And from that point the outcome seemed obvious, and we lost 94–88.

There were some mixed feelings in the locker room. It was positive that we'd been down by 20 late in the game and made a great run. It was a good lesson for the younger guys: anything is possible. Don't give up and don't quit. That will give us some confidence later in the season.

But most of us were still thinking about those disappointing first 35 minutes of the game. Actually, it was more the middle 30 minutes of the game. We played well in the first five and very well in the last five. That means we've had significant leads in our last three losses—George Mason, Gonzaga, and now Virginia Tech. I can't explain why it happens that way. For some reason, we break down as a team after the first few minutes. We don't get in our stance defensively, we don't play our principles, and we don't make the easy play on offense.

We took a bus home from the game, which meant a brutal trip. We watched the tape of the game—it's one of those things where you don't want to relive it but you do want to watch it again to see where everything went wrong. It hurts to watch film after a game like that. It hurts to see all the little things that we work on every day in practice being ignored. To watch a team dismantle us and play harder than we did is very difficult. In some ways, being on a bus was the best possible scenario. We had time to watch the whole tape and then another whole hour after that to stew about what happened.

When you lose a game, you always think back to see if you can identify the point where it went wrong. This is a very loose team. We are always joking around before games. There are a lot of personalities and characters on our team, and more than any group I've been around, we enjoy being around each other. It can be two minutes before Coach Williams's pregame speech and it feels more like we're hanging out at someone's house watching a game on TV.

I'm more on the serious side, and that's something the other guys give me a hard time about. It's hard for me to be that loose right before tip-off. I've tried to realize that everyone prepares differently. And when we're joking around in the locker room and then go out and win by 30, it's not a problem. But when you lose you start to examine things more closely. For just a second, I wondered if everyone was taking it seriously enough. But then I think about how hard we practice and how much of a commitment everyone makes to this team, and it's impossible not to take it seriously. I believe we have a team of competitors, even if we might show it in different ways.

Not everyone has the same sense of perspective, though. When you're 18 or 19 years old, it's difficult to look past next year—sometimes it's hard to even look past next week. You don't realize how fast it goes by. Coach Williams always tells us how fast our career will be over. I've tried to take the advice of past seniors when they talk about how fast it's over. But as a college student, it's almost impossible to have a true sense of appreciation. It's easier for me because I'm a senior and this is something I've wanted my whole life. It's harder for a freshman to be completely immersed in every single second. That's where having a young team might hurt us. It's not their fault. It's just that they don't understand. It doesn't matter how talented a freshman might be. They're still going to have trouble appreciating the moment—and therefore sometimes they don't realize the importance of the situation.

How important is it, really? That's not something we ask ourselves very often. It's the most important thing we do. Everyone we know wants to talk about basketball. We're on TV more than *Friends* reruns. So we're not pleased with the way we played in Blacksburg. It shouldn't be OK with anyone.

```
                              Game 17
#1/1 North Carolina 88
Virginia Tech 94
Jan. 13, 2007 • Cassell Coliseum, Blacksburg, Va.
```

UNC	FG	3FG	FT	REB	PF	TP	A	TO	B	S	Min
Terry*	2-6	1-3	0-0	1-2-3	1	5	3	2	0	2	16
Wright*	6-9	0-0	1-8	3-5-8	2	13	0	3	2	0	25
Hansbrough*	5-13	0-1	9-10	8-7-15	2	19	1	4	1	0	34
Ellington*	4-12	2-8	2-2	1-1-2	2	12	1	1	0	1	27
Lawson*	6-10	2-3	2-3	0-3-3	4	16	6	4	0	3	24
Ginyard	2-6	0-1	1-2	3-0-3	5	5	0	0	0	0	19
Frasor	0-1	0-1	1-2	0-1-1	1	1	1	1	0	0	6
Thomas	0-1	0-0	0-0	0-1-1	1	0	2	0	0	0	7
Green	1-5	1-4	0-0	1-3-4	3	3	0	2	1	1	14
Thompson	3-3	0-0	0-2	0-0-0	2	6	0	0	0	0	10
Miller	2-5	2-5	0-0	1-0-1	2	6	2	0	0	0	14
Stepheson	1-2	0-0	0-0	0-1-1	0	2	0	0	0	0	4
TEAM				3-2-5							
Totals	32-73	8-26	16-29	24-23-47	25	88	16	17	4	7	200
Pct.	.438	.308	.552	DB: 7							

FG: (1st half: 15-31, .484; 2nd half: 17-42, .405)
3FG: (1st half: 3-8, .375; 2nd half: 5-18, .278)
FT: (1st half: 4-9, .444; 2nd half: 12-20, .600)

VT	FG	3FG	FT	REB	PF	TP	A	TO	B	S	Min
Washington*	3-6	0-1	0-0	2-1-3	5	6	1	1	0	1	10
Lewis*	0-2	0-0	0-0	0-2-2	4	0	0	0	0	0	10
Collins*	4-6	0-0	4-4	2-3-5	2	12	0	1	2	2	29
Dowdell*	5-9	2-3	11-15	0-3-3	0	23	3	4	0	4	33
Gordon*	6-16	0-2	5-7	1-5-6	4	17	6	3	0	5	32
Munson	3-4	2-2	2-2	0-2-2	2	10	3	1	0	0	17
Krabendam	0-0	0-0	0-0	0-1-1	1	0	0	0	0	0	8
Sailes	0-0	0-0	0-4	0-0-0	1	0	0	0	0	0	11
Diakite	3-4	0-0	0-0	2-1-3	5	6	0	0	3	0	14
Vassallo	5-9	2-4	5-6	2-1-3	3	17	1	1	0	1	28
Tucker	1-1	1-1	0-0	0-0-0	0	3	0	0	0	1	8
TEAM				0-5-5							
Totals	30-57	7-13	27-38	9-24-33	27	94	14	11	5	14	200
Pct.	.526	.538	.711	DB: 5							

FG: (1st half: 17-33, .515; 2nd half: 13-24, .542)
3FG: (1st half: 6-9, .667; 2nd half: 1-4, .250)
FT: (1st half: 7-9, .778; 2nd half: 20-29, .690)

Officials: Mike Wood, Ray Natili, Sean Hull
Attendance: 9,487 • **Technical Fouls:** None

Score by Periods	1st	2nd	Total
North Carolina	37	51	88
Virginia Tech	47	47	94

At the same time, it's a college basketball game. That was reinforced to us on the day after the game, because we had our annual Special Olympics clinic. Coach Williams brought that tradition with him from Kansas, and Special Olympians come from all over the state to spend three hours with us going through a mini-clinic. It really puts the Virginia Tech game in perspective. In my time here, it's always been one of my favorite days of the season. One of the first things a couple of the Special Olympians in my group said was, "You guys sure didn't play very well last night." Then the very next thing they said was, "We still love you."

What can you say to that? They don't care whether we won or lost. All they care about is getting to play in the Smith Center and having a little bit of fun with us. It's amazing to see how happy they are and how much they enjoy life.

LUCAS: SPECIAL CLINIC FOR TAR HEELS

JAN. 14, 2007

William Graves hasn't played a single second for North Carolina this season.

But he picked up an assist on one of the biggest baskets of the year on Sunday.

The Tar Heels hosted their fourth annual Special Olympics clinic at the Smith Center on Sunday, bringing together 100 athletes from 21 local programs across the state. The group making the longest trip was the Watauga County organization, which left Boone at 9 a.m. to make sure they'd be standing at the doors when they opened at 1 p.m. That's exactly the response Roy Williams hoped for when he began the clinic at Kansas and then imported it to Carolina.

"My son Mieszko came in my bedroom at 6 a.m. this morning," said Jon Kwiatkowski, one of the Watauga volunteers and the parent of a Special Olympian. "It was like Christmas morning. He couldn't understand why we would still be in bed when it was such a big day."

The first hour of the two-hour clinic was devoted to skill stations. At least three Tar Heels were at every station. There was some skill instruction, of course. Marcus Ginyard and Dewey Burke and Marc Campbell instructed the athletes at the free throw station to bend their knees and follow through.

More importantly, though, there was fun. Made free throws were required to be accompanied by a loud, "Whoooossshhh!" from everyone at the station. Across the court, Wayne Ellington, Wes Miller, Alex Stepheson, and Surry Wood were hunkering down on defense and trying to prevent blow-bys as the Special Olympians worked on their dribbling. When one particularly adventurous participant chose to toss in a spin move, he was greeted with a multitude of high fives.

Steve Robinson concluded his shooting station by asking his charges, "Who here is a Tar Heel fan?" His repetition of the question drove one particular camper into a frenzy, who started bounding around like she was in the middle of a Tar Heel post-victory mosh pit. With that, the group moved to the next station; as Tyler Hansbrough escorted them to the passing area, he couldn't stop smiling.

Watching the stations, it was impossible not to be captivated by one particular Special Olympian. Durham's Tyler Coburn will turn 8 in May, making him by far the youngest participant. He's been to so many doctors in his young life that he usually bursts into tears whenever the Coburns come into sight of Duke University Hospital, even if they're just passing by.

The only medical conclusion so far is that he's developmentally delayed, which means his communication skills are extremely limited. His father, R.C., accompanied him from station to station. The dad stood right behind his son while Tyler worked on chest passes and followed closely behind at the dribbling station.

Graves, who is redshirting, was supposedly running layup lines. But he couldn't resist taking his students over to the lower goals beyond one Smith Center baseline. The rims there were about seven feet high.

That was still about four and a half feet too high for Tyler. He took the ball, ran up to the rim . . . and stopped. This was perplexing.

That's when Graves swooped in. He grabbed Tyler around the waist, hoisted him into the air, and suddenly Tyler was at eye level with the rim. The next step was obvious: the laughing 7-year-old slammed the ball through the rim.

Upon returning to earth, Tyler pumped his fist. He ran straight to his mother, striking a pose so she could capture the moment with her camera. Then he got back in line—on his next turn, he and

Graves threw down a vicious two-handed 360 dunk.

"This just makes your heart melt," said Tyler's father. "You want so badly for him to have as good an adult life as possible. He may not have the typical joys in life. He may not get his high school diploma. He may not go to college. He may not get married or go to the prom or drive. And as a parent, it's so terrific to see him get to enjoy things like this. You want to capture it and hold on to it."

He certainly captured the Tar Heels. At the shooting station, Bobby Frasor tried lifting him three straight times to make a shot on the 10-foot goal. All three shots bounded off the rim.

With the clock running down on the 8-minute segment of the clinic, Frasor picked him up one more time. This time, Tyler's aim was perfect. The ball swished through the net and the parents assembled in the nearby Smith Center stands burst into cheers that rivaled anything you heard at the Ohio State game.

After the stations, the campers and the Tar Heels split into teams for 5-minute half-court scrimmages. Play was fierce—after one participant swatted a blocked shot and accompanied it with a hearty yell, Ginyard said, "If I blocked a shot like that, I would *never* stop talking about it. Never."

Carolina players were reduced primarily to screeners and passers, clearing the way for the Special Olympians to rack up the baskets.

The scrimmages were followed by a 15-minute

autograph session. Every participant received a team poster, and most secured the autographs of virtually every player and coach. R.C. Coburn held his son's poster—with freshly inked Roy Williams and Reyshawn Terry signatures—for him as the duo walked off the Smith Center court.

"For me?" Tyler asked.

"This is all for you," his dad said.

His son's response was immediate and energetic. "Yesssssssss!"

We had the Special Olympics clinic Sunday and I was confident we were going to have a very tough practice on Monday. Our next game wasn't until the trip to Clemson on Wednesday, so Tuesday would be lighter, but I knew Monday would be rough. Coach came out with a simple attitude: "The way we played against Virginia Tech is not OK. I'm not going to condone it. I'm not going to accept it."

Coach got after us, and we needed it. We all needed to hear where our mistakes were coming from. Absolutely nothing slipped in practice on Monday. We either did it exactly the way the coaches demand or we repeated the drill. For this time of year, it was an extremely tough practice. If we're going to turn it around, the two practices before the Clemson game were going to be critical.

The Monday practice was almost critical for the wrong reason, because Tyler Hansbrough took an extremely hard fall. I was on the sideline for the play. He went up to dunk it and caught some contact going up. That contact flipped him sideways and he fell parallel to the ground directly on his back. It was one of the hardest falls I have ever seen. It felt like they probably should've felt the earth move on Franklin Street. There's a pretty simple rule with Tyler, because he takes a ton of contact: if he doesn't bounce right back up, something is wrong. He likes contact more than anyone I've ever seen. But after this one, he didn't jump right back to his feet. That's when everyone started thinking, "He better be OK." Fortunately, it was just the wind knocked out of him. We've had a ton of injuries at the guard positions but have been very fortunate with our big men. This wasn't the time to start having bad injury luck in the post.

The day before the game is the only time we think about our next opponent. It's the same routine every time: watch film of the opponent before practice. Then we go out on the court and go through some of their plays. Usually, those practices are a little more relaxed. That wasn't the case before the Clemson game. Monday had been such a hard practice, and some of those feelings were still lingering on Tuesday.

We had a really good drill in which Coach put six players on the Blue Team to simulate Clemson's pressing defensive style. They pressed five guys on the White Team to give the White Team a feel for how it seems like Clemson is all over the court after a made basket.

We finished practice with an unusually competitive drill. We hadn't done it in a long time and definitely not on the day before a game. It's pretty simple: we split into the Blue Team and the White Team and play halfcourt defense. The team with the most stops wins the drill. The White Team just kicked our butts. It wasn't like we laid down. We were competing hard, but they just blew us out. As a penalty for losing the drill, our Blue Team had to run a 68, which is 12 crossings of the court in 68 seconds. It's extremely difficult. We usually run 33's—six crossings in 33 seconds. This was double that drill, so the competitive juices were really flowing by the time we finished. There wasn't nearly as much joking. This was exactly the right time of the season to have a couple of very intense practices. I felt a marked difference in everyone as we stretched when it was over. The emotions were high—the White guys were happy they won and the Blue guys were ticked.

Will Graves was my roommate at Clemson, and I had heard worrisome reports that he was the biggest snorer on the team. But I finished Season 3 of *The Wire* on DVD, and when I went to sleep I didn't notice his snoring a single time. Does that mean I'm a big snorer, too? I was just happy it turned out to be untrue, because I was in dire need of good sleep and the last thing I needed was some trombone over there across the room keeping me awake.

Our game didn't start until 9 p.m., which makes for a very long day. Usually we sleep in a little and eat a late breakfast. We have roughly an hour of shootaround at the gym, come back to the hotel, and then it's time for pregame meal. Then we have a couple of hours until the bus leaves. It's a lot of sitting. The coaches try to break it up for us—we're never sitting there in our room for more than 90 minutes at a time. You can't let a group of college kids sit around a hotel all day without doing anything or they'll have trouble getting ready for the game.

This was my second trip to Littlejohn Coliseum. It's not an easy place to play and lately we haven't played very well there. Clemson has had a great start to the season, so we knew it would be loud—and it was. But around halfway through the first half, I felt their crowd lose some energy. At North Carolina, we love that feeling. We want to come into a hostile building and take the crowd completely out of it. One of the best joys in college basketball is sitting on the bench watching the home fans leave their seats early to beat the traffic in the parking lot.

We got a solid 22-point win. It was our first ACC road win, so we jumped around a little in the locker room. The mosh pit is one of the best experiences of the season. The bigger the win, the more we jump around. At this point, I've just accepted the mosh pit as part of Carolina basketball. It's something Coach Williams brought with him from Kansas. I don't even know how it started. I think the first time we did it must have been after the win over Connecticut during my redshirt year. Coach just started jumping around and the next thing I know, we were all jumping around.

Coach just said a couple words to us after the game. He told us how proud he was of the way we played. We said our prayer, and after we break following the prayer usually guys are just laughing with each other. All of a sudden somebody yelled out, "Danny got banged on!"

Poor Danny. He really did get dunked on pretty hard during the game, and that was the first thing that came up in the locker room after our normal victory routine. Poor guy. That shows you how tight this team is. They're not going to let you live anything down.

The last time he got dunked on, it was against Ohio State and it was my fault. This time, it wasn't me. As usual, Bobby can't hold things back so he blurted out, "And it was

Marcus's fault because he turned the ball over!" That doesn't help Danny, though. He's the one who will be on SportsCenter.

Game 18

#4/4 North Carolina 77
#19/16 Clemson 55
Jan. 17, 2007 • Littlejohn Coliseum, Clemson, S.C.

UNC	FG	3FG	FT	REB	PF	TP	A	TO	B	S	Min
Terry*	3-9	1-3	1-1	1-6-7	3	8	2	3	0	2	26
Wright*	8-10	0-0	1-3	1-3-4	2	17	0	1	4	1	29
Hansbrough*	5-10	0-0	6-8	3-4-7	2	16	1	2	1	1	31
Ellington*	5-8	1-2	0-0	0-3-3	1	11	4	2	0	0	23
Lawson*	1-4	0-1	0-0	1-0-1	4	2	3	7	0	2	22
Ginyard	0-1	0-0	0-0	0-2-2	3	0	1	3	0	3	15
Thomas	0-3	0-0	0-0	0-3-3	2	0	4	3	0	1	10
Green	3-5	1-2	3-4	1-2-3	2	10	0	1	1	0	13
Burke	0-0	0-0	0-0	0-0-0	0	0	0	0	0	0	1
Thompson	3-6	0-0	1-1	1-1-2	1	7	2	0	0	1	13
Miller	1-1	0-0	0-0	0-1-1	0	2	0	0	0	0	9
Wood	0-0	0-0	0-0	0-1-1	0	0	0	0	0	0	1
Stepheson	0-1	0-0	0-0	0-5-5	1	0	0	0	0	0	6
Copeland	2-2	0-0	0-0	0-0-0	0	4	0	0	0	0	1
TEAM				3-5-8							
Totals	**31-60**	**3-8**	**12-17**	**11-36-47**	**21**	**77**	**17**	**22**	**6**	**11**	**200**
Pct.	**.517**	**.375**	**.706**	**DB: 3**							

FG: (1st half: 16-31, .516; 2nd half: 15-29, .517)
3FG: (1st half: 3-5, .600; 2nd half: 0-3, .000)
FT: (1st half: 9-12, .750; 2nd half: 3-5, .600)

CU	FG	3FG	FT	REB	PF	TP	A	TO	B	S	Min
Perry*	1-5	0-0	0-3	2-4-6	0	2	1	3	2	3	16
Mays*	5-12	1-2	4-6	1-0-1	4	15	1	3	0	4	32
Booker*	2-7	0-0	0-2	2-3-5	2	4	1	3	8	0	22
Hamilton*	5-12	0-2	0-3	2-1-3	2	10	1	3	0	6	29
Hammonds*	6-13	2-7	1-3	1-4-5	1	15	3	3	1	3	32
Rivers	2-9	0-4	0-0	3-4-7	2	4	1	1	1	0	23
Tyler	0-1	0-0	0-0	0-0-0	0	0	1	0	0	0	4
Sykes	0-0	0-0	0-0	2-0-2	2	0	0	1	0	1	11
Potter	1-7	0-2	0-0	0-1-1	0	2	0	0	0	1	15
Morris	1-1	1-1	0-0	0-1-1	1	3	0	0	0	1	4
Powell	0-1	0-1	0-0	0-0-0	0	0	0	2	0	1	9
Petrukonis	0-0	0-0	0-2	0-1-1	0	0	0	0	0	0	3
TEAM				5-1-6							
Totals	**23-68**	**4-19**	**5-19**	**18-20-38**	**14**	**55**	**9**	**19**	**12**	**20**	**200**
Pct.	**.338**	**.211**	**.263**	**DB: 5**							

FG: (1st half: 12-34, .353; 2nd half: 11-34, .324)
3FG: (1st half: 3-12, .250; 2nd half: 1-7, .143)
FT: (1st half: 4-10, .400; 2nd half: 1-9, .111)

Officials: Mike Eades, Roger Ayers, Duke Edsall
Attendance: 10,000 • **Technical Fouls:** None

Score by Periods	1st	2nd	Total
North Carolina	44	33	77
Clemson	31	24	55

ESPN's COLLEGE GAMEDAY is in town this weekend. That means Hubert Davis is back in Chapel Hill, but he won't have to do much preparation to learn about our team. He practiced with us several times last year. We were short on bodies and Hubert was in town, so Coach asked him to join us. King Rice, a former point guard under Coach Smith, also was a regular, and on the first day Hubert showed up King gave me the following advice: "Watch Hubert, because he's never wrong."

He didn't mean that in the sense that Coach Williams would never get on a veteran (even though that's probably true). He meant that Hubert never made a mistake. Never. Any time Coach needed to make an example with someone,

Hubert was always the guy he used. That's why he was so successful and played in the NBA for so many years. This year he's done a great job on ESPN and I've enjoyed seeing him give us a couple shout-outs.

That's not the only ESPN coverage we received this week. A couple days ago, someone told me I definitely had to read the story on us in ESPN the Magazine. It's just one page: a big picture of Tyler and the headline, "Ten things you don't know about North Carolina."

I start reading the story, and what's number one?

"Wes Miller is a nerd."

It was a good prank. Even better than the joke itself was watching Tyler's face as he waited for me to get to that point in the story. He had been waiting for that moment all day. I'm sure he thinks it's the best prank he has pulled all year.

I don't think I knew I had a reputation for being a nerd. I do read the paper. If reading the paper makes you a nerd, then that's what I am. And of course he had to make a comment about my age, but being old doesn't make you a nerd, it just makes you experienced.

The good news is that with GameDay coming this weekend, I might have a good opportunity to get him back on national television. I don't think he wants me to bring Erin Andrews into this, but I will if necessary.

GameDay is an obvious way to show how much excitement is around the program. I watched it on television from my house—it looked like a great crowd. Anytime you have ESPN setting up on your home court with a couple thousand screaming fans behind them, it's obvious why anyone would want to play basketball at North Carolina. Marcus went to the Smith Center to watch part of the show, and he said he couldn't believe how loud and rowdy they were.

The highlight of the show came when a student made a halfcourt shot on his first try. I've always said with nobody guarding me, I can make 1-out-of-5 from halfcourt. If I take time to get my steps right and get my rhythm, that's the best I can do. This guy had on Carolina blue crocs, a toga, and didn't have an opportunity to get ready. As I watched, I thought, "This guy has no chance to make it." I was in one room and Preston Puckett, our head manager, was in another room, and as soon as it went in both of us started going crazy. It was a great way to start the day.

Oh yeah, and we also had to play a game. With all the talk about ESPN it was easy for the fans to forget about Georgia Tech. Not for us, though. They're 13–4, which is a couple more losses than people expected. But they are a very big, athletic, talented team. They are much better than their record. They also have some Carolina connections—Thaddeus Young visited here and really liked his visit, and Anthony Morrow attended Charlotte Latin. His high school coach works camp here every year. It always makes me nervous when the opponent has a couple players who had some interest in North Carolina. It means they're going to play that much harder.

Thaddeus is a special case, because when he visited it felt like he had a major interest in playing at Carolina. He's going to have a great college career and a great NBA career. He'll make a lot of money playing basketball. But his story also makes me realize how fortunate I am to play at Carolina. This experience is so unique. I'm sure on some level players who don't come here understand that they're missing out on something, but you don't realize how much until you're actually here. It's important not to take it for granted.

Game 19

Georgia Tech 61
#4/4 North Carolina 77
Jan. 20, 2007 • Smith Center, Chapel Hill

GT	FG	3FG	FT	REB	PF	TP	A	TO	B	S	Min
Smith*	2-6	0-0	2-6	2-3-5	1	6	2	2	0	2	27
Young*	10-16	2-5	0-0	3-0-3	3	22	0	3	0	2	32
Dickey*	3-6	0-0	0-0	1-3-4	4	6	0	5	2	2	33
Crittenton*	2-10	1-4	2-2	0-2-2	0	7	3	7	0	2	36
West*	0-5	0-2	2-2	4-2-6	4	2	2	1	0	3	19
Morrow	4-6	2-4	0-0	1-2-3	4	10	0	0	0	0	22
Peacock	2-5	0-0	0-0	0-2-2	3	4	2	1	0	1	14
Bell	0-0	0-0	0-0	0-0-0	0	0	0	0	0	0	5
Faye	2-6	0-2	0-0	1-2-3	4	4	0	0	2	0	11
Diaw	0-0	0-0	0-0	0-0-0	0	0	0	0	0	0	1
TEAM				1-5-6				2			
Totals	**25-60**	**5-17**	**6-10**	**13-21-34**	**23**	**61**	**9**	**21**	**4**	**12**	**200**
Pct.	.417	.294	.600	DB: 4							

FG: (1st half: 10-29, .345; 2nd half: 15-31, .485)
3FG: (1st half: 2-10, .200; 2nd half: 3-7, .429)
FT: (1st half: 1-2, .500; 2nd half: 5-8, .625)

UNC	FG	3FG	FT	REB	PF	TP	A	TO	B	S	Min
Terry*	7-9	2-2	0-3	3-1-4	0	16	0	3	1	1	25
Wright*	3-6	0-0	3-4	1-3-4	2	9	2	1	1	1	28
Hansbrough*	5-11	0-0	14-15	4-2-6	3	24	1	3	0	1	31
Ellington*	3-9	1-3	0-0	0-3-3	0	7	3	1	0	0	21
Lawson*	2-5	1-2	2-5	0-5-5	2	7	4	4	0	1	26
Green	2-5	1-2	0-0	1-3-4	1	5	2	1	1	1	15
Thomas	0-0	0-0	0-0	0-2-2	0	0	2	0	1	1	13
Thompson	1-2	0-0	0-0	2-0-2	0	2	1	2	1	3	13
Stepheson	0-1	0-0	0-0	1-1-2	0	0	0	0	0	0	6
Ginyard	2-3	0-0	0-0	1-0-1	1	4	0	2	0	1	12
Miller	1-3	1-3	0-0	0-0-0	2	3	0	2	0	0	7
Burke	0-0	0-0	0-0	0-0-0	0	0	0	0	0	0	1
Wood	0-0	0-0	0-0	0-0-0	0	0	0	0	0	0	1
Copeland	0-1	0-0	0-0	0-1-1	0	0	0	0	0	0	1
TEAM				0-1-1							
Totals	**26-55**	**6-12**	**19-27**	**13-22-35**	**11**	**77**	**15**	**19**	**5**	**10**	**200**
Pct.	.473	.500	.704	DB: 7							

FG: (1st half: 13-28, .464; 2nd half: 13-27, .481)
3FG: (1st half: 5-8, .625; 2nd half: 1-4, .250)
FT: (1st half: 3-7, .429; 2nd half: 16-20, .800)

Officials: Ted Valentine, Les Jones, Ray Natili
Attendance: 21,750 • **Technical Fouls:** None

Score by Periods	1st	2nd	Total
Georgia Tech	23	38	61
North Carolina	34	43	77

One way to avoid taking it for granted is playing hard all the time. I've always wanted to be someone who provides energy when I check into the game. I never thought I would be a starter or someone who plays 30 minutes a game—that happened to me at a point last year, and that was unbelievable. But it's not something I depended on. I've always wanted to bring something defensively, threaten defenses from the three-point line, and try to make good decisions. Playing tough defense is the best way to bring a spark to the game. Earlier in the season, there were times I felt I was trying too hard not to make mistakes. Now I'm playing more the way I want to play.

The Georgia Tech game never developed a flow because it was so physical. There was no chance to get on a run because someone was always shooting free throws or taking the ball out of bounds. The arena got quiet, and I was sitting at the scorer's table next to Danny Green waiting to check into the game. I looked at him and said, "Danny, we've got to pick this up." When we got on the floor, I focused on picking up defensively full-court and trying to turn their point guard. Those kinds of plays have two benefits: they tend to get my teammates more involved and then excite the crowd.

LUCAS: A NEW REPUTATION

JAN. 20, 2007

Maybe this will happen at some point before the end of the season: Carolina will be playing a big game against a quality opponent. The game will be broken down on national television. And at some point, one of the talking heads will say, "Well, (fill in opponent) better be ready, because Carolina is going to play very intense defense."

That's not going to happen, is it? I know it's not and you know it's not.

The storyline on the 2006–07 Tar Heels was written before the first basketball was tossed into the air, and it's the same one that will be used until the last game is played. It's simple—Carolina is the designated overwhelmingly talented team. The phrase "all that talent" is required to be used in any assessment of their play. You know the type:

"Sure, the Tar Heels won, but they've got all that talent."

"Well, they *should* win a bunch of games, they've got all that talent."

"Well, (fill in team) would be that good, too, if they had all that talent."

No one talks about Carolina's defense. No television wonks warn opponents that they'll be viciously guarded for 40 minutes when they play the Tar Heels.

So here's some news the nation won't notice. Carolina played another team with plenty of talent Saturday night. The Tar Heels ground Georgia Tech into a fine powder, 77–61. And they didn't beat them with high-flying acrobatics. They beat them with grit.

It's like finding out the best-looking girl in class is also a genius. She can't be smart. She's too pretty.

Roy Williams himself called the game "ugly, sloppy, bad in some ways for both teams." That's his frustration with the last five minutes— when Carolina had a chance to blow Tech out but instead let them hang around and nudge their shooting percentage for the game over 40.0—talking. This was not a Rick Barnes-era Clemson team the Tar Heels were playing. This was a talented, high-scoring Yellow Jacket squad that came into the game ranked second in the league in scoring offense.

They left with just 61 points, more than 20 under their season-long average. It was their lowest point total of the season and just the second time all year they've been held under 71. They didn't break 50 points until there were less than four minutes remaining.

Some of that was due to a poor shooting night. But at some point doesn't Carolina earn some credit for the bad opposing shooting nights that always seem to happen when they're on the floor?

The Tar Heels let Tech point guard Javaris Crittenton cross midcourt unimpeded for most of the evening. Then the harassment began. Every single pass was contested. Every single passing lane had a Tar Heel's arm waving through it. The frustration soon became apparent on Crittenton's face. His confusion was easy to read. These passes—these simple movements of the ball 35 feet from the basket—were supposed to be easy. Then why was he having to work so hard?

During one stretch, Georgia Tech went six minutes and 35 seconds without a basket. College basketball teams just don't go 6:35 without a basket. Not high-octane teams like Georgia Tech.

The maddening thing for the Jackets was that every time they drew closer, every time they threatened to chisel the lead below double digits, Carolina would simply go to the other end of the court and shoot a layup. The Tar Heel offense wasn't especially pretty, but it was pretty when it had to be.

Tech draws to 36–25 in the second half? No problem, Ty Lawson hits Brandan Wright, who is so wide open that he has time to actually look around and try to find a defender before he dunks.

Tech hits a 3-pointer to cut it to 46–36 with 13 minutes left? No problem, Reyshawn Terry just drives to the basket for a layup.

"We definitely slowed them down and limited their possessions on the offensive end," Terry said. "And they weren't able to get stops when they needed them. It's a no-win situation for them. You can't win a whole lot of ballgames when you're not getting a lot of possessions and not getting stops."

On the very first Yellow Jacket possession of the second half, Ra'sean Dickey was trying to post up so he could receive a pass from Mario West. Dickey spread his arms wide, calling for the ball. But West didn't think there was an opening and reversed the ball. Dickey rolled his eyes and shouted, "Come on, man!"

This is exactly the kind of communication you want to see as a defender.

"We wouldn't let them run their regular plays," Lawson said. "That put them in scramble situations. And when they got in those situations, we helped and stayed in our lanes."

When they are playing well, Georgia Tech can be beautiful to watch. Crittenton races down the floor and tosses the ball in the air, then waits for one of his athletic wings to launch into the air and slam it. Any team with Thaddeus Young—who scored 9 of his 22 points with less than 4 minutes remaining and the game decided—is accustomed to spending plenty of time above the rim.

Carolina wouldn't let the game be played that way.

"We put a body on them," Wright said. "Even if they had inside position, we gave them a little nudge. We knew they were a very athletic team that can jump and play above the rim. So we wanted to make sure we were sound with our defensive principles."

That sounds suspiciously like a team that might be developing a taste for playing defense. And—just maybe—earning a new reputation.

I love road trips. Coach Williams tells us, "If you play at North Carolina, you're going to travel first-class. You're going to eat at nice restaurants and stay at nice hotels." We're not spending crazy money, but there's no question we do things right. We don't stay at the Ritz-Carlton, but we stay at nice places. On the way out of town, we eat dinner at the Angus Barn or the Chop House. The best luxury of all, though, is that we travel on a private plane in most cases. That enables us to leave after 9 p.m. games and be in class the next day. We don't have to go through security or check our bags or do all those things that are required on a commercial airliner. You just get on the plane and take off—and sometimes you even bump into Ashley Judd while you're waiting to board, like we did last year after the Kentucky game.

Another advantage to road games as a player is the lack of

outside distractions. At home, we have lots of tickets and parking passes and friends and family to worry about. On the road, you just worry about the game.

Unless it's Duke or NC State, we travel to road games the night before the game. The routine is simple: late-night snack at 11 p.m., wake up and have breakfast, shoot-around, pregame, and then the game. It becomes second nature by this point in the season.

Late-night snack is great, because we always have ice cream and then one other snack—maybe chicken fingers or peanut butter and jelly sandwiches or fruit. Jonas Sahratian, our strength coach, is never a happy man at late-night snack. It's the one time that no one is eating healthy. Every road trip at around 11 p.m., you can count on Jonas looking miserable. I do try to eat healthily. I follow his nutrition guidelines.

But I love my ice cream.

Even Tyler usually gets a bowl of ice cream. He's a guy who eats the right way all the time, so I feel like if he's doing it, it must be OK. We usually have a choice between chocolate and vanilla and then there's a bowl of cookies. I've developed a little tradition: I break up the cookies in my ice cream. It's the greatest thing ever. It's the Wes Miller Special.

But we also have to go to class. The Wake Forest game in Winston-Salem was a Wednesday game, and we were leaving a day early for the weekend game against Arizona. So anyone with Monday-Wednesday-Friday classes was going to miss two of them this week. Coach Williams was concerned about that, so he talked to the staff and they decided if anyone missed class on Monday, we weren't going to leave for Wake until the day of the game. That means we would lose some big perks: no late-night snack and ice cream, no dinner at the Chop House, no night in a hotel.

You can probably guess what happens. One of us was late to class, and when the coaches checked attendance he wasn't there yet. So that meant we stayed in Chapel Hill Tuesday night. Losing the dinner at the Chop House was a big blow.

But I didn't lose my ice cream. Since we were in Chapel Hill unexpectedly on the night before a road game, Eric Hoots and I snuck over to Coldstone Creamery and I had them break up some cookies in my ice cream. That's probably confidential information. Jonas doesn't know about our Coldstone trip.

We have a new road tradition this year, and it's another one that revolves around food. It started before the Ohio State game in Chapel Hill. Coach told us we couldn't let anyone come into the Smith Center and take our brownies. We've run with it from there, so now anytime we go on the road we talk about taking the other team's brownies. Marcus started it, because when we run out of the locker room he starts yelling about how he wants some brownies. After the Saint Louis game, we had a box of brownies with "Saint Louis" written on it. After every away game we've won, Coach asks for the brownies and a manager hands them over. We've kept it in-house so far, and Coach has asked us not to talk with the media about it.

Of course, it's another thing Jonas probably isn't happy about. But since we do it as a team, he can't resist it. I'm going to tell him that to put it in his terms, someone taking our brownies would be like someone coming into his house and taking his vitamins. He'll understand it from that perspective.

Our next goal was to get some Wake Forest brownies.

That means it's time for the annual "Wes Miller plays at Wake Forest" storyline. Every year, a couple reporters talk to me at length about what it's like for me to play at Wake. It's true, I went to more games than I can count at Wake growing up. I've watched a lot of ACC games there from the stands. But as I got to high school, I became less of a Wake fan and more of a college basketball fan. That's what I wanted to do, play college basketball. It honestly was never about playing college basketball for Wake Forest. It was about having the opportunity to play.

I'm not going to lie, it's cool to look around and realize I'm playing at the same place I watched a lot of games. But that's happened to me in several arenas. I got to play at the Charlotte Coliseum, and that's a place I saw a lot of games. I've been able to play at the Smith Center and Cameron Indoor Stadium. I've played a lot of games in familiar places during my career.

The highlight of the game—other than the fact that we won—was that my three brothers sat courtside in my dad's seats. On one possession, I was running down the court and I could have reached out and touched them. That's a very unique experience. I glanced at them a couple times. Coming out of one timeout, we had a minute or so before the horn blew and Marcus walked over to chat with them. Especially my two little brothers, they eat that stuff up.

After the game, I thought we might have lost Ty. After an away game, we have a short period of time where we can talk to our families and then we have to board the bus. Especially in a place like Winston, where I've got some people there, Eric Hoots and I will be the last couple guys on the bus. Senior privileges, you know. If I was a freshman I'd probably be sitting right next to Super Dave, our bus driver, as soon as the game was over. You can't take any chances as a freshman.

Above: I always like to make a grand entrance — this one is from Late Night 2005. Below: One of the perks of my famous Roy Williams impression at Late Night was the chance to give my teammates some coaching pointers.

Jim Bounds (2)

Eric

Above: Our 2005 team hanging out in Maui during the Maui Invitational. RIGHT: Defending Illinois' Dee Brown was one of my biggest early challenges during the 2005-06 season.

Robert Cra

BELOW: I'm looking for Tyler inside — an easy way to get an assist.

Peyton Williams

Eric Hoots

ABOVE: Jackie Manuel decked out his grooms-men — here featuring Eric Hoots, Sean May, and me — in sharp vests and tennis shoes for his wedding. RIGHT: At some moments you can feel it when you take a big shot — with almost everyone in the Smith Center standing, this was one of them.

Ke

Peyton Williams

LEFT: Playing solid defense is the quickest way to earn playing time from Coach Williams. BELOW: After Coach Williams won his 500th game, we celebrated on the floor with a video retrospective of his career.

Brian Fleming

BELOW: I'll never forget leaving the Smith Center court for the last time on Senior Day against Duke. RIGHT: I'll also never forget having to give a speech at midcourt after the game.

Bob Donnan

Peyton Williams

John

One of the biggest challenges of Senior Day was rounding up enough tickets for all my family and friends.

John Lyon

ABOVE: For a kid who grew up going to the ACC Tournament, being able to celebrate with my teammates after we won it in 2007 was a great moment. **LEFT:** I'm pretty sure I was the first person to start calling Dewey Burke "Biscuits" because of all the times he helped us hit the 100-point mark.

Bob Donnan

Reyshawn, Dewey and I celebrated our graduation with Dean Smith and Chancellor James Mo

Game 20

#4/4 North Carolina 88
Wake Forest 60
Jan. 24, 2007 • Joel Coliseum, Winston-Salem, N.C.

UNC	FG	3FG	FT	REB	PF	TP	A	TO	B	S	Min
Terry*	3-9	0-3	0-0	1-4-5	3	6	0	1	1	3	17
Wright*	6-9	0-0	0-0	0-7-7	4	12	1	2	3	1	29
Hansbrough*	5-7	0-0	3-5	1-8-9	1	13	1	2	1	0	27
Ellington*	8-12	2-5	0-0	1-3-4	0	18	1	1	1	1	23
Lawson*	5-8	2-4	3-4	0-1-1	3	15	5	3	1	3	21
Ginyard	1-1	0-0	2-2	1-1-2	0	4	2	0	0	2	12
Thomas	0-1	0-1	1-2	0-2-2	1	1	6	5	0	0	14
Green	3-6	3-5	3-4	1-2-3	1	12	0	1	1	0	20
Burke	0-0	0-0	0-0	0-0-0	0	0	0	0	0	0	1
Thompson	1-1	0-0	0-0	0-1-1	3	2	0	0	0	0	14
Miller	0-2	0-1	2-2	0-1-1	1	2	0	1	0	0	11
Wood	0-0	0-0	0-0	0-0-0	0	0	0	0	0	0	1
Stepheson	1-1	0-0	1-2	2-6-8	1	3	1	2	0	0	9
Copeland	0-1	0-0	0-0	0-1-1	0	0	0	0	0	0	1
TEAM				0-0-0				1			
Totals	**33-58**	**7-19**	**15-21**	**7-37-44**	**18**	**88**	**17**	**19**	**8**	**10**	**200**
Pct.	**.569**	**.368**	**.714**	**DB: 4**							

FG: (1st half: 17-30, .567; 2nd half: 16-28, .571)
3FG: (1st half: 3-10, .300; 2nd half: 4-9, .444)
FT: (1st half: 5-7, .714; 2nd half: 10-14, .714)

WFU	FG	3FG	FT	REB	PF	TP	A	TO	B	S	Min
Swinton*	2-5	0-0	0-1	3-2-5	3	4	1	2	0	1	11
Drum*	1-8	1-5	0-0	1-4-5	3	3	1	2	0	1	29
Visser*	6-10	0-0	4-7	2-3-5	1	16	1	0	0	2	31
I. Smith*	4-8	1-3	0-0	1-0-1	5	9	5	3	0	1	25
Williams*	3-10	0-2	0-1	6-0-6	2	6	0	5	0	3	21
Dukes	0-3	0-0	0-1	0-0-0	1	0	0	1	0	0	9
Hale	2-9	2-4	0-0	1-1-2	2	6	1	3	0	0	15
Stanley	0-3	0-3	0-2	1-2-3	0	0	1	1	0	0	12
McFarland	0-0	0-0	0-0	0-1-1	0	0	0	0	0	0	4
Lepore	0-0	0-0	0-0	0-0-0	0	0	0	0	0	0	1
M. Smith	1-1	1-1	0-0	0-0-0	0	3	0	0	0	0	1
Skeen	2-5	2-5	1-2	1-3-4	1	7	0	0	0	1	22
Gurley	1-5	1-3	0-0	0-0-0	0	3	0	0	0	1	6
Weaver	0-1	0-0	0-2	1-0-1	3	0	0	1	1	0	10
Crawford	1-3	1-3	0-0	0-0-0	0	3	1	0	0	0	2
Hoekstra	0-0	0-0	0-0	0-1-1	0	0	0	0	0	0	1
TEAM				1-3-4				1			
Totals	**23-71**	**9-29**	**5-16**	**18-20-38**	**21**	**60**	**11**	**19**	**1**	**10**	**200**
Pct.	**.324**	**.310**	**.313**	**DB: 4**							

FG: (1st half: 14-36, .389; 2nd half: 9-35, .257)
3FG: (1st half: 6-13, .462; 2nd half: 3-16, .188)
FT: (1st half: 3-5, .600; 2nd half: 2-11, .182)

Officials: Gary Maxwell, John Cahill, Brian Dorsey
Attendance: 14,351 • **Technical Fouls:** None

Unless you're Ty Lawson. I was going to the bus and knew I was the last one. Then I see Ty going the other way. I asked him where he was going and he said something about getting his parents to sign a form. In normal Ty fashion, he wasn't in a big hurry. He ended up on the concourse, just kind of wandering around, while his parents were standing down by the tunnel. We yelled at him to hurry up, and he sped up from a walk to a slow-paced trot. That's about as fast as you can get him to move off the court. He is a real character. He's got his cartoons and his crazy socks and sometimes you wonder if he's paying attention, and then he gets on the court and he's one of the best point guards in the country. He pays better attention than he will admit.

And he did finally make it on the bus. I'm sure Coach had a couple things to say to him, but after a win there's a little more leeway for postgame escapades.

LUCAS: ANGRY ALL THE TIME

JAN. 24, 2007

WINSTON–SALEM—Here was the mission: watch Tyler Hansbrough.

That was the goal Wednesday night. You always walk away from a Carolina game with the nagging feeling that the Tar Heel sophomore is taking a beating. So for one night, while Carolina stretched out to an eventual 88–60 victory over Wake Forest, it was all Tyler, all the time.

After watching him for 27 minutes, I walked into the locker room convinced he would be bloodied and angry. Maybe a black eye or two. Scratches on his biceps.

And here sat Hansbrough, wearing a pink button-up shirt. Pink? Yes. With a Carolina blue tie and gray pants.

It looked sharp. As if you would tell him anything else.

So, Tyler, that was pretty rough, right? Very physical down there in the paint, huh?

"Eh, not that bad," he said.

Really?

"Nah," he said. "Towards the end some things happened. But I'm fine with them happening. It was the flow of the game at the time. Whatever happens, happens."

Here is the thing about Hansbrough: he infuriates people. He infuriates opposing players and coaches. He infuriates opposing fans. Your buddy who likes Duke or State? Ask him, he'll tell you that Hansbrough infuriates him, too. Just reading that quote probably caused the teeth of at least a couple non-Tar Heels to grind.

I have tried to look at this through non-Carolina lenses. I see a player who hustles constantly, who treats the basketball like treasure, and who has a knack for scoring even with three opponents draped on him.

That does not infuriate me. What am I missing?

It probably has something to do with, as Bruce Pearl said earlier this year, the way Hansbrough "takes it to the contact." Two months later, it's still not exactly clear what that means. But know this: when he has the ball, there's usually contact.

It's become clear that the book on the Tar Heels is to be as physical as possible with Hansbrough and try to tip him over mentally. The fact that this has worked perhaps once in his entire college basketball career doesn't seem to bother anyone.

Don't believe it? Here, try this:

Tyler, have you noticed how mad you seem to make people? Have you heard the fans cheering when you take a hard foul under the basket and seen the signs and watched the coaches pirouetting on the sideline after you ram through another hoop?

"Apparently not."

Not at all?

"No, not really."

The fact that he's completely oblivious to the anger just makes it worse. It's a red-faced, eyes-bulging, spit-flying kind of anger. Just mention his name and watch the blood pressure rise across the ACC.

To appreciate what goes on, you can't just watch him when he has the ball. You have to watch him set screens and be screened. You have to watch him post up and box out. This was an actual sequence—which should have been accompanied by Batman-style cartoon graphics and sound effects (Pow! Bam! Smack!)—late in the second half as Carolina's lead got out of hand:

Hansbrough and Visser were entwined as a Wake Forest jumper approached the rim. Visser wrapped an arm around him, Hansbrough banged back. On the next Carolina possession, as a shot went up, Hansbrough was standing alone under the basket prepared for an offensive rebound . . . until Visser spotted him and backed over him like a dump truck. Both players ended up in a heap on the floor. Twenty seconds later, Visser missed a shot over Hansbrough and fell to the floor, swatting the hardwood. He labored up the court, never crossing the center stripe while pleading his case to the officials.

Meanwhile Danny Green was busy with a fast break opportunity.

None of this is to imply that Visser is dirty. He isn't. He's a good player who has made himself a quality contributor, and like everyone else in the league, he's physical. So is Hansbrough. And when they crash together, the reverberations can be felt throughout the lower level.

To non-Tar Heels, those shockwaves can be infuriating. Hansbrough leaves a trail of anger in his wake like a vapor trail behind a 737.

"I guess I could make them a lot madder," Hansbrough said with a raised eyebrow.

Really? How is that even possible?

"I could lose my head. But I'm not going to do that. The only way I would lose my head would be for someone to hit me in the face. I would not like that."

Just then, Wes Miller happened by. He caught the tail end of the conversation.

"I made him lose his head the other day," Miller said. "I called him soft in practice. I took a charge from him and jumped up and called him soft."

There they stood, the senior and sophomore, facing each other, Miller about a head shorter. It seemed an unlikely practice showdown, even in the ultra-competitive Carolina environment.

Wes, you really called him soft?

Miller stared straight ahead, no smile on his face. He was completely serious.

"This guy?" Miller said. "No way."

And he laughed. The mere idea was humorous.

WEEK SEVENTEEN

PLAYING BASKETBALL AT NORTH CAROLINA has big perks. We play in one of the best arenas in the country. We're on television every week. We know we're going to be in the NCAA Tournament every year.

But the off-court perks are as good as the on-court advantages. We do things most of us would never get to do otherwise. Our trip to Arizona was a great example of the benefits of playing for Carolina.

First off, that's the longest midseason trip we've had during my career. We left a day early because of the strange game time (11 a.m. local time) and the long distance. I downloaded four episodes of *24* onto my iPod and thought that would last the whole trip. Instead, I had watched all of them by the time our plane landed in Oklahoma City to refuel. We arrived late to the hotel, and the next day we followed a normal routine, including practice at the McKale Center.

Things really got interesting after practice. Coach Haase's brother is stationed at an air base in Tucson. So after practice we got a behind-the-scenes tour of the base. Especially with everything going on in the world today, it was fascinating to get a glimpse of our military that most Americans don't get to see. My favorite movie as a kid was *Top Gun*. I used to pretend to be Goose and Maverick. It's even more impressive in person. We were on the runway when F-16's took off right in front of our face. We saw one take off and then go vertical up to 15,000 feet. We sat inside the cockpit and saw all kinds of different bombs.

The coolest thing was getting in the actual flight simulators pilots use to train and trying to fly. I crashed on my landing, which was disappointing. That's why my brother wants to be a pilot and not me. They also took us into a completely dark room and then handed us night-vision goggles. The whole experience was unreal, and it's all because we're Carolina basketball players.

It also had a personal side to me. My brother is being recruited by Air Force to play football. If he goes there, he's very interested in becoming a pilot. I was able to talk to some pilots who attended the Air Force Academy. When my brother goes on his recruiting visit next weekend, I'll have a good idea of what he is experiencing.

We usually have one of these extended trips per season. My

first eligible season, we went to Oakland to play Santa Clara and then on to Maui. Last year we went to Los Angeles a couple days early to play Southern Cal. Our hotel was right on the beach and we took a couple trips to Venice Beach. This year, we went to New York City over Thanksgiving for the NIT.

See any common traits on those trips? We've lost every time. So you can see why I was nervous about this trip. I decided this one was different, though, because we only went one night early. And it wasn't like we had a lot of down time—when we weren't at practice or eating, we were at the air base. It felt more like a regular road trip than some of our other long-distance trips.

We went to dinner as a team on Friday night. Brandan didn't feel great, but he seemed OK to me. Later, at late-night snack, he wasn't there. Someone told me he was sick. In previous years, that would have been disastrous. We could not have afforded to lose our starting four-man who averages 15 points per game. But this year we have more depth.

It just so happened that my roommate on the trip was Deon Thompson, who we needed to step up and fill Brandan's role. I really like Deon. He reminds me a lot of Sean May—one of those big guys who is a big teddy bear. He's the happiest, most loving guy in the world. But I was a little worried because he had so much of his family in town, plus his girlfriend was there. It was the closest thing he's had to a home game since he's been at Carolina, and he was playing in front of people he hadn't seen in a long time. Now we're not just asking him to play, we're asking him to start. That's a lot going on for anyone, much less a freshman. But he handled it as well as anyone could. He spent quality time with his family, but he was also ready to play. The morning of the game, he seemed loose and confident.

Being loose was even more impressive because the game tipped off at 11 a.m. Tucson time. Usually, our pregame meal is four hours before tipoff. Coach Williams hates to change anything about our routine, but he knew a 7 a.m. pregame meal might not have been much fun. So he bumped it back to 7:30, which is the earliest pregame we've had since I have been here.

Right about that same time, we realized Marcus wasn't feeling well. He was Brandan's roommate and came down with the same virus. That's the exact circumstance where it pays off to play as much depth as we've played this year. There are other teams that never go beyond the eighth man on their bench. We feel comfortable going 12 or 13 players down our bench, and when two are out, we just wait for two more to step up.

I wasn't sure what to expect when we arrived at the arena because it was so early. We had been told it would be very loud, but I thought at 9:30 in the morning it might be a little more laid-back.

It wasn't.

I couldn't believe how crowded the student section was the first time we came out of the locker room. Our tunnel was right next to the students, so we had to run right by them. I had never seen anything like that in a game that wasn't played in Raleigh, Durham, or College Park.

During warm-ups, I was shooting at the basket closest to the students. There were about 10 students who were harassing me the whole time. They were yelling my name and telling me I needed to be on the JV team. It went on for the entire early warm-up period, so it was a good 20 minutes. I looked at Hoots and Preston and Q and said, "I've never gotten this kind of attention before." It's a great compliment. I'm someone who didn't know if anyone would know who I was, and now I've got the Arizona student section telling me

I suck. This will sound strange, but for a basketball player, that's quite a compliment.

Coach addressed the fact that we were missing two key players during his pregame talk in the locker room. "We don't have Marcus and we don't have Brandan," he said. "But other than the Santa Clara game, I've never had a team that was a player or two down where everyone else didn't raise their level of play.

"That doesn't mean, Tyler, that you have to play over your head. That doesn't mean, Wayne, that you have to play over your head. It just means everyone has to play well. It means we have to play the way we're capable of playing."

I thought that was a good message. It eliminated the possibility of any one player thinking they had to pick up for Brandan or Marcus all by themselves. We've had a lot of 30-point wins this year, but I think all of us expected the Arizona game to come down to the last couple of possessions. We were as surprised as anyone with the way it unfolded, especially since it was in their gym. They missed some shots and we were able to run a lot, and we were very effective in transition.

They made one second-half run, but we were able to withstand it. A big play in that sequence happened to come when I was in the game. In our system, the two-guard goes to the long rebounding spot when a teammate takes a shot. I'm not much of an offensive rebounder, and I'm also worried about getting back on defense and being a second guard to help the point guard.

We missed a long shot, and as I was getting back I saw Ty fall. That gave Arizona a 3-on-1 fast break, and I was the only one back. There was a big guy trailing down the middle. Coach always tells us that giving the ball to the big guy trailing in that situation is a cardinal sin because it invites a charging call. So as soon as they dropped it to the big guy, I thought, "I might have an opportunity to take a charge here."

I knew he was going to try and bulldoze me. He put his knee right in my chest. In his mind, I think he thought he was going to go over me and put me on SportsCenter. In the moment after he hit me, the first thing I thought was, "That really hurt." The next thing I thought was, "Don't be a baby. I can't act like it hurts, so let's get up and go." I tried to run down the court like I was completely fine, but inside I was hurting.

Coach made a point of singling me out during the next timeout and saying it was a great charge to take. When we got home, he said in practice it was one of the two best charges he's seen in his coaching career. That's a huge compliment. I just wish some more planning had gone into it so I could talk about how I meant to do it. Instead, it just fell into my lap—almost literally.

We won 92–64. After the game when I was running off the court, I tried to find those guys who were screaming from the student section during warm-ups. I just wanted to give them a little wink and a smile. They weren't there, though. I think they had already left to beat the traffic.

Coach doesn't say much in the postgame whether we win or lose. I knew we would be jumping around after the Arizona game because that's what we do after big wins. This was the kind of game where I'll always remember the locker room. I remember the locker room at Kentucky after we beat them and at Duke after we beat them. I remember all the locker rooms from the 2005 NCAA Tournament. Those are the moments when you realize how much bigger the entire team is than any one individual. So I knew this would be a memorable one.

But even before we started jumping, Coach walked to the board and wrote one word: "Team."

"That's what we are," he said, "and that's what we just did."

It's funny, because during that stretch in New York, the big problem was that we had some guys who were trying to do it on their own. It wasn't because we were selfish, it was because we just hadn't come together yet. Now we're at a point that we can do things as a team, and we accomplish so much more that way. We would not have beaten Arizona playing as individuals—not without Brandan and Marcus. As a team, though, we played a very impressive game.

Game 21

#4/4 North Carolina 92
#17/19 Arizona 64
Jan. 27, 2007 • McKale Center, Tucson, Ariz.

UNC	FG	3FG	FT	REB	PF	TP	A	TO	B	S	Min
Thompson*	7-8	0-0	0-1	1-5-6	4	14	0	0	1	1	23
Terry*	5-10	2-4	3-3	3-3-6	3	15	4	3	0	1	32
Hansbrough*	5-12	0-0	4-5	1-5-6	4	14	0	4	0	1	26
Ellington*	6-15	2-6	0-1	1-4-5	1	14	1	2	0	1	28
Lawson*	8-14	1-5	1-2	1-2-3	2	18	8	1	0	4	30
Thomas	1-1	0-0	0-0	0-2-2	1	2	2	0	0	0	10
Green	2-5	0-3	1-1	0-3-3	4	5	0	0	0	1	17
Burke	0-1	0-1	0-0	0-0-0	0	0	0	0	0	0	1
Miller	0-3	0-3	0-0	0-0-0	0	0	0	0	0	0	14
Wood	0-0	0-0	0-0	0-1-1	0	0	0	0	0	0	2
Stephenson	5-7	0-0	0-0	2-4-6	5	10	0	2	0	0	15
Copeland	0-0	0-0	0-0	0-0-0	0	0	0	0	0	0	2
TEAM				2-3-5							
Totals	**39-76**	**5-22**	**9-13**	**11-32-43**	**24**	**92**	**15**	**12**	**1**	**9**	**200**
Pct.	**.513**	**.227**	**.692**	**DB: 1**							

FG: (1st half: 18-39, .462; 2nd half: 21-37, .568)
3FG: (1st half: 3-11, .273; 2nd half: 2-11, .182)
FT: (1st half: 4-7, .571; 2nd half: 5-6, .833)

UA	FG	3FG	FT	REB	PF	TP	A	TO	B	S	Min
Williams*	2-4	0-2	0-0	0-3-3	1	4	1	3	0	1	20
Budinger*	5-13	0-5	6-7	4-3-7	4	16	0	1	0	0	21
Radenovic*	3-12	0-4	6-9	0-8-8	2	12	2	2	0	0	35
McClellan*	1-6	0-3	2-4	2-1-3	1	4	1	1	2	0	30
Shakur*	4-11	1-4	6-8	0-6-6	1	15	4	8	2	1	39
Dillon	0-1	0-1	0-0	0-0-0	1	0	2	1	0	1	12
Wise	0-5	0-4	0-0	0-1-1	0	0	0	1	0	1	11
Onobun	0-0	0-0	0-0	1-2-3	0	0	0	0	0	0	5
Hill	5-7	0-0	3-4	5-5-10	4	13	0	3	1	1	20
Brielmaier	0-0	0-0	0-0	0-0-0	0	0	0	0	0	0	7
TEAM				2-0-2			0				
Totals	**20-59**	**1-23**	**23-32**	**14-29-43**	**14**	**64**	**10**	**20**	**5**	**5**	**200**
Pct.	**.339**	**.043**	**.719**	**DB: 2**							

FG: (1st half: 10-28, .357; 2nd half: 10-31, .323)
3FG: (1st half: 0-10, .000; 2nd half: 1-13, .077)
FT: (1st half: 5-8, .625; 2nd half: 18-24, .750)

Officials: Bryan Kersey, Mike Eades, Mike Wood
Attendance: 14,596 • **Technical Fouls:** None

Score by Periods	1st	2nd	Total
North Carolina	43	49	92
Arizona	25	39	64

That doesn't mean we can coast until March. In practice, Coach said, "We're exactly where we want to be. We are leading the ACC. But we can't get fat and happy." He says "Don't get fat and happy," all the time. Watching the tape of the Arizona game, we saw what he meant. We played great and got a big win. But there were so many things we could have done better. When you beat a team like Arizona by 28 points on the road and can still do a lot of things better, you realize the sky is the limit with this team.

LUCAS: LISTEN

JAN. 27, 2007

TUCSON—Listen.

You saw the game. You don't need me to tell you what I saw in Tucson as Carolina completely dismantled Arizona 92–64 on Saturday afternoon.

But let me tell you about what I heard. This was a game about sounds, about intense noise . . . and thunderous silence.

It is an hour before the game. The Tar Heels' depleted roster is making their way onto the floor. No Brandan Wright. No Marcus Ginyard.

The "Zona Zoo," the name for the Wildcat student section, doesn't care. The sign outside the student entrance says students are permitted to begin lining up four hours before tipoff. But at 6:30 a.m., four and a half hours before the 11 a.m. tip, there's already a healthy line of red-clad students. Soon, they plug in a mammoth speaker, and the bass thumps throughout campus.

Students are admitted beginning two hours before the game. Some try to catch a quick nap. But when the Tar Heels arrive and trickle onto the court, everyone awakens. Every player has to walk through the tunnel nearest the student section as they take the floor. The students lean over the rail—everything they say is clean, but it's obvious they've cultivated an intense dislike for their visitors.

Listen to this:

"Wayne!" screams one guy whose body is painted red. He is wearing a red wrestling mask with green flames and purple suspenders. "Wayne! You are going down, Wayne! Down!"

Ellington smiles. He rocks his arms back and forth and smiles.

"I love this," he says with a wink and a smile, just subtle enough so Mask Guy can't tell he's been heard.

It is a little disarming. You want to pull him aside and explain the situation. Here's the deal, Wayne: you're missing two of your most critical pieces. You're on the road against a team that hasn't lost a nonconference home game in five years. Today's sports section refers to this as the "biggest day of the year on the Arizona sports frontier."

You're not supposed to love it. You're supposed to tremble.

So then Ellington goes out and makes his very first three-pointer and the points start tumbling.

Listen to this:

Every time Arizona narrows the gap in the first half, one of Carolina's big men responds with a basket. No surprise there. That's what the Tar

Heels do—feed the post and squash teams into submission.

But these are different big guys. This is Alex Stepheson and Deon Thompson, and every time they score a rowdy bunch of their family members stand and cheer behind the Carolina bench.

This is a testament to the recruiting of Roy Williams. He went into California, into a place where the Tar Heels have never put much effort into recruiting, and found the rarest of college basketball gems: big guys. Talented big guys. Big guys who were willing to spurn the local schools and travel all the way across the country because they believed what the gray-haired coach with the funny accent was telling them.

Throughout the preseason, Williams was asked what he planned to do with all his depth.

All that worrying, all those questions, and now the answer looks pretty simple, doesn't it? What's Williams going to do with all that depth?

Well, he's going to play it.

Now Stepheson and Thompson are close to home for a day and loving it, and their only worry is hurrying through the throng of postgame media so they can share a quick hug with their families. Just a month ago, both freshmen became visibly nervous when they had to speak live on the radio to Woody Durham after a Tar Heel victory. Now they look like veterans, their ties knotted perfectly, smiling and joking with the horde of tape recorder-wielding writers.

Listen to this:

With a minute left in the first half, Carolina has stretched the advantage to 39–23. Ty Lawson works his way into the lane, into a dicey situation with three Wildcats around him. Somehow he wriggles through them, and all you see of him is his right arm lofting the ball against the backboard and dropping it through for a 41–23 lead.

The crowd has already gone from frenetic to stunned. And when Lawson tosses in his spinner, they make this sound: "Awwwwwwuugghhh."

It is as if they simultaneously do not believe what just happened and also believe it all too well.

Listen to this:

By now, the game is well in hand. Carolina leads 67–44 with 9 minutes remaining, and the only remaining drama is the margin of victory. Around this same time, Arizona staffers bring a sheet of paper to the media headlined "Worst McKale Center losses under Lute Olson." The leader is a 12-point defeat to Tennessee. This game has not been as close as 12 points since four minutes were left in the first half.

Danny Green gets the ball on the break and feeds Tyler Hansbrough for a forceful slam dunk. Some aggression comes out in the slam, and the crowd is awed into complete silence by the play.

Suddenly, a noise:

"Thwack!"

Hansbrough has just delivered a high five that would shake Mount Vesuvius to the right hand of Ellington. With the silence, the smack echoes throughout the lower level.

"He had some force behind that one," Ellington will say later, wincing at the memory. "My hand is still hurting a little bit."

Finally, it is over. The two teams shake hands, and each Tar Heel runs back through the same tunnel through which they'd entered the court. Mask Guy is gone. Most of the students remain.

Listen to this:

The sound of every Arizona student leaning over the rail as Carolina left the floor. Not yelling, not any more. Now they were applauding. As Ellington passed, one student in a red t-shirt nods, as if to acknowledge what he had just seen.

"That was why I was saying, `I love it,' at the beginning," Ellington said. "All I could do was smile. I knew we were getting ready to come out, play hard, and show what we can do."

He said it so softly you had to lean in to hear him.

But for some reason it came out like a roar.

One other funny thing happened at Arizona. We drove up the day of the game for the previous road game at Wake Forest. For some reason, C.B. McGrath wore his suit pants, his suit shoes, and a white t-shirt to shootaround. Then we went back to the hotel for pregame meal, and he came downstairs wearing the same outfit. At home, we dress up for pregame, but on the road anything goes.

Apparently, at the table where the coaches were sitting, Coach made a comment about C.B.'s outfit. So we get to pregame meal in Arizona, and it's 7:30 in the morning.

Everyone looks like they just rolled out of bed. Then here comes C.B. and he has on a full suit and tie and looks like he is going for an interview at Goldman Sachs. He was perfectly dressed and had his hair slicked back. I'm sure he thought he would get a great reaction from Coach Williams, because Coach's comment at Wake had obviously had a big impact on him. And here's exactly what Coach said:

Nothing. Not a word.

As far as I know, Coach never acknowledged it at all. There's a rumor that C.B. is going to wear a full tuxedo to the next road pregame meal. I'm just glad he listened to Coach and ditched the white undershirt.

I shot two airballs against Miami. I'm pretty sure if I added up all my airballs from high school until right now, I could probably count them all on two hands. A miss is a miss, it doesn't matter how badly you miss them. But I wasn't pleased with two airballs in the same game. The odd thing was that I took four shots: two of them swished through cleanly and the other two were airballs. Usually, if you tell me I'm going to take four shots and none will hit the rim, then I'm going to assume they're all swishes and I have 12 points. Instead, I had six points.

That summed up the first half for us. Miami isn't a marquee name and our fans weren't excited. We're so spoiled by how great it is playing for North Carolina that I don't even feel right complaining about it. It's hard to whine about it not being loud for warm-ups 30 minutes before tip. But as players, we do notice. Bobby always makes jokes about it. He'll say, "Looks like another packed house," when we're about to take the floor 30 minutes beforehand and the stands aren't filled yet. We know they'll be filled eventually, but we also know that if it's not a marquee game we may have to generate some enthusiasm ourselves instead of relying on the crowd. Marcus, especially, does a good job of creating that enthusiasm. Against a capable team like Miami, if you're still waiting for enthusiasm five minutes into the game, there's a good chance they're going to beat you.

This is a good window into the way Coach Williams thinks: at halftime, we were ahead 41–24. But he was still upset about the way we were playing.

"I'm not going to look at the score," he told us in the locker room. "I'm not going to tell you it's OK because we are ahead by double figures against an ACC team. We're leaving our feet defensively and we're not playing our scramble very well. We can play much better."

That kind of attitude trickles down through a team. We are more talented than some teams and that can carry us to some wins. But it won't carry us to a national championship. He is going to coach every possession of every single game regardless of the score. He expects us to play the same way.

The highlight of the Miami game for me was the play of Quentin Thomas. He had 8 assists and 1 turnover in just 11 minutes. Two of those assists came on my two 3-pointers. When we were sitting on the bench later, I told him, "Thanks, man, you know how much I needed those."

He said, "You know I'm always coming to you." That's exactly how I feel—when I'm on the floor with Quentin, I feel like I'm always going to get a good shot. He finds people in a position where they can score.

Game 22

Miami 64
#3/3 North Carolina 105
Jan. 31, 2007 • Smith Center, Chapel Hill

UM	FG	3FG	FT	REB	PF	TP	A	TO	B	S	Min
Gilbert*	0-4	0-1	0-0	1-1-2	1	0	0	1	0	1	11
Collins*	1-5	0-0	0-0	1-1-2	5	2	1	0	0	0	20
Asbury*	2-10	1-4	1-2	2-1-3	0	6	1	1	1	2	30
Harris*	5-10	3-4	5-6	0-3-3	3	18	3	3	0	1	28
Clemente*	2-6	0-1	1-2	0-1-1	2	5	4	4	0	2	32
Hicks	4-6	0-0	2-2	1-3-4	5	10	0	1	1	0	27
McClinton	6-14	3-6	0-1	0-1-1	1	15	1	1	0	2	29
Dews	2-6	1-3	0-0	0-0-0	3	7	0	0	0	1	17
Copeland	0-1	0-0	1-2	0-0-0	1	1	0	1	0	0	6
TEAM				2-6-8			0				
Totals	22-62	8-19	12-17	7-17-24	21	64	10	12	2	9	200
Pct.	.355	.421	.706	DB: 3							

FG: (1st half: 10-28, .357; 2nd half: 12-34, .353)
3FG: (1st half: 1-5, .200; 2nd half: 7-14, .500)
FT: (1st half: 3-4, .750; 2nd half: 9-13, .692)

UNC	FG	3FG	FT	REB	PF	TP	A	TO	B	S	Min
Terry*	3-5	2-4	2-2	2-5-7	3	10	1	1	0	0	15
Wright*	3-5	0-0	2-4	2-5-7	1	8	1	5	4	2	27
Hansbrough*	7-13	0-0	8-12	6-7-13	2	22	1	1	1	0	25
Ellington*	5-9	3-5	1-1	0-3-3	0	14	4	1	0	2	20
Lawson*	5-8	3-5	0-0	0-0-0	3	13	3	4	0	0	20
Green	3-6	1-2	5-5	0-1-1	1	12	3	0	1	2	13
Thompson	3-4	0-0	0-0	0-4-4	1	6	0	0	1	0	15
Stepheson	0-0	0-0	2-2	1-3-4	0	2	0	0	0	0	10
Ginyard	2-3	0-0	1-1	1-4-5	1	5	2	1	0	1	19
Thomas	0-1	0-1	0-0	0-1-1	0	0	8	1	0	0	11
Frasor	0-0	0-0	0-0-0		1	0	2	2	0	0	9
Miller	2-5	2-5	0-0	0-0-0	2	6	1	0	0	0	12
Copeland	2-3	0-0	0-2	2-0-2	0	4	0	0	0	0	2
Burke	1-2	1-2	0-0	0-0-0	1	3	0	0	0	0	1
Wood	0-0	0-0	0-0	0-1-1	0	0	0	0	0	0	1
TEAM				0-1-1							
Totals	36-64	12-24	21-27	14-35-49	16	105	26	16	7	7	200
Pct.	.562	.500	.778	DB: 2							

FG: (1st half: 14-28, .500; 2nd half: 22-36, .611)
3FG: (1st half: 6-12, .500; 2nd half: 6-12, .500)
FT: (1st half: 7-8, .875; 2nd half: 14-19, .737)

Officials: Karl Hess, Mike Kitts, Bob Donato
Attendance: 21,132 • **Technical Fouls:** Miami bench (2)

Score by Periods	1st	2nd	Total
Miami	24	40	64
North Carolina	41	64	105

WEEK EIGHTEEN

I HAVE NEVER SEEN COACH WILLIAMS as upset, for a single moment, as he was at halftime of the NC State game.

Let me back up.

During my career at Carolina, I've always felt good about playing State. We were 6–0 against them in my first three years. Duke-Carolina gets all the national attention, but locally State-Carolina is taken just as seriously. This is probably more of a senior's mentality, but we only get so many chances to go into venues where people truly hate us and shut them up. At most, guys on our team will go to the RBC Center four times. It is consistently one of the rowdiest environments we see each year. At Duke, they're right on top of you but there's usually a certain element of humor. At State, it's malicious. They say things that make you think, "How could anyone say that about another person in public?" They will talk about your mother, your girlfriend, and lots of other things we can't write in this book. The tickets for player parents are directly in front of the student section and it's not unusual for the students to be yelling at a player about his parents—with the parents sitting right there.

They also make all kinds of crazy signs. The video board there encourages it, because the more crass a sign is, the better chance they'll show it on the video board and everyone will cheer. That's the kind of crowd it is. The craziest thing I have seen there happened during my redshirt year. Rashad McCants was at the free throw line. He dribbled a couple times and all of a sudden you could hear this cheer: "S-T-D."

I was close with Rashad at the time, and there wasn't any reason for them to be chanting that. He stopped in the middle of his free throw routine and his jaw dropped. He couldn't believe it and none of the guys on our bench could believe it. But hey, that's NC State for you.

So usually once you walk into the building, it's not hard to find motivation to play well. But I never felt that edge from our team against them. We felt like we were just going to walk out there and win by 20 or 30 points. We've done that throughout the year several times, and that's what we thought was going to happen against State. They were 12–8 and 2–5 in the conference and maybe some of our younger guys were fooled by their record.

After watching the film, State really played well. They made big shots and we didn't. Sometimes you just run into a team that makes big shots. But there was another element to our loss: there were times we just weren't into it mentally.

I have played for Coach Williams for four years. One thing he can't stand is letting someone dribble the length of the floor for a layup. The last time it happened was at home against Duke my redshirt year, when Chris Duhon made a shot at the buzzer to win the game. It happened again against NC State, as Gavin Grant went the length of the court just before halftime to give State a 38–36 lead.

At halftime, usually Coach spends a period of time with the assistants before he talks to us. At State, the coaches' locker room and our locker room are separated by one of those plastic dividers. While we were sitting there waiting for him, we could hear him yelling and screaming. He was irate. That's not characteristic of Coach Williams, but that's how upset he was—not just about the last play, but about our intensity level in the first half. He eventually opened the divider and stormed in to express his displeasure. That's as upset as I've ever seen him in a single moment. Then he went back into his locker room, closed the divider, and we went about the normal half-time routine. When he came back into our locker room for the second time, he was still upset, but it was more about making adjustments to fix what we had done wrong.

I've watched the tape and there's only one conclusion for how one player can beat five defenders all the way down the court: it takes a breakdown from all five defenders. Unless we're in our "24" (full-court) defense, everyone should be in the line of the ball. If the ball is behind you, it's your job to sprint back and get at least in line with the ball. Two of our guys were up hugging their men, and as soon as the ball came in to Grant they were behind the ball. That took them out of the play.

That created a 3-on-3 game. He beat his man, and the two other defenders who were left never stepped in. It's pretty simple defense: if your teammate is beaten and the clock is running down, step in and protect the goal. Force them to make at least one extra pass rather than just cruising to the basket. We never did that. It's impossible to point to one player and say, "That layup was his fault." All five defenders bear some responsibility.

The second half wasn't much better. We were eventually down by 12 points, and even though we closed it to three points with a minute left, we didn't play well enough to win the game. No surprise—when the final buzzer sounded, the crowd stormed the court.

Being on the floor as the losing team in a court-storming situation is very unusual. You're already upset about the loss, and then you have to deal with all these people who are so happy about the victory. It reinforces the missed opportunity. It's a compliment, of course, because fans don't storm the court when they beat a nobody.

We are always taught that as soon as we shake the hands of the other team, we should get off the court. Whether it's a win or a loss, we sprint off the floor as soon as possible. A couple people said things to me as I was trying to get off the court, but I straight-lined towards the exit and didn't pay attention to what they were saying. When you play the way we played, there's not much room to discuss the game.

We don't have long postgame talks from Coach Williams. He gets that from Coach Smith—I've read that Coach Smith often said he didn't say much in the postgame because he wanted to have a chance to fairly evaluate his team on tape rather than say something emotional in the heat of the moment. So I knew we wouldn't get a long speech after the game. But even by the standards of short Coach Williams speeches, this was a short one. He walked into the locker room and said, "They were better than us. They outplayed us. They beat us. They played harder than us. Bring it in."

You know how when you do something wrong as a kid and you know your parents are going to yell at you? One of the most painful things they can do, rather than yelling and screaming, is say, "We're very disappointed in you." That's how it was to hear those words from Coach Williams. It's one thing to make physical mistakes, but it's another thing entirely to be outhustled.

Game 23

#3/3 North Carolina 79
NC State 83
Feb. 3, 2007 • RBC Center, Raleigh, N.C.

UNC	FG	3FG	FT	REB	PF	TP	A	TO	B	S	Min
Ellington*	3-9	2-7	3-4	1-1-2	1	11	2	1	0	1	26
Terry*	1-3	0-1	0-0	0-0-0	5	2	1	0	0	0	15
Lawson*	8-12	2-4	3-4	0-0-0	3	21	7	1	0	1	31
Wright*	6-12	0-0	3-4	3-3-6	4	15	2	0	1	1	31
Hansbrough*	9-16	0-0	6-6	3-5-8	4	24	0	4	0	2	32
Ginyard	2-3	0-0	0-0	1-1-2	1	4	2	0	0	2	20
Frasor	0-2	0-2	0-0	0-0-0	0	0	0	1	0	1	6
Thomas	0-1	0-0	0-0	0-0-0	1	0	0	2	0	0	4
Green	0-1	0-1	0-0	0-1-1	2	0	1	1	0	0	10
Thompson	1-2	0-0	0-0	0-1-1	2	2	0	2	0	1	12
Miller	0-0	0-0	0-0	0-2-2	1	0	0	0	0	2	9
Stepheson	0-1	0-0	0-2	0-0-0	1	0	0	0	0	0	4
TEAM				3-0-3							
Totals	**30-62**	**4-15**	**15-20**	**11-14-25**	**25**	**79**	**15**	**12**	**1**	**11**	**200**
Pct.	.484	.267	.750	DB: 2							

FG: (1st half: 14-26, .538; 2nd half: 16-36, .444)
3FG: (1st half: 1-5, .200; 2nd half: 3-10, .300)
FT: (1st half: 7-9, .778; 2nd half: 8-11, .727)

NCSU	FG	3FG	FT	REB	PF	TP	A	TO	B	S	Min
Fells*	8-11	4-5	1-2	0-4-4	2	21	1	0	3	2	35
Grant*	5-10	2-3	4-6	2-1-3	2	16	2	8	1	1	39
Atsur*	2-3	1-2	7-7	1-1-2	3	12	10	4	0	3	38
Costner*	4-11	1-5	6-9	3-8-11	3	15	4	3	2	2	38
McCauley*	6-6	0-0	5-8	0-4-4	4	17	2	2	1	0	28
Nieman	0-1	0-0	0-0	0-3-3	2	0	0	1	0	1	8
Horner	1-1	0-0	0-0	0-0-0	5	2	0	3	0	0	15
TEAM				1-3-4				1			
Totals	**26-43**	**8-15**	**23-32**	**7-24-31**	**21**	**83**	**19**	**22**	**7**	**9**	**201**
Pct.	.605	.533	.719	DB: 5							

FG: (1st half: 13-26, .500; 2nd half: 13-17, .765)
3FG: (1st half: 4-9, .444; 2nd half: 4-6, .667)
FT: (1st half: 8-9, .889; 2nd half: 15-23, .652)

Officials: Bryan Kersey, Ray Natili, Curtis Shaw
Attendance: 19,700 • **Technical Fouls:** Hansbrough (UNC)

Score by Periods	1st	2nd	Total
North Carolina	36	43	79
NC State	38	45	83

After Coach got the box score, he walked back in and wrote the number of points State scored in the second half (45) and their second half field goal percentage (76.5) on the board. He walked out without saying a word.

I hate citing inexperience for losses. In this case, however, it was probably true. I've been doing some shooting in the mornings and a couple days later when I went into the locker room, Coach Robinson was writing the Duke scouting report on the board.

"Watching that State clip tape was one of the most painful film sessions we've had," I said. It was true. It was disgusting to watch us make constant mistakes.

"It was tough, but we had some pretty tough ones your first year, too," he said. That was my redshirt year, which was also Coach Williams's first year at Carolina.

"But now we know better," I said. "Back then, we didn't understand. Now we shouldn't have any excuses, which makes it even more painful."

His response was a good one: "Some of these guys don't understand yet, either."

That's a great point. I've been here long enough to know a performance like the one against NC State was unacceptable. Not everyone knows that. Our freshmen don't know that. Maybe some of our sophomores don't even know that. I can't always assume everyone has the same background as I do.

And we're so much further along than his first team. That team had a lot to overcome in every area. We had more problems than just playing hard and playing the right way. We've won on the road this year and that team couldn't win on the road at all. We've been at the top of the ACC. We've won some big games. In order to make sure we don't turn into that team, we have to make the NC State game the exception rather than the rule.

I was expecting a brutal practice after the State game. I should have known better. Coach knew it wouldn't be smart to run us too hard a couple days before we went to Durham. Instead, we watched 45 minutes of film. That's a substantial amount for us, and the clips they selected highlighted the mistakes we made.

"I'm not going to kill you at practice," Coach said. "But we do have to get better. And we are going to get better starting right now."

LUCAS: PASSION PLAY

FEB. 3, 2007

RALEIGH—Carolina arrived at the RBC Center Saturday afternoon ready to play a game.

NC State arrived at the RBC Center Saturday afternoon ready to contest a rivalry.

The difference showed.

It's been a nice almost decade-long hiatus for this particular rivalry. During that time, the Carolina-Duke battles exploded into a national phenomenon. Several cycles of UNC students have come and gone from Chapel Hill without fully appreciating the Carolina-State rivalry.

There wasn't much to appreciate. In the early 2000s, the Tar Heels fell from their familiar perch atop college basketball. Once the ship was righted, State was being led by Herb Sendek, who approached the Carolina game exactly like the other 30 on his schedule.

That's not how the rest of Wolfpack nation sees it. Never has been. Never will be.

The only people surprised by Saturday's outcome were those not up on their Carolina-State history, a group that—up until Saturday at about 6 p.m.—evidently included most of the Tar Heel players.

Surprised? Try this:

1992. Carolina's starting lineup: George Lynch, Hubert Davis, Eric Montross, Pat Sullivan, Derrick Phelps. State's starting lineup: Tom Gugliotta, Donnie Seale, Curtis Marshall, Kevin Thompson, Mark Davis.

The outcome? A 99–88 State victory. The Wolfpack went on to lose their next 9 games, including a home loss to East Tennessee State. They broke the losing streak against Carolina, with a 99–94 victory.

1995. Carolina's starting lineup: Jeff McInnis, Donald Williams, Pearce Landry, Jerry Stackhouse, Rasheed Wallace. State's starting lineup: Lakista McCuller, Ishua Benjamin, Bryant Feggins, Todd Fuller, Ricky Daniels.

The outcome? An 80–70 State victory.

1998. Carolina's starting lineup: Ademola Okulaja, Antawn Jamison, Vince Carter, Shammond Williams, Makhtar Ndiaye. State's starting lineup: Kenny Inge, Ron Kelley, C.C. Harrison, Ishua Benjamin, Cornelius Williams.

The outcome? An 86–72 State victory.

Sure, all of that is history, and none of it had any impact on Saturday's game.

Or maybe it did. State played the game like it meant something in a grander historical context. Carolina played the game like it was the last one they had to get out of the way before going to Duke on Wednesday night. Five or 10 or 15 years from now, we'll list the starting lineups from this game and they'll look just like the above—like a walkover on paper.

We're officially back to the days when the State game is a tossup no matter what the relative strength of the two teams competing in the game. Sidney Lowe gets it. He has the same purebred hatred for Carolina that Roy Williams has for State. For the last three seasons, the Tar Heels have thrived on Williams's passion because there wasn't an equal amount of emotion coming from Raleigh. That's over now. No one has any idea what kind of success Lowe will have at State, whether he'll be there for five years or 50 years. But for every single one of those years, he will burn to beat Carolina.

If you're Carolina coming into Raleigh, you have to expect someone to have a career day from the 3-point line (Courtney Fells, 4-for-5). You have to expect an unsung player to shine (Ben McCauley, 6-of-6 from the floor and 17 points). You have to expect the fluky, the bizarre, and the weird. Because that is what happens in Carolina-State games.

"They had much more passion for the game than we did today," Williams said.

That's a good word for it—passion. Ty Lawson was asked about the team's lack of passion after the game. This was the exchange:

Ty, Coach said the team lacked passion. Did you think so?

"I thought I played with intensity. In the beginning you could tell they had more intensity than us, though."

See, that's the thing. Intensity means focus. Let's accept that the Tar Heels had that.

Passion means you can't bear the thought of losing the game. Passion means the mere sight of the other team's uniforms makes your pulse quicken. Passion means you've known the date of the game since the schedule was released.

Only one side had passion on Saturday.

The current Tar Heels don't know this rivalry. They grew up at various towns in America weaned on Carolina-Duke. No matter where they lived, no matter what kind of cable package they had, they've always watched Carolina-Duke. The nation watches that game.

The state watches Carolina-State. These Tar Heels don't know about Vinny Del Negro in 1987 or the sheer joy (and relief) at finally beating David Thompson in 1975.

There was a play with one minute to go in the first half. Brandon Costner got the ball at the top of the key against Tyler Hansbrough and Lowe asked everyone else to clear out and let Costner operate. As the other four Wolfpack players moved aside, a buzz built in the RBC Center.

This is what State fans love. This is their scrappy underdog against Carolina's All-American. This is the perfect embodiment of exactly how they picture the rivalry in one nice, neat package. You could feel it. When Costner lofted a 3-pointer, no one wearing red had any doubt that the ball was going straight through the hoop. When it bounded off the rim, there was an audible, "Awww . . . ," as if someone had just ripped off Santa's beard.

That's how much they care.

"It seemed like everyone in our locker room understood this was a big game," Wes Miller said.

"But I know everyone understands it now for sure."

DUKE

THE DUKE GAME is just another game on the schedule.

Yeah, right.

Granted, it's not the national championship. And a victory just counts for one win in the race for the ACC title. But every player on this team, whether they grew up in North Carolina or Illinois or California, remembers as a kid stopping what they were doing two times per season to watch Duke-Carolina. So when we take the floor, we know people all over the country are doing the same thing.

I pay attention to Duke even when we're not playing them. They're eight miles down the road and they're our rivals. They've also been good every year I've been here, so their performance usually impacts us in the ACC race. I watched at home when they lost their last game to Florida State. Hoots and Preston and I were watching in different rooms, and when Duke didn't score on their last possession, we all started cheering. It's nothing against the individuals on this year's Duke team. It's just that when you're a Tar Heel, you don't cheer for the Blue Devils. You just can't do it.

It's the rare game that's about more than just the game. It's also about the night before and the day of the game. I couldn't sleep at all the night before we went to Durham this year. I started thinking about all the Duke-Carolina games I watched as a kid. It's almost like Christmas Eve. All those moments you see on TV all the time were running through my mind: Eric Montross bleeding, Jerry Stackhouse's dunk, Jeff Capel's half-court shot. I remember watching Rashad play in the Duke-Carolina game for the first time when I was at James Madison. I couldn't believe I knew someone playing in the country's greatest rivalry. Playing in one of those games isn't just being a part of a basketball game. It's being a part of history.

As a senior, I knew this would be my last time playing in Cameron. I'd always dreamed of playing in this game and this was going to be my last chance. I visualized things that could happen. It was a long, long night. There haven't been many times this year that I've been conscious of this year being my last chance at Carolina. This was one of those times.

Fortunately, the day of the game I had two classes. That helps time move faster. Duke-Carolina games during the week are always at 9 p.m., and that can make for a very slow day if your class schedule is light. I went to Naval Weapons at 9 a.m. and had my golf class at noon, so I was able to relax and hit some golf balls. Even in class, though, it's the only thing people are talking about. Everybody wants to say,

"Good luck," or ask a question about the game. Everybody knows when it's game day in Chapel Hill. But when it's game day and it's the Duke game, everybody knows *and* they want to talk about it.

The bus ride to Durham was quiet. I always wear headphones on the bus ride. I put on some jazz and listen to Miles Davis—that's been my routine since high school. It's a short bus ride, but it was obvious everyone was focused. There are times with this team that I've been worried about our focus before a game. Not this time. It never crossed my mind to worry about whether we'd be ready to play. I actually had the opposite worry: whether anyone would be too pumped up.

Their crowd contributes to the atmosphere. They tend to be more clever than mean, and usually I can get a laugh out of it even if it's aimed at me. In warm-ups, I always try to listen to the chants and read the signs. The funniest thing I've seen in my four years happened my redshirt year. A couple students had a cheeseburger attached to a fishing pole, and they threw it on the court near Sean May. When he got close, they started reeling it in. That's the kind of joke we'll talk about later—especially if we win.

They had a couple good ones this year. Dewey, Ty, and I were the first three out to shoot an hour before the game. The crowd started chanting, "Short and stumpy." I thought that was pretty funny. Later Jonas was stretching out Tyler. Tyler was lying on his stomach and Jonas was behind him, and the students started chanting, "Use protection." That was funny. If it's clever rather than mean, I don't mind getting a laugh out of it.

It's important to take a minute to soak in the crowd and all the extracurricular stuff around a Duke-Carolina game. Otherwise you're just playing in a normal basketball game. But once we went back into the locker room, all the outside stuff was forgotten. The first time I went into the visiting locker room at Cameron I thought, "Man, this is really cramped." Now I don't think twice about it because it feels so comfortable to me. Some great memories came back, including jumping around like crazy after beating them on Senior Day last year.

It's special to beat Duke because they have a very good program. Defensively, they try to take you out of your game. They apply pressure on the ball. They don't let you throw the ball around the perimeter, because they step into passing lanes and switch all screens. That's a unique approach—not many teams pressure as hard as they do while switching all screens.

Playing that way opens some driving lanes. That's the area we want to exploit when we play Duke. We'd worked on our spacing in practice, but in the first half we didn't do a great job. In the second half, we did a better job of spreading out and letting Ty and Bobby and Marcus get in the gaps. We also were able to spread the floor and work inside to Tyler and Brandan. Duke takes away so many things defensively, but anytime you take something away on defense, you have to accept giving up something else. We were able to take advantage of what they were giving up in the second half.

I spent the opening minutes of the game watching Greg Paulus from the bench. He was playing very well, and I remember thinking, "When I get in the game, I'm going to change the way he's playing. I'm going to eliminate his looks and make it difficult for him." I wanted to make him earn every shot he took while I was in the game.

Once Coach put me in the game, the first thing I did was

increase my pressure on Paulus. I could tell right away he was uncomfortable. It took him out of his rhythm, and it gave me more confidence because I felt like I was making a contribution to the game. At the same time, my teammates began to feed off my defense. Marcus and Bobby were also playing great defensively, so our entire team's defensive intensity was elevated.

After Reyshawn didn't get a single rebound against State, Coach had been on him in practice this week. It was no surprise that Reyshawn had a great first half. He got tangled up with Duke's big guy, Brian Zoubek, early in the game on the baseline and they were wrestling hard for the ball. It set the stage for the game: neither side is backing down. That was a very important play because it provided an example to our younger guys of the kind of play required to win a Duke-Carolina game. If Reyshawn didn't have the big first half that he had, we would have been down by more than five points at halftime.

The halftime locker room was much different than against NC State. There wasn't a sense of worry. Marcus said a couple times, "We have to do a better job on the guards and we have to do a better job on the ball screen." Coach talked about the same things. We needed our big guys to hedge better on the ball screen and we needed our guards to get over the top better.

Coach Holladay and Coach Robinson pointed out the success their guards were having offensively. "This is on you," Coach Robinson told the guards. "You have to step up and defend in the second half." I took that personally. I'm a guard. I don't want to be the reason Duke's guards are having career days. That was the biggest adjustment I wanted to make in the second half.

We were down 50–41 when Coach went with an unusual lineup: Bobby, Tyler, Marcus, Reyshawn, and me. That's not a group that has been on the floor together much this year. At the time, I didn't think about how much experience that lineup had. That's not the kind of thing you think about as a player when you're in the flow of the game. Coach tells you to go in the game, and you go in. The only thing you think about is who you're guarding and what you're supposed to be doing offensively.

Bobby and I were at the scorer's table together, and I looked at him and said, "Let's pick this up. We're going to do it right now."

I could feel a change when we got on the court together. Those first couple of minutes, all five guys on the court were very intense defensively. It wasn't until the first media timeout when we were on the floor together that I had a chance to process which players were in the game. My first thought was, "This group hasn't been in much at all together this year." My second thought was, "These are all guys who have a lot of confidence in each other."

During that stretch in the second half, I got into a zone. It's no one's fault but my own, but there have been times this year that every time the horn blows I look up to see if I'm coming out of the game. It's my fault, and I know I should just play, but I've fallen into that habit. In the second half of the Duke game, though, I never once looked to see if I was coming out. All I could think about was who I was guarding. It was as focused and confident as I have been all year.

We closed it to 52–47 and tried to play some four-out, one-in with Tyler in the middle. It was a familiar setup, because we played a good bit that way last year since David Noel was more of a perimeter player as our four-man. I saw the ball go inside to Tyler and he was double-teamed. I was sitting there helpless on the wing, and I knew from the angle that he couldn't kick it out to me.

But suddenly he split the double and it was like the Red Sea parted. I was wide open. He kicked it to me and without even thinking, I stepped into it and let it fly. As soon as the shot went in, I knew it was a big shot. It was as exciting a moment as I've had this year. I looked at the bench and thought, "We're doing this." My parents were sitting right behind the bench and they said they could see it in my eyes. They said they thought it was as focused as I've been all year, and I definitely felt that way.

With a few minutes left, that focus was tested. We were up 66–63 and I went to the free throw line. Someone told me later the crowd was chanting, "Walk-on." I honestly had no idea. I can tell you everything about their pregame chants and signs but nothing about what happened during the game. Once I knocked the first one in, I knew the second one was going in. When I miss free throws, it's always the first one, not the second one. On the second, I thought my release and stroke were good, but I didn't get enough legs into it. It bounced away, and we had a four-point lead.

There was a timeout with 32 seconds left and we were up by seven points. At that moment, I looked around and thought, "We're really going to win the game." As soon as that thought entered my mind, I thought, "Stop thinking that. Things can still happen. This is Duke-Carolina." I didn't even want to celebrate in my head. Finally, during another timeout with under 10 seconds left, I felt more comfortable showing some outward emotion about winning the game.

It was a happy, happy locker room. We have always wanted to do our celebrating in the locker room rather than on the court, so we didn't hang around on the floor after the game. I'll never forget this: as we were jumping around, I almost had to step back out of the mosh pit. It was the first time I realized I was exhausted. I can't describe how I felt inside after that game. It was as satisfied as I've been after a game in a long time, and it was also as tired as I've been after a game in a long time. I could barely speak because of the combination of physical and mental exhaustion. I'm not sure anyone saw it, but I even had a couple tears of joy running down my face. The interviews I did after the game were some of the worst of my life, because I just didn't have anything else left to give.

Duke is unique in that everyone kind of gathers on the court for a few minutes after the game. By the time I got back out there, my family was standing there near center court. John Lyon, a photographer who goes to all our games, happened to be standing there, and my dad asked him if he would take a couple pictures. It was a really neat moment. I didn't want anyone to perceive it as me mocking Duke. It was just a moment I want to remember. My last game at Cameron, our second straight win there, and I was able to contribute to the victory. I grew up watching this rivalry and I want to have a memory of the last time I was able to participate. I don't know if I ever want to go back to Cameron Indoor Stadium, and if I don't I want to remember how I walked out the last time.

The bus ride home was exciting. They played the last eight minutes on the bus televisions. We all had pizza and we were all talking about going to Franklin Street to see what the students had done. I try not to eat pizza because it's not healthy, but when I do I love Hawaiian pizza from Domino's. The night before, Preston had told me he was getting Domino's for the postgame. I said, "Preston, there would be nothing better in the world than getting on the bus after beating Duke and eating Hawaiian pizza." That's exactly what I did.

I doubt I'll ever forget that pizza—or anything else from that night.

Game 24

#5/5 North Carolina 79
#16/16 Duke 73
Feb. 7, 2007 • Cameron Indoor Stadium, Durham, N.C.

UNC	FG	3FG	FT	REB	PF	TP	A	TO	B	S	Min
Terry*	4-8	2-3	0-0	1-9-10	2	10	3	5	1	1	26
Wright*	9-12	0-0	1-2	1-8-9	1	19	0	2	1	0	24
Hansbrough*	5-9	0-0	6-6	1-2-3	3	16	1	2	1	1	34
Ellington*	2-8	0-2	0-0	0-1-1	2	4	1	0	0	1	18
Lawson*	6-12	0-2	3-4	2-6-8	3	15	4	3	0	1	25
Ginyard	1-2	0-1	3-4	2-0-2	0	5	3	0	0	0	18
Thomas	0-1	0-0	0-0	0-0-0	2	0	1	0	0	0	3
Green	2-4	0-1	0-0	1-1-2	1	4	0	0	1	0	11
Thompson	0-1	0-0	0-0	0-0-0	2	0	0	1	2	0	8
Miller	1-2	1-2	1-2	0-0-0	1	4	0	0	0	0	17
Stephenson	0-0	0-0	0-0	0-0-0	0	0	0	0	0	0	4
Frasor	1-2	0-1	0-0	0-2-2	0	2	1	0	0	2	12
TEAM				2-0-2							
Totals	31-61	3-12	14-18	10-29-39	17	79	14	13	6	7	200
Pct.	.508	.250	.778	DB: 1							

FG: (1st half: 15-34, .441; 2nd half: 16-27, .593)
3FG: (1st half: 2-8, .250; 2nd half: 1-4, .250)
FT: (1st half: 2-2, 1.000; 2nd half: 12-16, .750)

DU	FG	3FG	FT	REB	PF	TP	A	TO	B	S	Min
McClure*	0-3	0-0	0-0	3-2-5	1	0	0	2	3	1	22
Henderson*	6-13	1-3	1-1	2-2-4	1	14	2	1	1	1	25
Zoubek*	0-0	0-0	0-0	0-2-2	0	0	3	2	0	1	11
Paulus*	5-17	1-4	4-4	0-3-3	5	15	4	0	0	1	37
Scheyer*	8-18	4-10	6-8	1-0-1	5	26	0	2	1	1	38
McRoberts	3-5	0-0	0-2	3-8-11	4	6	3	4	1	1	30
Pocius	0-0	0-0	0-0	0-0-0	1	0	0	0	0	0	1
Davidson	0-0	0-0	0-0	0-0-0	0	0	0	0	0	0	0+
Nelson	5-6	1-1	1-4	0-2-2	0	12	1	4	1	2	25
Thomas	0-1	0-0	0-0	1-0-1	1	0	0	0	0	1	11
TEAM				1-3-4							
Totals	27-63	7-18	12-19	11-22-33	18	73	10	16	9	8	200
Pct.	.429	.389	.632	DB: 4							

FG: (1st half: 13-31, .419; 2nd half: 14-32, .438)
3FG: (1st half: 4-10, .400; 2nd half: 3-8, .375)
FT: (1st half: 9-9, 1.000; 2nd half: 3-10, .300)

Officials: Ted Valentine, Gary Maxwell, Reggie Greenwood
Attendance: 9,314 • **Technical Fouls:** Thompson (UNC)

Score by Periods	1st	2nd	Total
North Carolina	34	45	79
Duke	39	34	73

LUCAS: SENIOR MOMENTS

FEB. 7, 2007

Wes Miller is having a moment.

An hour after Carolina had dispatched Duke 79–73 at Cameron Indoor Stadium, Miller was lugging his travel bag to the Tar Heel bus. To get there, he had to walk across Coach K Court.

He was intercepted by his family and girlfriend. They hugged and they high-fived, not necessarily in that order.

Photographer extraordinaire John Lyon happened to walk by, and he snapped a photo of the happy Millers. Their toes were just touching the center jump circle with the royal blue "D." Their arms were around each other. And they were smiling—broadly.

The moment made you want to run down to Miller and make sure he soaked it in for just a second longer. For the next 50 years, he'll look at that picture and remember the night he closed out his Cameron Indoor Stadium career with a victory. Can you imagine what that would feel like?

He almost didn't get that feeling. Down 50–41 with 14 minutes to play, it's OK to admit that you didn't believe. All day, this game had been looming with a curious sense of excitement and dread.

Excitement, because it was Duke. Because Carolina won in Durham last year when no one believed it was possible and because this was a chance for a 2-game winning streak in the rivalry and because it was an opportunity to deepen Duke's misery by sending them to a three-game losing streak overall. And because you looked at these two teams on paper, compared the stats and the rosters and the results, and you thought, "*We* can't lose to *them*." And you smiled, because you were confident.

But not confident enough to jinx anything, of course.

Dread, because, well, it was Duke. They are tough and they are gritty and they make everything difficult. They play good defense and they dive for loose balls and they slow the tempo. And you looked at all the close games they had played and the imposing specter of Cameron Indoor Stadium, and you thought, "We *can't* lose to them." And you grimaced, because you were nervous.

But not nervous enough to be scared of those dastardly Dukies, of course.

But at 50–41, it was time to stop being nervous and start shouting. It was time for these Tar Heels to decide if they were content to be a very talented group of basketball players that won some games or if they wanted to be a winning basketball team.

"It was time," Bobby Frasor said, "to get down and dirty."

Exactly. This is the lineup Roy Williams deployed: Frasor, Tyler Hansbrough, Marcus Ginyard, Reyshawn Terry, and Miller. That is perhaps the slowest, shortest, least athletic lineup Carolina has available.

But it's also one of the most experienced lineups available. At Monday's practice, Williams stopped practice and pointed at Terry. "He's won at

Cameron Indoor Stadium," he said. Then he pointed to Miller. "And he's won at Cameron Indoor Stadium." The process continued until he'd singled out every player with a win in Durham. The implication was clear—Carolina might have some talented freshmen, but they were entering uncharted waters.

And with the game in the balance, all five players on the floor could claim a road win over Duke.

But they weren't out there simply because they were older. They were out there because they were the most effective.

Understand that this season has been difficult for Miller. He is a good shooter who for some reason is shooting 28.8% from the 3-point line. That is not how the storybook senior season is supposed to go.

About three weeks ago, he made a commitment to himself: no matter what was happening with his shot, when he got into the game he was going to play the type of vigorous defense that turns games around. He was going to move his feet, clap his hands, and be an all-around pest.

That is what he wanted to do to Greg Paulus.

"I wanted to bother him," Miller said. "I didn't want him to feel like he could make a pass without thinking twice about it. I didn't want anything to be easy for him."

To that point, Paulus was 4-for-9 with 13 points.

He would hit just one of his last eight field goal attempts.

The storyline will be that Paulus was fatigued. Does anyone ever think to ask how he got that way? The answer is simple—defense. Intense, game-changing defense.

This is why we keep watching sports. Because on a court with remarkable raw talent, with future NBA Draft picks battling at almost every position and even holding down a few spots on the bench, it was the (allegedly) 5-foot-11 Miller who changed the game.

"They were playing such hard defense," said Ty Lawson, who watched from the bench and then returned refreshed later in the half. "We needed everyone to play defense the way Wes, Bobby, and Marcus were playing defense. They took Duke's guards out of the game." Lawson would be the beneficiary of that defense. By the time he returned to the game, the gap had tightened and the Carolina spark was reignited.

Eventually, the Tar Heels would push the lead to 75–70 with 11 seconds left. Hansbrough was on the free throw line for two shots, and he converted them both. They were the shots that basically sealed Duke's fate, and they led to a Carolina timeout.

As he walked to the Tar Heel huddle, Miller almost let a smile cross his face. Instead, he settled for just pumping his fists, shouting, "Yeah!"

"It was such an indescribable feeling," he would say moments later. "There are no words to describe what it's like to come into this hostile environment and win. It's one of the greatest things about being a college basketball player. This was my last time at Duke, and I went out with two wins. It feels . . ."

His words trailed off, like he wasn't sure he could do his feelings justice.

"Amazing. It feels amazing."

So maybe it was wrong. Maybe Wes Miller wasn't having just one moment.

Maybe he just had a whole night of them.

THE REUNION

One of Coach Williams's favorite sayings is, "Carolina Basketball is much bigger than any of us. It's bigger than any of you and it's bigger than me."

The weekend of the Wake Forest game, we got to see a living example.

To celebrate the 25th anniversary of the 1982 title team and the 50th anniversary of the 1957 team, every member of those teams was invited back to Chapel Hill. Almost every person attended, and it turned into quite a spectacle.

My first introduction to the 1957 team came during my redshirt season. During that season, Coach Williams organized a letterman's reunion, which had speeches from every era and featured almost 250 Tar Heel basketball lettermen. Hearing the stories of that undefeated '57 team and the great scoring of Lennie Rosenbluth was a treat for a basketball junkie like me.

But Coach never talks about their 32–0 record or even their triple-overtime championship win over Wilt Chamberlain. He talks about the bond that team has. With all the living members in attendance, it was very evident how close that team remains. They're still like brothers. Even when they haven't seen each other for a couple years, they can get together and pick up just like they're in college. It makes me feel good inside. It also makes me wonder if our 2005 team will be the same way. And I can't help but wonder if one day the 2007 team might have that same bond, too.

The 1982 team was one that had a major impact on the game of basketball. For players of my generation, we grew up on an NBA that featured Michael Jordan, James Worthy, and Sam Perkins. All three of those players were on the '82 team. I had met a couple of those guys briefly, but looked forward to spending more time with them. I also thought it was important for our current team to have the opportunity to spend time around a couple of championship teams. I wanted the young guys to see the kind of bond those teams had—and still have. Hopefully, that will motivate us to follow the same path.

It was the only time in my Carolina career that I've gotten the sense from the crowd that the game is almost secondary. The players from both teams were seated behind one of the baskets, and when Michael Jordan walked to his seat I felt the hairs on the back of my neck stand up. There's something about his presence—even if you're not watching him, you can feel it.

We didn't get to see the halftime ceremony because we were in the locker room. It's a pretty long tunnel from the floor to the locker room, but we could still hear the roar as all the players and coaches from '57 and '82 were introduced.

Game 25											

Wake Forest 67
#5/5 North Carolina 104
Feb. 10, 2007 • Smith Center, Chapel Hill

WFU	FG	3FG	FT	REB	PF	TP	A	TO	B	S	Min
Skeen*	2-6	1-3	4-4	2-4-6	3	9	1	0	0	0	27
Visser*	4-10	0-0	3-5	1-2-3	5	11	1	1	0	0	26
Williams*	4-9	0-2	1-1	1-0-1	2	9	1	1	0	0	22
Hale*	2-6	1-3	0-0	0-0-0	3	5	2	2	0	1	17
Smith*	3-7	0-0	0-0	0-6-6	4	6	6	5	0	2	34
Drum	2-5	1-2	0-0	1-1-2	3	5	0	0	0	0	15
Weaver	1-3	0-0	2-3	1-0-1	2	4	0	1	0	0	11
Gurley	4-12	2-6	2-4	0-2-2	0	12	0	1	0	1	19
Dukes	0-1	0-0	0-0	1-1-2	0	0	1	3	0	1	5
Swinton	2-3	0-0	2-2	1-2-3	2	6	0	1	1	1	9
Stanley	0-1	0-1	0-0	1-0-1	0	0	0	2	0	1	8
McFarland	0-2	0-0	0-0	1-1-2	1	0	0	0	1	0	4
Crawford	0-0	0-0	0-0	0-1-1	1	0	0	0	0	0	3
TEAM				2-1-3							
Totals	24-65	5-17	14-19	12-21-33	26	67	12	17	2	7	200
Pct.	.369	.294	.737	DB: 3							

FG: (1st half: 11-34, .324; 2nd half: 13-31, .419)
3FG: (1st half: 2-8, .250; 2nd half: 3-9, .333)
FT: (1st half: 8-10, .800; 2nd half: 6-9, .667)

UNC	FG	3FG	FT	REB	PF	TP	A	TO	B	S	Min
Terry*	7-8	3-3	6-6	1-7-8	4	23	0	0	0	0	17
Hansbrough*	4-6	0-0	8-9	0-3-3	2	16	1	0	0	0	21
Wright*	7-7	0-0	1-2	2-5-7	1	15	5	1	0	2	22
Ellington*	3-7	1-4	4-4	0-1-1	1	11	5	0	0	0	21
Lawson*	3-7	1-2	0-0	0-2-2	1	7	6	2	0	0	21
Thompson	3-8	0-0	0-2	3-4-7	3	6	1	2	0	1	20
Frasor	1-2	1-2	0-0	0-0-0	0	3	1	1	0	2	8
Green	0-3	0-3	4-4	0-1-1	0	4	0	3	1	1	10
Ginyard	2-5	0-2	1-1	3-2-5	0	5	3	0	1	1	17
Stepheson	1-3	0-0	0-0	1-3-4	3	2	0	3	0	0	13
Thomas	0-1	0-0	2-2	0-0-0	0	2	1	3	0	0	11
Miller	2-4	2-4	0-0	0-0-0	1	6	1	0	0	0	9
Copeland	1-2	0-0	1-2	1-1-2	1	3	0	0	0	1	4
Wood	0-0	0-0	0-0	0-1-1	0	0	0	0	0	0	3
Burke	0-1	0-1	1-2	1-0-1	0	1	0	1	0	0	3
TEAM				1-0-1							
Totals	34-64	8-21	28-34	12-31-43	17	104	24	13	5	8	200
Pct.	.562	.500	.778	DB: 2							

FG: (1st half: 17-28, .607; 2nd half: 17-36, .472)
3FG: (1st half: 3-8, .375; 2nd half: 5-13, .385)
FT: (1st half: 14-17, .824; 2nd half: 14-17, .824)

Officials: Les Jones, Roger Ayers, Bernard Clinton
Attendance: 21,750 • **Technical Fouls:** none

Score by Periods	1st	2nd	Total
Wake Forest	32	35	67
North Carolina	51	53	104

It would have been a major downer on a special occasion for us to lose to Wake Forest. Fortunately, we won 104–67, and the margin of victory created a nice moment at the end of the game. With about 20 seconds left, Coach Williams walked down the bench and looked up where the former players were seated. He gave them a standing ovation and everyone on our bench followed his lead. It was a subtle gesture, but people who know Coach Williams understand what a big deal it was. He is a coach who values every second of every game. Whether we are behind by 30 or up by 30, he coaches like it's a one-possession game. For him to take some time out from the game to acknowledge the former players was another example of how special the weekend was for him.

LUCAS: ONE EXTRAORDINARY DAY

FEB. 10, 2007

Michael Jordan is in the kitchen making coffee.

Where else, other than Jordan's house, do they say those words?

Saturday, that's exactly what the man who came to Chapel Hill as a lanky basketball player and exploded into a worldwide brand was doing. This is to be considered normal at Carolina. You walk into the basketball office a couple of hours before the game, and there's an all-time great taking cream and sugar.

Can this be considered normal? On this day, in this place, at this time, it was.

Days like this don't happen anywhere else. You know that, right?

It takes a really remarkable day to be extraordinary in Chapel Hill. This is a place where NBA All-Stars roam the halls in the summer and players from one of the nation's best college teams can often be found playing ping-pong in the basement.

But Saturday was extraordinary.

It started with the dedication of the newly-named Bill Guthridge Locker Room, as the Tar Heel locker room was renamed for one of the most dedicated Tar Heels ever. The ceremony was held in the tiny hallway outside the locker room, with a podium wedged against the door and attendees standing shoulder-to-shoulder.

Roy Williams likes to bring his team in tight before they take the floor in a big road game, so they can feel the energy and the closeness. It was the same way for the dedication. There was the entire living roster of the 1957 title team on that side of the podium. Here was the 1982 team on this side. It was like walking through a Carolina Basketball Encyclopedia.

"It's a great thrill for me to pull up in the parking lot and see the Dean Smith Center," Roy Williams told the small crowd. "And it will be a great thrill for me to walk into this locker room and see the Bill Guthridge Locker Room."

Guthridge is best-known by some Carolina fans for his calm sideline demeanor, crunching ice while directing the Tar Heels to two Final Fours in three years as a head coach. Few outside the locker room ever got to see the passion that burned behind that façade.

He started out with his trademark dry wit, saying, "I have to pinch myself. Usually this only happens to people when they're dead. So I wanted to make sure I was OK."

Then the tears came. As he tried to thank his family, the tears came, and they wouldn't stop.

But it wasn't uncomfortable. Everyone pressed together in that small space knew how much he'd given to Carolina, how much his time in Chapel Hill had meant to him. In a bigger setting, it probably would have been cause for some applause to pick him up. In this environment, though, it was OK to soak in the feelings.

Eventually, he recovered. "You know, I could beat anybody running the golf course," Guthridge said, "except for Michael Jordan. He wouldn't lose."

That's when you heard a familiar deep chuckle. And standing right next to you was Michael Jordan.

Do I lose professionalism points by telling you that it made my stomach flip?

Jordan, of course, was the picture of calm. "I couldn't lose," he said. "I would've had to run again."

So do you see why highlights won't work for this day? It was about relationships and hugs and the ties that bind.

The '82 team is a bunch of rock stars. Really, they are. They have a handful of members who need just one name—Jordan and Perkins and Worthy and Coach Smith. In most places, they would be the show. The beauty of Saturday was that they were as enthralled by the 1957 team as everyone else was by the '82 squad.

"Don't get me wrong, I want to see the guys from my class," Perkins said. "But I also wanted to see the history that came before me. Those '57 guys, they are so close. And it's great to see that."

The 37-point win over Wake Forest was perhaps

the most anticlimactic ACC basketball game in conference history. This story is supposed to be about
the game. Do you mind if we just skip that part?

For the first time ever, no one left their seats at
halftime. And when the '57 and '82 teams took the
floor together, flashbulbs popped like the first
pitch of the World Series.

They were saluted with videos put together by
Jones Angell, Ken Cleary and Justin Burnett.
Maybe you were part of the crowd of 21,750 that
watched the videos along with the players. But if
you took just a moment to take your eyes off the
screen and watch the players, you saw something
that would make you shiver:

Several of the 1957 players were crying. They
played in an era with no television, no internet,
and only the barest of radio. And now, 50 years
later, they were being greeted with a roar from
over 20,000 people who still appreciated what
they had done.

Will anyone remember what you've done today
50 years from now? And if so, can you imagine
how good it would feel?

And then, the '82 introductions. Perkins, Worthy,
Jordan and Smith on the end of the line. This was
not just a moment for Carolina basketball—it was a
moment for the entire basketball world. And when
you looked over at the tiny Wake Forest rooting section behind their bench, you couldn't help but
notice that almost every single one of them had
out their cameras or cell phones, snapping photos
so they could prove they were there, too, on a very

memorable day. It's impressive, sure, when you're loved by your own. It's even more impressive when you're respected by your foes.

Jordan threw his left arm around Smith and planted a kiss on the top of his head as the head coach—he'll always be the head coach, even if Roy Williams officially bears the title now—was introduced. It was a spine-tingler. The greatest basketball player of all time and the regal coach who often kept his emotions hidden, for one brief second open for the entire world to see.

We hear and read about the Carolina basketball family. In that moment, Jordan and Smith cracked the door for all of us to actually *see* it.

"Sometimes, on a day-to-day basis, we get so wrapped up in the next practice that we don't take time to look at the rafters at the jerseys or banners and think about the history here," Wes Miller said. "We've got it around us with pictures and banners. But to actually have the people who are part of that history come back, and to see them so involved with the program, it shows how special Carolina basketball really is."

Tonight, Miller and the rest of his teammates will join the '57 and '82 players at a banquet where they'll get another taste of the history they are living. The current Tar Heels were in the locker room as the halftime ceremony ended. They didn't see the '57 and '82 teams embrace. One-by-one, they shook each other's hands—Rosenbluth and Black, Brennan and Worthy, Jordan and Kearns.

They've gone their own way and made their

own reputations and lived separate lives. But in that moment, on the Smith Center floor, they greeted each other like brothers.

Like, yes, a family.

"It puts it into perspective," Bobby Frasor said. "It shows you how big North Carolina basketball is. It makes you so happy you're a part of it.

"We're lucky. We don't always think about it, but we're very lucky."

Before the letterman's banquet in 2004, Coach Williams gave the current players a simple instruction: "Don't be cool." He meant he wanted us to really pay attention to what was being said at the banquet. As college students we might have had a tendency to be blasé about what a great night it was. Coach wanted to make sure we appreciated how lucky we were for that one night.

He didn't give us the same "cool" speech before we attended the Saturday night banquet with the 1957 and 1982 teams. But he did explain what a great opportunity we had—not just to be in the presence of some great basketball players, but to soak in what it's like to be a part of an all-time great team.

Before the speeches began, the official photographer wanted the current team to pose with the '82 and '57 teams for a group picture. To be honest, it felt awkward to me. I didn't feel like we belonged. We're fortunate that we happened to be the current team when their anniversaries rolled around. But we haven't accomplished anything yet. The 1982 team had a trophy and the 1957 team had a trophy and we had nothing . . . yet.

I really enjoyed getting to stand on the stage with them. During the group photo, I was standing next to Wayne Ellington and Michael Jordan put his hand on Wayne's shoulder. I looked at Wayne and he had this crazy look on his face. I told him later, "I don't know what I'd do if Michael Jordan had his hands on my shoulders for a minute. Probably never wash that jacket again."

We're college athletes for one of the top programs in the country. When people see us around town, sometimes they're excited to see a basketball player. In our locker room, you'll hear guys say they would never be that excited just to meet another person. But when Michael Jordan walks in the room it doesn't matter who you are. Every guy on our team would say that in that moment they were back to being the seven-year-old kid who watched "Come Fly With Me" while wearing a number-23 jersey and then went out in the back-yard and practiced the moves.

For that reason, it was very exciting to be on the stage with the all-time greats. But I want to earn the right to stand beside them because we earn a championship.

Everyone who spoke at the banquet was very impressive. My favorite speech was Jordan's—not because it was Michael Jordan, but because he was concise and had a good message. He spoke about how Carolina Basketball had not only prepared him for his basketball career, but it built on the lessons his parents had taught him to be prepared for life in general.

His points about the 1982 team were not about basketball or about specific games. Instead, he told us he still felt all his teammates were his brothers. He looked right at us and told us this was our only chance to play with this group of team-mates. We'll never have this opportunity again, and it's important to take advantage of it.

That's a powerful message. When it's coming from the greatest basketball player of all time, it's even more impressive.

I happened to walk out of the Alumni Center with Eddie Fogler, an assistant coach on the 1982 team. I introduced myself and he said, "Wes, I know who you are. I really enjoy watching you play." Comments like that surprise me every time. I can't put into words what that means to me. At the letterman's reunion my first year, I almost didn't feel like I belonged. I was just a redshirt and I'm pretty sure not even all the guys on the current team realized I was on the team—much less any of the former players. This year, I felt more like a part of it. Jimmy Black approached me and said he liked the way I played the game. Sam Perkins introduced himself. And Eddie Fogler said he liked the way I play.

I'm a guy who would go to AAU tournaments as a high schooler and be amazed at all the college coaches who were there recruiting. I remember playing at an event at Fork Union and Coach Guthridge was there watching Jason Parker. Every 30 seconds I'd sneak a glance at him to see if he noticed me. Honestly, I don't think he did.

But now people like Coach Fogler know who I am and compliment my style of play. Not many people get to truly experience a dream come true. That's what I'm doing right now as a Carolina basketball player.

LUCAS: ONE EXTRAORDINARY NIGHT

FEB. 10, 2007

There is one room in the United States where Michael Jordan walks to the podium in front of a capacity audience and does not get a standing ovation. OK, maybe one room in the entire world where Michael Jordan walks to the podium in the front of a capacity audience and does not get a standing ovation.

Saturday night, that room was inside the Carolina Club on the UNC campus. Jordan was the last of four speakers to address a banquet honoring the 1957 and 1982 teams. And as he made his way to the front of the room, something remarkable happened—everyone clapped . . . while staying in their seats.

That's remarkable to you and to me. If Jordan walks to a podium in front of us, we stand on the chair and wave our hands above our heads and generally act like Julia Roberts in the polo scene from "Pretty Woman" (Woo woo woo!).

But in front of the '57 and '82 teams, Jordan is something he is nowhere else in the world—he is among peers. To some of them, he is still Mike Jordan. To all of them, he's simply family.

His presence was important because he was a key member of Dean Smith's first national championship. But as was mentioned several times during the night, and although history tends to obscure it, he was not *the* key member.

"I heard through the grapevine that Michael didn't want to speak tonight," said Jimmy Black, the point guard and co-captain from 1982 who was the first member of that team to address the gathering. "But Michael, with all you have accomplished, you can't step on any toes. I'm happy and proud to call you a teammate."

"This is our family," Roy Williams said as he

opened the evening. "And we always want our family to feel good about coming back."

On nights like tonight, they wouldn't have any choice. Fifty years of Tar Heel history was in the room, from the full living roster of the '57 squad to the '82 team to the current team. Williams usually gives his current players one simple instruction at reunion events: "Don't try to be cool." It means he doesn't want them to send text messages during the speeches, doesn't want them to check their watches, and doesn't want them to guess how much longer the speaker will be at the podium.

Pete Brennan, the versatile forward from the '57 team, was the night's first speaker and he addressed the current Tar Heels directly.

"Guys, I want you to listen to this," he said. "In 1957, we all realized Lennie Rosenbluth was the best shooter we had. So the rest of us knew we had to become a better rebounder, or a better defensive player, or a better passer. We had to struggle with that through our sophomore years.

"And when we understood that and became a team during our junior years, that's when we won a national title."

That title is familiar to many Carolina fans but not always easily accessible to the current team. This is a generation that considers the '91 Bulls-Lakers NBA Finals to be a historic game. So it was instructive to watch Danny Green raise an eyebrow at Marcus Ginyard as the details of the '57 squad's back-to-back triple overtime wins in the Final Four were recounted.

"Being from the West Coast, I think I'm missing a part of that whole Carolina tradition," freshman Alex Stepheson said. "I wasn't able to live in that moment and in that time. So I'm excited about getting a taste of everything."

The day's earlier events included the unveiling of a new banner honoring the perfect 32–0 record of the '57 team and head coach Frank McGuire. To some fans, it might have been simply another banner. But to the '57 Tar Heels, it was recognition they had been seeking for decades. Not for themselves, but for McGuire.

"Frank McGuire meant everything to us," said the night's second speaker, '57 reserve Bob Young. "Getting him the recognition he deserved was the highlight of the day."

It was a testament to the events of the evening that everyone could have probably identified a unique highlight. One of them came next, as the '82 team was saluted with a special '82-centric version of the now traditional "One Shining Moment" video. February 10 will be remembered for many different things in Chapel Hill. But it will be hard to forget the opportunity to watch Jordan, Worthy, and Perkins watching much younger versions of themselves while the current Tar Heels bobbed their heads to the song every player hopes to watch from the NCAA podium after accepting a championship trophy.

"Hey," Black said when he took the microphone, "I can probably make my mile time after watching that video."

Ever intent on sharing the credit, Black also called co-captains Chris Brust and Jeb Barlow to the podium. Barlow's final words perfectly captured the spirit of the night.

"I didn't play a single minute in the championship game," he said. "That was my last college game. And in the locker room after the game, Coach Smith came to my locker while my dad was sitting there and apologized for not getting me into the game.

"That is Carolina basketball and that is Dean Smith."

Jordan's speech was the shortest of the night, but its brevity made it crackle. Imagine that you're a 2007 Tar Heel. You're one of the five best teams in the country. But you're also very, very young.

And then the world's greatest basketball player stands at the front of the room, looks at each of you, and says the following:

"The memories I have with the '82 team can never be replaced. It's like no other team I played with.

"For the 2007 guys, this is the only time you will ever be on a team like this. The things you laugh about, the things you joke about, are the same things you'll talk about when you get together 25 or 50 years from now. That's what this program means.

"This will never be replaced in my memory. And this will always be home for me."

At exactly that moment, there was not a single college basketball player in the entire United States who wouldn't have wanted to be a Tar Heel. Only a select few get the opportunity. And they were all beaming.

"I love Carolina basketball," Williams told the room. "And that means I love the people in this room. That's why every single day I make sure I do every bit of work that I possibly can to make sure I don't cheat you."

Before the group disbanded, they made time for photos. One shot brought together all three teams. Wright and Perkins, Rosenbluth and Jordan, Worthy and Hansbrough.

The photo was exactly what it looked like:

A family portrait.

WEEK TWENTY

COMING OFF THE REUNION, there were times I'd allow myself to think about the possibility of earning another national championship ring. Not often and never for very long, but when I was standing up there with those other championship teams I couldn't help but think about it. We have one month until the NCAA Tournament begins, and there are times it seems so close.

And then there are times it feels so far away, like after we lost again to Virginia Tech. It was our fourth loss of the season and second in ten days. At this level, it's hard to distinguish between losses in terms of which is more disappointing. But losing at home to Virginia Tech, a team that had already beaten us once, is tough to live with. The way they beat us was even more disheartening, because they came into the Smith Center and out-toughed us. They were more physical than us and it seemed like they wanted to win more than we did.

I can't accept that.

We had a six-point lead with three minutes left in regulation. That's a situation we have practiced since the first day of practice. We go over it constantly—how we want to defend, how we want to execute, how we want to play.

I'm starting to realize how young we are. Some guys don't realize how great it is to go through an entire season and play close to your potential every single time. We came close during the national championship season. When we had a rare breakdown, it was fixed quickly and it wasn't repeated.

We haven't had that same instinct this year. Some of our key players are just so young. It's not their fault and there's not much that can be done to fix it. A good example happened late in regulation. We were up six and Virginia Tech was making a run. Ty had given the tired signal and he was on the bench sitting next to me. He was talking to me and seemed fine. So I said, "Ty, are you ready?"

"Yeah," he said.

"You have to go tell Coach," I told him. "You have to go back in the game."

I honestly think he had forgotten. He doesn't realize yet how important it is that he's our point guard and when he gives the tired sign he has the obligation to tell Coach when he is ready to go back into the game. He's our point guard. We depend on him and the other guys need him on the court.

I've played point guard in this system and I know how hard it is. Coach Williams will tell you how hard it is because he is very demanding of his quarterback. It eventually becomes instinctive, but there's a long learning curve. Even

Raymond Felton, as great as he was, had that year-long learning curve. Ty is still in the middle of that learning process. I can't wait to see how well this team clicks when he learns to run the team with that instinctive feeling.

It's hard for me to be critical of Ty because I also made big contributions to the loss. When we lose, there's usually one play that makes me unable to sleep. This time it happened in overtime. I was guarding Zabian Dowdell, who is a very good player. I was tight on him in the corner because I knew he wanted to make a play. He gave me a head fake and I rose up just a little. As soon as I left my feet, he went by me on the baseline and eventually drew a goaltending call on Brandan.

Not leaving our feet on defense has been one of the most emphasized points of this entire season. I know it better than anyone else. And in a crucial moment, I broke down. That cost us two points and we lost by one point. It turned out to be a game-changing play and it's on me. That's tough to handle.

Coach Williams came in the locker room after the game and said, "This loss is on me." He was upset with the way he managed the game down the stretch.

When he said that, the first thing I thought was, "No way." The second thing I thought was that when he went back to watch the tape, he was going to see how much we contributed to the loss. He can't say the loss is on him when we were in the exact situation we practice every week and didn't execute.

This team is very nonchalant. It's bothered me before but the natural reaction is to say it's just some individual person-alities, and when we get on the floor everyone plays hard. I can't expect them to act like me in pregame just like they can't expect me to act like them in pregame. I'm more focused and serious but everyone prepares differently, and that's what I've told myself throughout the season.

But looking at the way we've played over the last two weeks, maybe it's not acceptable anymore. That makes me feel guilty because I'm someone who is supposed to be a leader. I have to voice my opinion more often. We can't let it slide anymore.

Game 26

#-/25 Virginia Tech 81
#4/4 North Carolina 80 (overtime)
Feb. 13, 2007 • Smith Center, Chapel Hill

VT	FG	3FG	FT	REB	PF	TP	A	TO	B	S	Min
Washington*	5-15	2-4	0-2	6-8-14	3	12	4	4	2	2	33
Witcher*	1-2	0-0	2-2	5-1-6	4	4	0	0	0	0	9
Collins*	3-12	0-0	1-1	1-5-6	5	7	0	1	0	0	31
Gordon*	5-11	0-2	0-0	0-3-3	5	10	4	1	0	1	36
Dowdell*	7-15	2-4	17-19	0-3-3	1	33	2	3	1	2	41
Diakite	4-6	0-0	1-2	2-4-6	1	9	0	0	1	1	17
Vassallo	2-10	1-3	0-0	0-1-1	3	5	0	1	0	0	36
Sailes	0-0	0-0	0-2	0-0-0	0	0	0	0	0	0	12
Munson	0-0	0-0	1-2	0-0-0	1	1	1	0	0	0	7
Tucker	0-0	0-0	0-0	0-0-0	0	0	0	0	0	0	1
Krabbendam	0-0	0-0	0-0	0-0-0	0	0	0	0	0	0	2
TEAM				1-3-4							
Totals	**27-71**	**5-13**	**22-30**	**15-28-43**	**23**	**81**	**11**	**10**	**4**	**6**	**225**
Pct.	.380	.385	.733	DB: 5							

FG: (1st half: 12-37, .324; 2nd half: 13-29, .448; OT: 2-5, .400)
3FG: (1st half: 2-8, .250; 2nd half: 3-5, .600; OT: 0-0, —)
FT: (1st half: 4-4, 1.000; 2nd half: 14-20, .700; OT: 4-6, .667)

UNC	FG	3FG	FT	REB	PF	TP	A	TO	B	S	Min
Terry*	4-9	1-3	0-0	2-4-6	5	9	0	1	1	2	21
Hansbrough*	4-10	0-0	14-18	3-5-8	4	22	1	1	0	0	32
Wright*	3-7	0-0	0-2	1-6-7	1	6	0	1	2	1	26
Ellington*	4-13	1-6	5-7	2-1-3	1	14	1	1	0	1	30
Lawson*	6-14	1-4	0-2	1-2-3	3	13	5	1	0	0	39
Green	2-4	0-2	2-2	1-3-4	0	6	1	1	0	1	17
Thompson	1-2	0-0	2-2	0-2-2	2	4	0	0	0	0	13
Ginyard	1-2	0-0	2-2	1-2-3	2	4	1	1	0	0	24
Stepheson	1-2	0-0	0-0	0-0-0	1	2	0	2	0	0	7
Frasor	0-1	0-1	0-2	0-1-1	0	0	0	0	0	0	5
Miller	0-1	0-1	0-0	0-2-2	0	0	1	0	0	0	10
Thomas	0-0	0-0	0-0	0-1-1	2	0	1	0	0	0	1
TEAM				3-2-5							
Totals	**26-65**	**3-17**	**25-37**	**14-31-45**	**21**	**80**	**11**	**9**	**3**	**5**	**225**
Pct.	.400	.176	.676	DB: 10							

FG: (1st half: 13-30, .433; 2nd half: 12-29, .414; OT: 1-6, .167)
3FG: (1st half: 3-7, .429; 2nd half: 0-8, .000; OT: 0-2, .000)
FT: (1st half: 5-9, .556; 2nd half: 15-20, .750; OT: 5-8, .625)

Officials: Jamie Luckie, J.B. Caldwell, Curtis Shaw
Attendance: 21,750 • **Technical Fouls:** UNC bench

Score by Periods	1st	2nd	OT	Total
Virginia Tech	30	43	8	81
North Carolina	34	39	7	80

The first change has to come with our practice habits. Lately, it seems like practicing is a chore for some of us. If we go into practice with that attitude, we're not going to get the results we need. I know practice is hard. But we have to find pieces of it that excite us. I always look for the full-court part of practice, because it's fun to go up and down. It's not the fault of the young guys that they don't know how to practice. It's mine, because I'm a veteran and I'm supposed to help them through this difficult time.

Every loss this season has been because of the wrong mindset and focus. It's not an issue of talent or personnel. In sports, there are times you lose a game because the other team is better. I can deal with those losses. I can't deal with it when I have to look in the mirror and think I had control of the situation but didn't do the right thing.

LUCAS: WHAT COMES NEXT

FEB. 13, 2007

The easy storyline from Carolina's 81–80 overtime loss to Virginia Tech will be Roy Williams's postgame comments.

"Congratulations to Seth (Greenberg) and his staff and his kids," the head coach said. "They played very well. Zabian Dowdell was really something . . . I've been coaching for 19 years, and that's the worst coaching job I've ever done. I did a poor job. I did the worst job I've ever done in my entire life."

The Tar Heel head coach said it publicly. He said it privately, telling his team in the locker room that at least 90 percent of the blame for the loss was on his shoulders. And he was still saying it an hour after the game, continuing to assert that the loss belonged to him.

Sadly, it's big news when a major college

basketball coach takes responsibility like that. Columns will be written and ESPN will buzz.

Maybe that was the story for this night, although like Williams, you have to temper the blame with some credit for Virginia Tech, a team that nearly ran Carolina out of the gym in Blacksburg and then punched them square in the nose in Chapel Hill.

But the story for the rest of the season was happening outside the Carolina locker room. That's where Marcus Ginyard was sitting in a white t-shirt and a pair of jeans, rubbing his head as if massaging his brain might help him make sense of what he'd just seen.

He was provided with a handy excuse. A few days ago, Williams had called his team too "fat and happy." This was an easy explanation that fit perfectly with the theme that has been bestowed on the 2006–07 Tar Heels—a young team with a lot of talent. Probably, it was suggested to Ginyard, they just got too full of themselves. Maybe they thought they were a little better than they really are.

The Carolina sophomore disagreed. And in doing so, he turned a floodlight on this year's team.

"I don't think that's it," he said. "I think it's the opposite. We don't understand how good we really are. Because of that, we're not holding ourselves accountable for games like this. I don't feel like people are taking a game like this to heart as much as they need to. We can play so much better than the way we're playing. So much better. But I don't think everyone knows that."

This is where this column should end, because

that's the most insightful comment you're going to read about this game. Sure, part of the problem was late-game execution and a series of three straight possessions in the final two minutes of regulation when Tyler Hansbrough never touched the ball and the Tar Heels never got the ball below the free throw line. But that's just a symptom of the problem. And Ginyard's comments cut straight to what ailed the Tar Heels on this particular evening. It's been what ails them ever since Gonzaga, when a handful of players chuckled in the locker room after losing a stunner.

It's maddening to you and to me because we know a collection of talent like this doesn't happen very often. We look at the roster on paper and see raw talent and potential.

But not everyone has that sense of perspective. It was fashionable early in the season to compare this team to the 2005 team. There's one enormous difference: a sense of urgency. The 2005 team had at least five players (the three seniors, Raymond Felton, and Rashad McCants) who knew it was their last chance at college basketball. They didn't just want to win. They *had* to win.

This team wants to win, and don't let anyone suggest otherwise. But they haven't yet pondered what it might be like to lose a heartbreaker in the NCAA Tournament and have to live with it—maybe even live with the idea that they could've or should've made a deeper run—all summer.

Someone will have to explain that feeling, and it might be Ginyard.

"Every time we lose a game like this it's because someone else wanted it more or someone else could take the bump more or someone else was willing to shove us and we backed off," he said. "We have to get it together some way, somehow."

"That's the thing. Nobody expects anybody to take the lead on getting it together. I feel like we keep approaching the point where we say, `OK, now we're playing our best basketball.' And then we have a let-up like this and it makes it hard to get back into the flow. We can't have those let-downs now. We have to go straight up."

That sounds suspiciously like a leader emerging.

At his leadership class Monday night, Ginyard was asked what his team could do better. His response:

Take practice more seriously.

The Tar Heels practiced poorly the last two days. Little things went undone, box-outs were missed, and Williams had to repeat himself multiple times. Those transgressions eventually resulted in extra running.

They also might have resulted in Tuesday's loss.

"When coaches are having to yell at you to pick up the intensity in practice, you shouldn't wonder why they have to yell the same thing in the games," Ginyard said.

Right now, in the wee hours of Wednesday morning, the stories from Tuesday's game are Zabian Dowdell's superstar performance and Roy Williams's postgame comments.

That will last exactly 24 hours, long enough for

Carolina to take an off day from practice Wednesday.

Beginning with Thursday's practice and extending over the next seven weeks, the biggest story will be what leadership emerges from the wreckage of this game. If it's just a loss, then the same thing will happen sometime in March.

If it's a learning experience, team dynamics may shift.

It looks like it might start with Ginyard.

"Somebody's got to do it," he said. "Every day I'm thinking I need to do something better. Someone has to step up, and maybe it's me."

✦

We had an off day after Virginia Tech and then Coach wanted to meet with the entire team right before our next practice. We knew what was coming. We've been so inconsistent the last two weeks, and I think we've reached that now-or-never point in our season. We can't continue to play soft. We can't continue to make mental mistakes.

The first thing we did was watch the game film. On the very first play of the game, we didn't box out Deron Washington. We talked about him on the scouting report and in our pregame meeting, and the focus was simple—put a body on him every time because he goes to the offensive glass. That's one of his best offensive assets. And on the very first play, we didn't box him out.

That's the kind of game it was. And it made me believe even more strongly that the loss didn't belong to Coach Williams, no matter what he said after the game. He told us what to do. We didn't do it. Whose fault is that? There were several other clips of missed box-outs.

Improving game habits starts with practice habits. "We practiced like we didn't care for two days before the Virginia Tech game," Coach told us. The worst part is that he's right. They might have been our two worst practices of the year and it carried over to the game. One of Coach Williams's favorite sayings about Michael Jordan is, "He's the only person I've ever seen who could turn it on and off, and he never turned it off." Anybody who has played here has heard Coach say that at least 100 times. His message is simple: you can't turn it off in practice and expect to turn it on against an ACC opponent. If you do, you'll lose.

After we watched film, Coach addressed everyone in front of the team. He had written down some thoughts for every player. "These are things you're thinking that you probably shouldn't be thinking," he told us. He told certain guys they were acting selfishly. He told certain guys he knew they were mad at their teammates for not playing hard. He told certain guys he knew they had friends or family in their ears telling them they should play more.

When he came to me, he said, "Wes, you're mad at the way you're playing and mad at everyone else for not working as hard as you." I thought he hit it on the head. I don't feel like I've been selfish. I'm critical of myself and I'm not happy with my play. The work ethic of certain players does frustrate me and I feel I have to do a better job as a leader of getting them to work hard. In talking to my teammates, everyone seemed to feel there was truth in what Coach said to them in the locker room.

That can be a tricky situation. You have to have people who are able to take criticism and respond positively to it. It's not easy to be criticized that strongly in front of your peers. It was helpful that Coach was saying things we all had thought at some point. As a teammate, though, you can't always say them out loud. You don't want anyone to think you have ulterior motives. But when Coach says it, we all know his only motives are winning basketball games and making us a better team. It diffuses the chances of anyone getting defensive. We have guys with good character on this team, and from what I have heard everyone took the comments the right way. Being that blunt with us definitely set the right tone for practice.

It wasn't a punishment-type practice. But it was a long practice and there was lots of competition. There wasn't a lot of yelling and screaming. Instead, I think the theme from the meeting carried over—we didn't play up to our potential against Virginia Tech. There are areas we need to fix. Let's start fixing them. We can't let anyone outplay us anymore. We can't be outhustled. We can't have defensive breakdowns. We should all understand that if that's the way we want to play, we have to practice that way too.

<hr />

The day before the Boston College game, we arrived at the Smith Center thinking it would be a normal day. We'd watch some clips of BC, have practice, and then head for dinner and the airport.

Then Coach Holladay walked in and said, "Some of the NBA guys are back in town during the All-Star break. We want you to listen to them for a little bit. The coaches are going out of the room and when they're finished talking to you, we'll watch scouting film."

Then David Noel, Marvin Williams, and Sean May walked in. It turned into one of the most beneficial talking sessions our team has had this year. It gave us three guys in the locker room who instantly were respected by everyone. They reiterated everything Coach Williams has been saying, but they did it from the perspective of someone who was exactly where we were a year or two ago.

The first thing Sean talked about was the importance of playing for North Carolina. He told us how special a situation it was to play somewhere where the only thing that mattered was winning, and he said this would probably be the last time in our lives that we'd play for a team like that. "The NBA is about individuals," he said. "It's not about a team anymore. It's about getting your paycheck and who has the biggest contract. If you don't take seriously the opportunity you have to play for North Carolina, it will be a major regret for you in the near future."

Those words probably shocked some of the guys on our team. The goal throughout high school and college basketball has become making it to the NBA. It's the basketball utopia. To hear someone who is living in that so-called utopia say it's not as perfect as everyone thinks was an eye-opener. "The first and the fifteenth of every month are great because I get my paycheck," Sean said. "But my fondest memories of playing basketball my whole life will be at North Carolina because of the pride we had in playing for our team."

Dave and Marvin followed the same message. "I like getting paid," David said. "But I would do anything to be back in your shoes playing for Coach Williams."

Marvin told us, "If you can't play for Coach Williams, you can't play for anybody."

It was definitely one of those only-at-Carolina experiences. When I see Sean, David, and Marvin I think of them as friends. I played with them and I've heard them talk thousands of times. I respect what they say, but I can hear them say it any-time. I talk to them on the phone and I go out to eat dinner with them.

I realized as I was walking to practice that there were only two other people on our team who feel the same way—Reyshawn and Q. We're the only ones who went through those experiences with them. Everyone else in the room watched Sean May's Final Four performance on television. Everyone else saw David Noel's dunk at Kentucky or Marvin Williams's shot against Duke on the SportsCenter highlights. The young guys look up to them not only because of what they've accomplished, but because of where they are now.

As I looked around the locker room, I saw complete focus. Part of being 18 or 19 years old is occasionally having so much going on in your head that you lose focus for a couple minutes at a time. During the 25 minutes the NBA players were addressing us, I never saw a single current player lose focus. Walking out to the court, I even heard a couple guys say, "That was really cool." That's a good sign. It means the words had an impact.

The night before, I had dinner with Sean. I started talking to him about Deon. It would be hard to find a nicer kid than Deon Thompson. He reminds me of Sean, because he gets along with everyone. But he also reminds me of Sean for another reason—he has the talent to do almost anything he wants on the basket-ball court. When both guys arrived on campus, they had all the raw ability they needed to be a success. I'm worried that Deon hasn't shown that work ethic that could take him to Sean's level. So we talked about that at dinner and I asked Sean if he would talk to Deon about it.

One of the first things Sean did when he addressed the team was look straight at Deon and talk about how much potential he had if he would dedicate himself to playing and eating and working out the right way. Deon absolutely soaked it in. It wouldn't have meant as much coming from Reyshawn or me or anyone else on the team. To have it come from Sean May, a guy whose jersey is in the rafters, was very beneficial for him. It's something I think will pay dividends not just this year, but several years from now.

⚬

I roomed with our other freshman Californian, Alex Stepheson, on the Boston College trip. We call him "Big Art" because his middle name is Arthur. He's kind of out there. You never really know what he's thinking. I like him a lot, because he makes me laugh all the time.

I'm pretty sure Alex was a little surprised by the Boston weather. Everyone kept talking about how cold it was. But for three years I went to prep school farther north and more in the mountains than Boston, so it didn't seem that bad to me. My sister goes to Middlebury College in Vermont, so she was able to make it for one of the few times in my Carolina career, which was nice.

Boston College is a very unique team. Coach Haase had the scouting report on them last year, which was the first time I'd ever been involved in a Boston College game. He told us they run the flex offense, which is fairly common. Maryland runs a flex cut, so we see that all the time. But Boston College wants every single pass to be inside the three-point line.

That seems contrary to everything most players know about basketball. At every level, coaches talk about spacing. Spacing opens the floor. Set a screen and widen out. Pass and move away. But here was a team that wanted to decrease spacing instead of increase it.

I don't think we fully understood it until we played them the first time. The tighter they are, the better. It's a different style of play than I've ever seen before and it's a very smash-mouth style. They excel at making close passes with everyone bunched together. This year, we felt we were more prepared for their style because we experienced it last year.

Game 27

#4/4 North Carolina 77
#21/21 Boston College 72
Feb. 17, 2007 • Conte Forum, Chestnut Hill, Mass.

UNC	FG	3FG	FT	REB	PF	TP	A	TO	B	S	Min
Terry*	4-9	2-3	0-1	3-3-6	3	10	2	3	0	1	29
Wright*	6-7	0-0	1-1	1-2-3	1	13	0	3	3	1	30
Hansbrough*	6-12	0-0	5-6	2-5-7	3	17	1	2	2	1	36
Ellington*	5-8	2-4	0-0	0-1-1	1	12	3	1	0	0	25
Lawson*	4-6	1-2	4-4	1-5-6	3	13	7	3	0	1	33
Ginyard	0-1	0-0	2-2	0-3-3	1	2	0	0	0	0	17
Frasor	0-1	0-0	0-0	0-0-0	0	0	2	1	0	0	5
Thomas	0-0	0-0	0-0	0-0-0	1	0	1	0	0	0	1
Green	1-4	0-2	3-4	1-0-1	1	5	0	0	0	0	8
Thompson	2-6	0-0	1-2	3-0-3	2	5	1	2	0	1	12
Miller	0-0	0-0	0-0	0-0-0	0	0	0	0	0	0	3
Stepheson	0-0	0-0	0-0	0-0-0	0	0	1	0	0	0	1
TEAM				2-1-3				1			
Totals	**28-54**	**5-11**	**16-20**	**13-20-33**	**16**	**77**	**18**	**16**	**5**	**5**	**200**
Pct.	.519	.455	.800	DB: 3							

FG: (1st half: 17-32, .531; 2nd half: 11-22, .500)
3FG: (1st half: 3-7, .429; 2nd half: 2-4, .500)
FT: (1st half: 7-9, 0.778; 2nd half: 9-11, .818)

BC	FG	3FG	FT	REB	PF	TP	A	TO	B	S	Min
Dudley*	7-11	1-4	7-13	2-1-3	3	22	3	2	0	2	33
Spears*	1-3	0-0	0-0	3-0-3	3	2	1	2	1	2	16
Oates*	3-4	1-2	0-0	2-4-6	3	7	1	1	2	0	33
Rice*	8-18	2-7	2-3	0-3-3	0	20	5	2	0	0	40
Marshall*	6-12	0-4	2-4	2-1-3	2	14	2	4	1	2	37
Haynes	1-2	1-1	0-0	0-0-0	0	3	1	1	0	2	9
Roche	0-1	0-0	0-0	0-0-0	0	0	0	0	0	0	7
Blair	2-3	0-0	0-1	1-3-4	5	4	0	1	1	0	25
TEAM				1-2-3							
Totals	**28-54**	**5-18**	**11-21**	**11-14-25**	**17**	**72**	**13**	**13**	**5**	**8**	**200**
Pct.	.519	.278	.524	DB: 5							

FG: (1st half: 13-22, .591; 2nd half: 15-32, .469)
3FG: (1st half: 5-8, .625; 2nd half: 0-10, .000)
FT: (1st half: 7-11, .636; 2nd half: 4-10, .400)

Officials: Karl Hess, Earl Walton, Ray Natili
Attendance: 8,606 • **Technical Fouls:** BC bench

Score by Periods	1st	2nd	Total
North Carolina	44	33	77
Boston College	38	34	72

Their level of emotion makes them unique also. They celebrate a lot after big plays. They'll scream in your face. Your first inclination is to think they are a bunch of punks. But as I watched them play more regularly, I realized something: they're much better than they get credit for. They do play with an edge. But they also make big-time plays at all the key moments. Their emotion level makes it more fun to beat them, because that's the type of guys you want to see go quiet.

Just as we expected, it was a very tight game. ESPN GameDay was there, so their students were very loud. It's a unique arena, though, because Boston is mostly a pro town. Their fans tend to react like pro fans—they wait for something to happen before they react rather than trying to make something happen with their emotion.

Coach always tells us there are no must-win games at this stage of the season. But Boston College was about as close as it gets, because we couldn't go out and have another bad performance. We needed to reassert ourselves in the league race. And I felt we needed to respond positively to the last couple days of practice, because they wouldn't have been as beneficial if we'd played poorly in our next game.

LUCAS: NO DOUBT ABOUT IT

FEB. 17, 2007

CHESTNUT HILL—Maybe this wasn't meant to be.

Boston College's Tyrese Rice had just thrown in a shot while parallel to the hardwood. The circus leaner brought the Eagles within 73–72 with 30.1 seconds left. A previously slumbering Conte Forum crowd was suddenly roaring, ghosts of close games lost in the recent past were stirring, and it was time for some armchair coaching. You know you were doing it.

Over the past three days, Carolina's late-game strategy has been a popular topic of conversation from the coffee shop to the internet to Franklin Street.

Everyone wants to be a coach. Even on the Tar Heel bench.

Before Carolina inbounded the ball, Bobby Frasor—the son of a coach—leaned over across a couple teammates and within earshot of the coaches.

"Should we put Wayne in to shoot free throws?" he said.

The implication was obvious. Ellington would come in for Marcus Ginyard.

But the substitution wasn't made. Ginyard had attempted just one field goal all night and was shooting 71.9 percent from the line. Ellington, the team's smoothest shooter, hits at a 76 percent clip.

The Tar Heels have to inbound the ball. And as the teams line up to trigger the play, one of the Eagles looks at Danny Green and says, "We're not fouling you."

It was probably sound strategy. Green had been the player chosen by Roy Williams earlier in the game to shoot a pair of technical foul free throws, and he makes over 90 percent of his charity tosses.

Apparently, there were several players Boston College didn't want to foul, because Carolina had the chance to cycle the ball up the court for eight seconds. As soon as the ball hit Ginyard's hands, the cry went up from the BC bench:

"Foul *him*!"

Green came out. On the bench, he relayed the Eagle comments to Frasor. The Illinois sophomore responded by telling him his substitution suggestion just a few seconds earlier.

As Ginyard toed the stripe, Frasor and Green were wearing subtle grins.

When the shot dropped through the net, the subtle grins turned into toothy smiles.

⚇

There has never been a North Carolina player like Reyshawn Terry.

It's a fan's compulsion to try and compare players. You know the drill—Brandan Wright reminds me of Sam Perkins. Wayne Ellington reminds me of Joseph Forte.

But Terry is in his own category. There's never been one like him.

Who else would make a mistake by throwing the ball to Wright 22 feet from the basket on a fast break . . . and then turn around and nail a three-pointer at one of the game's biggest moments?

Who else would make what Roy Williams described as one of the game's biggest shots, a three-pointer that put the Tar Heels up 73–66 . . . and then foul Jared Dudley in the act of shooting a three-pointer on the other end?

Just as you're getting ready to bellow, "No, Reyshawn!" he's on the other end making a crucial play. It's dizzying.

Sometimes literally.

When Terry hit the trifecta that gave Carolina a 64–61 lead, it prompted Williams to exhort his team defensively. He was screaming, he was clapping his hands—and then he was down. Crouched in front of the Tar Heel bench rubbing his temples, experiencing one of the periodic head rushes that mark his most intense of moments, he had his head in his hands. Had he been a boxer, it would have been time for the corner man to come over and squirt water on his face. Instead, it was up to Steve Robinson to hop out of his seat and grab Williams's shoulders to make sure he was steady.

That's what kind of game it was. And that's what kind of year it's been for Terry. Moments of sheer euphoria tempered with the heavy responsibilities of being a senior in the Carolina program.

"Being a senior has definitely been harder than I thought it would be," he said. "It's been a real task for me, and it's still challenging to this day. I'm still learning how to do it, and it's a great deal to learn."

What's enabled him to succeed is that he's a different player than he was his first three years. Now he hustles. Now he wins defensive awards. Now he balances the frenzied errors with rebounding. He is not perfect and wouldn't claim to be. But over the past couple of months, there have been flashes of a true senior.

His coach has noticed. Two sentences into his postgame press conference, he singled out the Winston-Salem native.

"I couldn't be more proud of Reyshawn," Williams said.

"He's successful when he lets the game come to him," says Green, who watches Terry's every move when he's on the bench to try and pick up pointers. "And there have been more times this year when he's let the game come to him. It's more natural, and that's why he gets better results."

For the first part of his Carolina career, Terry measured those results largely in points per game. It's no coincidence that as he's discovered other categories on the stat sheet, he's earned more rope from his head coach. There was a time when a play like the pass to Wright would have earned a laser-beam stare from his head coach.

Saturday night, though, Williams was standing right next to Terry when he made the play. He clapped, nodded his head, and called out the next defense.

Williams didn't like the play, of course. But he couldn't yank Terry because his senior was too important.

For all the right reasons.

The Tar Heels had jumped around in their spacious Conte Forum locker room to celebrate the crucial road victory. And now there was just one thing left for Bobby Frasor to do.

He approached Ginyard, his fellow sophomore.

"Hey, man," Frasor said. "I knew you had those free throws. I never doubted you."

He pounded his teammate on the back.

And then he laughed.

WEEK TWENTY-ONE

FOR THE SECOND STRAIGHT WEEK, we had a chance to get a home win against a team that had beaten us on the road. This time the opponent was NC State, and we had the added incentive of knowing we'd taken over first place in the ACC with the win over Boston College.

But we weren't very good in the first half. It was the reverse of our problem against Virginia Tech. Against them, we weren't fired up enough. Against State, we may have been too fired up. Everyone wanted to do it all, and the result was that no one was very effective. I contributed, because I made a silly foul defensively 40 feet from the basket. I was trying to do too much and force things to happen, and that's when I get in trouble.

The coaches picked up on the way we were playing. At half-time, Coach Robinson talked to us about playing more intelligently. "You don't have to hit a home run on every single play," he said. "Make the extra pass. Make the easy play."

Coach Williams reinforced that message at the first media timeout in the second half, and we eventually went on a good run to put State away. This time no one stormed the court at the end of the State-Carolina game, which was a nice change.

Game 28

NC State 64
#5/5 North Carolina 83
Feb. 21, 2007 • Smith Center, Chapel Hill

NCSU	FG	3FG	FT	REB	PF	TP	A	TO	B	S	Min
Grant*	6-13	0-2	2-2	1-4-5	3	14	3	2	1	1	39
Costner*	6-10	3-4	3-3	2-4-6	5	18	1	7	1	0	30
McCauley*	1-3	0-0	1-2	0-7-7	4	3	0	6	2	0	36
Fells*	3-12	2-5	1-2	0-3-3	1	9	3	0	1	2	39
Atsur*	4-9	3-5	5-6	2-0-2	2	16	4	1	0	1	40
Horner	1-3	0-1	2-2	0-0-0	3	4	0	0	0	1	12
Nieman	0-0	0-0	0-0	0-0-0	0	0	0	1	0	0	2
TEAM				0-0-0							
Totals	21-50	8-17	14-17	5-18-23	18	64	11	17	5	5	200
Pct.	.420	.471	.824	DB: 3							

FG: (1st half: 12-28, .429; 2nd half: 9-22, .409)
3FG: (1st half: 2-8, .250; 2nd half: 3-5, .600)
FT: (1st half: 4-4, 1.000; 2nd half: 14-20, .700)

UNC	FG	3FG	FT	REB	PF	TP	A	TO	B	S	Min
Terry*	1-2	0-0	0-0	0-1-1	2	2	0	0	0	0	17
Hansbrough*	7-14	0-0	6-6	2-5-7	2	20	0	4	0	1	34
Wright*	9-12	0-0	6-9	3-3-6	2	24	1	1	3	3	30
Ellington*	2-9	0-3	2-2	1-5-6	0	6	3	0	0	1	27
Lawson*	2-5	1-2	0-1	2-2-4	3	5	5	1	0	1	20
Green	3-6	2-3	0-0	4-4-8	1	8	2	2	3	1	17
Thompson	3-6	0-0	0-0	3-2-5	0	6	0	0	1	0	12
Stepheson	0-1	0-0	0-0	0-1-1	0	0	0	1	0	0	2
Ginyard	1-2	1-1	1-2	0-1-1	3	4	1	3	0	1	13
Frasor	1-3	0-1	1-2	0-0-0	1	3	4	1	0	1	14
Miller	1-1	1-1	0-0	0-0-0	1	3	1	0	0	0	8
Thomas	1-1	0-0	0-0	0-0-0	1	2	2	0	1	0	6
TEAM				1-1-2							
Totals	31-62	5-11	16-22	16-25-41	16	83	19	13	6	9	200
Pct.	.500	.455	.727	DB: 2							

FG: (1st half: 15-29, .517; 2nd half: 16-33, .485)
3FG: (1st half: 2-2, 1.000; 2nd half: 3-9, .333)
FT: (1st half: 9-14, .643; 2nd half: 7-8, .875)

Officials: Bryan Kersey, Mike Eades, Patrick Adams
Attendance: 21,750 • **Technical Fouls:** none

Score by Periods	1st	2nd	Total
NC State	40	24	64
North Carolina	41	42	83

꘎

I'm trying to bury any discussion of officiating deep in this book. I never want anyone to think I'm trying to use officiating as an excuse. But it's a part of college basketball, and I want to address as many parts of college basketball as I can.

At the college level, officiating is inconsistent from game to game and sometimes within a game. Some games everything is called extremely tight. When I'm guarding someone on the perimeter I know I can't touch them at all. But there are other games when anything goes. For some reason, the game always seems to be called that way when we play at Cameron—and it might help us, so it's not an excuse.

As a player, it's easy to adjust to the way a game is being called. What's not easy to understand is when a game is called differently in the first half and second half. Take the first game against State. The whole game was called very loosely. Then all of a sudden with a minute to play I'm called for a hand check. There's no question my hand was on him. I've seen it on film. But my hand was on him during other possessions also and nothing was called. Why call it in the last minute?

Players will tell you inconsistency is their main beef about officiating. At the same time, we realize it's a very difficult job. Anything involving humans will have human error. If I could eliminate human error, I'd make all my shots. One thing I appreciate about most of the officials—probably 80 percent of them in our league—is that you can talk to them. They'll explain why they made a call. In many cases, they'll warn you before they make a call to alert you about what you're doing wrong.

In my last two years, I've developed a rapport with many officials. It doesn't mean I get calls I shouldn't get, but I feel it gives me a better understanding of how they're going to call a game. Some players see the officials as adversaries. I don't look at it that way. If I can figure out a way to work with them rather than against them, everyone benefits. As long as you don't embarrass them, they will help you be a more effective player. If, for example, an official tells me, "Wes, you have to do a better job of keeping your hands off defensively," I can make that adjustment before it hurts my team.

There are definitely certain officials who have a certain style. That doesn't mean you can always predict what they'll do, though. Some nights we have an official who has a reputation for calling a very tight game, and that night the crew will let everything go. The way they call a game can change from night to night.

What rarely changes is the way they handle a game. Teddy Valentine will always be in control of the game. You do not want to say anything to him when he's making a call. You can go talk to him about it later, but when he's in the process of making a call and reporting it to the scorer's table, leave him alone. He's in control and it's his show. Mike Wood is an official who will always talk. No matter what is happening in the game, if you are polite he will explain any situation. As a player, I appreciate officials with that outlook.

The Maryland game was a debacle. We were up by 12 with seven minutes to play and lost 89–87. It was basically a carbon copy of our other losses—no focus, no intensity, botched execution on the final play.

I don't know how to describe it any differently than the other losses. It was very, very frustrating.

Other than the game, it was a classic road trip. I realize that's like asking Mrs. Lincoln how she liked the play other than the incident with her husband, but these really were classic moments.

Game 29

#5/5 North Carolina 87
Maryland 89
Feb. 25, 2007 • Comcast Center, College Park, Md.

UNC	FG	3FG	FT	REB	PF	TP	A	TO	B	S	Min
Ellington*	6-14	3-7	2-2	2-3-5	3	17	6	1	0	1	25
Terry*	2-7	0-3	2-2	0-3-3	2	6	1	0	1	0	22
Lawson*	3-7	1-2	0-1	1-4-5	4	7	9	1	0	0	23
Wright*	6-12	0-0	0-4	5-2-7	1	12	0	2	1	2	33
Hansbrough*	10-15	0-0	2-4	2-2-4	4	22	0	2	0	2	28
Ginyard	0-3	0-1	2-2	1-3-4	1	2	3	1	0	3	18
Frasor	2-5	1-3	0-0	0-2-2	1	5	3	0	0	2	14
Thomas	0-0	0-0	0-0	0-0-0	0	0	0	0	0	0	3
Green	2-4	0-1	0-0	1-0-1	2	4	0	2	1	0	8
Thompson	2-4	0-0	0-0	0-0-0	4	4	0	1	1	0	11
Miller	2-3	2-3	0-0	0-0-0	0	6	0	0	0	0	8
Stephenson	1-1	0-0	0-2	1-0-1	3	2	0	0	0	0	7
TEAM				1-0-1							
Totals	**36-75**	**7-20**	**8-17**	**14-19-33**	**25**	**87**	**22**	**10**	**4**	**10**	**200**
Pct.	**.480**	**.350**	**.471**	**DB: 5**							

FG: (1st half: 17-35, .486; 2nd half: 19-40, .475)
3FG: (1st half: 5-11, .455; 2nd half: 2-9, .222)
FT: (1st half: 5-7, 0.714; 2nd half: 3-10, .300)

UM	FG	3FG	FT	REB	PF	TP	A	TO	B	S	Min
Strawberry*	12-18	2-3	1-1	1-3-4	2	27	4	0	0	0	36
Gist*	5-11	0-1	2-2	1-8-9	3	12	2	1	1	0	28
Vasquez*	4-10	0-2	2-3	1-2-3	2	10	6	6	1	1	32
Jones*	8-17	1-6	1-2	2-2-4	2	18	1	2	1	2	29
Ibekwe	1-4	0-0	7-8	6-2-8	4	9	0	1	2	1	24
Hayes	0-1	0-0	0-0	0-5-5	1	0	5	5	1	0	20
Brown	0-0	0-0	0-0	0-0-0	0	0	0	1	0	0	3
Bowers	0-1	0-0	2-3	1-2-3	0	2	0	0	2	0	10
Bambale	3-4	0-0	5-7	4-5-9	2	11	1	1	0	0	18
TEAM				1-0-1							
Totals	**33-66**	**3-12**	**20-26**	**17-29-46**	**16**	**89**	**19**	**17**	**8**	**4**	**200**
Pct.	**.500**	**.250**	**.769**	**DB: 3**							

FG: (1st half: 15-38, .395; 2nd half: 18-28, .643)
3FG: (1st half: 1-6, .167; 2nd half: 2-6, .333)
FT: (1st half: 10-13, .769; 2nd half: 10-13, .769)

Officials: Gary Maxwell, Tom Lopes, Karl Hess
Attendance: 17,950 • Technical Fouls: none

Score by Periods	1st	2nd	Total
North Carolina	44	43	87
Maryland	41	48	89

First, we were at shootaround the day before the game and there was a Chipotle around the corner. Jonas Sahratian idolizes Chipotle. I ate there a couple years ago and didn't think it was great, but he talks about it all the time. Somehow during shootaround Jonas said he could eat three Chipotle burritos in 30 minutes. Eric Hoots told him to prove it.

The next day, Hoots and a couple other guys got a ride on the team bus to Chipotle and picked up three burritos. Before pregame, a bunch of us gathered in the meeting room to see if Jonas could pull off his great eating feat. When I walked into the room, he was on his third burrito and he was really struggling. I've never seen Jonas look weak before, but he looked like he was fighting the burrito for his life. It probably didn't help that Hoots was standing there with a stopwatch.

"Three minutes left!" he would shout. And when some rice and beans fell out the side of the burrito, he'd yell, "You have to eat that too! You can't just eat the burrito. You have to eat everything."

With about 90 seconds left, the whole team was in there watching Jonas try to defeat the burrito. I didn't think he was going to make it. Somehow, though, he was able to down every bit of it. Coach had pity on him and told him he didn't have to stay for pregame, but he was still in pain three hours later when he was stretching me out at the Comcast Center. He wouldn't admit it because Jonas is a tough guy, but it was obvious he was having issues. It affected him for a couple days afterward, but it was worth it. It was an amazing feat of eating prowess.

We also had some weather issues. The day we arrived, College Park had a big snowstorm. My teammates on the bus were trying to act like College Park was in Alaska and it snows all the time there. Even Associate Athletic Director for Communications Steve Kirschner joined in with them. I distinctly remember the phrase, "This happens five or six times a year up here," being said.

They were jumping all over me like I was some maniac who had just walked in from Hawaii and knew nothing about the weather. I lived in New Hampshire for three years. I know what snow looks like. This was an intense snowstorm, and having spent some time in the Washington D.C. area, I knew this wasn't a regular occurrence.

When we got to the hotel, everyone started a big snowball fight. I even saw Coach Williams pegging Ty with a couple of snowballs. But I wasn't interested. I was losing my mind about this weather issue. I walked straight to the front desk of the hotel and asked them if these were normal weather conditions.

"Of course not," said the desk clerk. "It doesn't snow much at all in this area."

I thought I was vindicated. But even after talking to the people at the desk, the Snow Crew on our team—Bobby, Hoots, Preston, and Steve Kirschner—still didn't believe them. I'm sure Steve still thinks I am crazy to this day.

I couldn't decide if I was angrier that I missed the snowball fight or that we had people on our bus who think College Park is at the same latitude as the North Pole.

LUCAS: GETTING EMOTIONAL

FEB. 25, 2007

COLLEGE PARK—Emotion was pouring out of the Comcast Center.

Maryland had just sealed a remarkable 89–87 victory over North Carolina. Suddenly, it was clear exactly how much the win meant to the Terrapins. Fans were streaming onto the court. Greivis Vasquez was bouncing through the tunnel cradling the game ball, his arms over his head, smile stretching from ear to ear. In a back hallway, D.J. Strawberry sprinted toward the Maryland locker room.

"Great job, D.J.," a Maryland fan said.

Here was Strawberry's answer: "Oh yeah!"

The Comcast Center walls are constructed of cinderblocks painted a dull gray. Roy Williams walked to the podium to address the media on the other side of those walls from the Terp locker room. As he began his opening comments, one sound was audible: a very happy basketball team roaring in celebration of a season-making win.

Pure emotion, college basketball style.

It was easy to tell exactly how much the game had meant to them. But there were other ways, too.

Look at rebounding—specifically, offensive rebounding. It is a stat that is made up almost entirely of effort. The ball bounds off the rim, and usually the player closest to the rim gets it. Sometimes, though, the inside player simply gets outworked.

Now, consider these stats from the first half of Sunday's game: there were 25 rebounding opportunities off missed Maryland shots. The Terps grabbed 15 offensive rebounds, leaving just 10 defensive rebounds for Carolina. The leading Tar Heel defensive rebounder was Ty Lawson with four.

That is startling.

"They were more aggressive than we were," Roy Williams said. "They went after the basketball harder than we did."

The Tar Heels were averaging giving up 11 second-chance points per game. Maryland rolled up 17 on second-chance opportunities in the first 20 minutes alone.

When the head coach walked into his locker room after the game, he wrote two simple stats on the white board in black marker:

64% in second half.

46–33 in rebounds.

Williams didn't say much to his team. He didn't have to, because the stats said it for him. Williams-coached teams simply do not allow opponents to shoot over 60 percent from the field in the second half of a crucial league game. They do not get outrebounded.

For the first time all year, there was a legitimate pall over the locker room. It felt like a loss was supposed to feel. On February 25, with just one week in the regular season, it felt like the Tar Heels finally realized what was slipping away.

"We're blowing opportunities," Bobby Frasor said. "Every time other teams lose and put us at the top of the league, we give it right back and give everyone else a shot. There's no way other teams should be competing for the league crown with us. This team should not have four (ACC) losses."

He's right . . . and he's wrong. On paper, he's right. On the court, he's wrong.

There are flashes. There was a first-half spurt that built a 13-point lead. There was a similar stretch early in the second half that built the lead back to ten. In some ways, that's what makes it so frustrating. The potential is there: it's Brandan Wright jamming through a follow dunk so forcefully that the Maryland crowd involuntarily shivers, "Ooohhhh." It's Tyler Hansbrough scoring over three Terp players—again. It's Wayne Ellington dropping in two early three-pointers.

But through 29 games, those flashes simply haven't been maintained. This is a team that loses to Virginia Tech and reassembles two days later for practice talking about how they have to practice and play with renewed intensity. Then, 10 days later, the head coach is saying things like this: "It's the same things we keep saying—intensity, attention. Early in the first half they kicked us about as hard as you can be kicked."

This team is dangerously close to graduating from "inconsistent" to "consistently inconsistent."

Twice this season Williams has drawn up game-winning or tying plays, only to watch a different player each time wander to the wrong spot on the floor. Down two with seconds left, the play wasn't designed to put Wright in a situation where he could be fouled. It was a foolproof call that would have replicated a play that had worked perfectly earlier in the half. But a mixup left Wright vulnerable to a hack, and his free throws were no good.

Watching this team play can be breathtaking. And it can be maddening. Watching Maryland celebrate the win, there was a nagging feeling that it was the kind of emotional display this Carolina team wouldn't make.

But there, in the locker room, was Frasor. He was in the corner, already dressed in his suit. His head was in his hands, and he wasn't moving.

And there, in that corner, emotion was pouring out of Carolina's tiny corner of the Comcast Center. Just a little too late.

WEEK TWENTY-TWO

THE BOXSCORE WILL TELL you what happened in the Georgia Tech game. It's pretty simple: we were bad. We were down seven at halftime and they shot 62 percent in the first half. We never got closer than four points in the second half and lost 84–77.

In other words: we were bad.

Things got worse at the airport because there was some bad weather in the area. We were checking through security and I heard Tyler say, "What?" They told us it was going to be a bad, bumpy flight. I've flown enough that a little turbulence doesn't bother me. I didn't realize until halfway through the flight that Tyler had decided to take the bus home. He is not a good flyer.

I don't mind a little turbulence. But this was not a little turbulence. It was as bad a flight as I've ever been on in my life. The plane was rocking side to side and up and down. Some of us were holding on to the ceiling. Other than a couple of occasional screams, it was completely quiet. No one was talking. After we landed—and it was a rough landing—someone said, "I bet Tyler is glad he missed this." Coach Williams said, "Tyler is the smartest one of all of us."

Tyler had a long bus ride. But he made a good decision.

In a situation where we just lost a game, I'm usually consumed with how bad things seem. A flight like that puts everything in perspective. Georgia Tech was just basketball. The flight was life or death. Especially after a loss, when we pray after a game, Coach always says, "Even in times like this, we do realize we're more fortunate than others." He always says, "We realize we're more fortunate than others," but after losses he adds, "Even in times like this." A situation like that flight emphasizes exactly how right he is.

Coach does an amazing job dealing with the different backgrounds we have on this team. We've got all kinds of different beliefs and religions. I'm sure Coach has his set of beliefs, too, but he never forces them on anyone. We do say the Lord's Prayer before every game and Coach prays after every game. We say the blessing at every meal, whether it's something silent to yourself or as a team. It's not overboard, but it's just enough to convey a certain set of values.

In pregame meal, the seniors say the blessing. I've been nervous about that my entire career. Before the first exhibition game, Coach called on Reyshawn to say the blessing. I was so glad it wasn't me, and I consciously made a note to memorize something really good before the next game.

But I forgot. It's pretty tense in the room at that time, and when I was called on before the second exhibition game I literally started shaking. The only prayer I could remember at that exact moment was, "God is great, God is good, let us thank Him for our food." I was pretty sure that wasn't appropriate.

So I just started rambling. I think I blessed the food, I'm not sure. When I finished, everyone had a big smile on their face. Ever since then, I'm under the microscope every time it's my turn to say the blessing. Even if I do it right, they still give me a hard time. Hoots's dad is a minister and I thought maybe he could help me. So I asked Hoots if he could get me some help. He wouldn't do it. That's what kind of friend he is. I think he's enjoyed my struggles too much. At any pregame when someone says it's my turn for the blessing, everyone goes, "Yes!"

We were boarding the plane after the game and I was sitting in the back with Reyshawn and Dewey Burke. Reyshawn said, "Do we need to get these guys together tomorrow to talk?"

At that point, I was still ticked about the game. I was tired of talking. "I don't know if it will do any good," I said. "It's just talk. Right now we need to play. But it can't hurt, so let's give it a try."

Dewey agreed. We decided the best time was after practice, because everyone would already be there and no one had to worry about being on time or having somewhere else to go.

After practiced, all the players gathered in the locker room and we started with an open floor. We wanted anyone who was frustrated or had anything they wanted to say to speak up. Marcus, Quentin, Reyshawn, and I spoke the most. Danny and Bobby also spoke a little. Everyone else mostly listened. It was a very, very positive talk.

I tried to make two points. First, I emphasized how special this next month could be. During the 2005 season, Al Wood spoke to us. He told us what a unique opportunity we had because we had a chance to win a national title. He said he enjoyed his Final Four experience, but that he would always be sorry he never won a title. He is a great speaker, and he went on to say he would always regret not doing all those little things and he wondered if they could have made a difference in a championship.

I want our team to be completely devoted to a championship for the next month. If that means going to bed early or eating differently or putting aside girl problems, that's what we need to do. I want everyone to be able to look in the mirror in April and say, "I did everything possible on and off the court to help us win a national championship." Sometimes younger guys don't realize they impact the team on the court with what they do off the court.

My other point was that I didn't feel like we were playing with the enthusiasm we needed. We're expected to win every game we play. When we go on the road and win, it's like, "Oh, this is what we're supposed to do." But when we lose it's a major catastrophe.

"When was the last time you saw guys celebrate after a big play?" I said. "When is the last time we had a big celebration after a big win?"

The last time I think we were completely into it emotionally was the game at Duke. That was almost a month ago. I think we have such high expectations that sometimes we forget to enjoy it when we play well.

The freshmen are not a vocal group, but I think they're listening. A couple of the older guys said in the meeting, "You younger guys aren't saying much. Is there anything at all you want to say? Are you frustrated, are we missing something, anything at all?"

It's natural for the sophomores to compare this year to last year. That's their only frame of reference. A couple of them said, "Last year we had fire. If anyone was going to beat us, they had to beat us. We weren't going to give in."

To a certain extent, that's true. But I didn't want the freshmen to perceive it as everyone ganging up on them and accusing them of being the problem. So I said, "The young guys have to understand that last year at this time, things were going better than they are now. That's not because you guys are here. We're all responsible for all of the mistakes. We're probably even more responsible than you, because we're supposed to be the leaders. Don't think for one second that it's us against you. Our point is this: we're not playing the way we're capable right now. It's a collective problem. And we want to solve it, and we know you do too."

To everyone's credit, the meeting never turned into a finger-pointing session. And talking to guys after they left, everyone felt very positive about it.

Reyshawn was the last person to speak. He got very emotional. He was crying so hard he could barely talk. That was exactly what the team needed. They needed to see how much it meant to him. They needed to realize that he was a senior and he could see the end of his Carolina career. That's an important realization for the freshmen and sophomores, because they think this lasts forever. To see how much it meant to Reyshawn had a profound impact on everyone in the room.

I don't know if the meeting means we will play better. I don't know if it will help us in a game when we need a basket. But I do know it didn't hurt, and everyone left the room feeling better about the basketball team than they felt when they walked in the door. It wasn't about playing better because the Duke game was next. It was about playing better because we're not playing up to our potential. What I think this team has taught us is that when you have a group with seven new guys, seven is a huge number. It's important to check periodically and make sure everyone is on the same page. That's not something anyone could have anticipated. It's something we have learned as the season has progressed.

Game 30

#8/8 North Carolina 77
Georgia Tech 84
March 1, 2007 • Alexander Memorial Coliseum, Atlanta, Ga.

UNC	FG	3FG	FT	REB	PF	TP	A	TO	B	S	Min
Terry*	1-3	0-1	5-8	1-2-3	3	7	1	3	1	0	17
Wright*	8-10	0-0	6-9	3-2-5	1	22	0	1	1	1	32
Hansbrough*	4-6	0-0	8-12	2-8-10	3	16	1	1	1	2	33
Ellington*	5-12	2-5	2-2	0-2-2	0	14	3	2	0	1	31
Frasor*	1-2	1-2	0-0	0-1-1	3	3	1	0	0	0	9
Ginyard	0-1	0-0	2-2	1-0-1	2	2	1	2	0	1	17
Lawson	2-6	0-2	2-2	1-1-2	3	6	8	3	0	1	25
Thomas	0-0	0-0	0-0	0-0-0	0	0	0	1	0	0	6
Green	2-4	0-2	0-1	0-0-0	2	4	1	2	0	1	12
Thompson	1-3	0-0	1-2	0-1-1	0	3	1	0	0	0	8
Miller	0-2	0-2	0-0	0-0-0	0	0	0	0	0	0	5
Stepheson	0-0	0-0	0-0	0-0-0	1	0	0	0	0	0	5
TEAM				1-3-4							
Totals	24-49	3-14	26-38	9-20-29	18	77	17	15	3	7	200
Pct.	.490	.214	.684	DB: 6							

FG: (1st half: 14-25, .560; 2nd half: 10-24, .417)
3FG: (1st half: 2-6, .333; 2nd half: 1-8, .125)
FT: (1st half: 12-16, 750; 2nd half: 14-22, .636)

GT	FG	3FG	FT	REB	PF	TP	A	TO	B	S	Min
Smith*	1-2	0-0	0-0	2-4-6	5	2	2	0	1	2	25
Young*	10-18	5-6	0-0	2-2-4	2	25	1	2	0	3	27
Dickey*	4-5	0-0	1-3	1-5-6	5	9	2	1	1	1	25
Crittenton*	4-12	0-3	5-8	2-1-3	0	13	11	5	0	2	34
Morrow*	6-12	4-10	2-2	1-2-3	4	18	1	3	0	0	27
West	1-1	1-1	2-2	0-1-1	3	5	1	2	0	1	11
Faye	0-1	0-0	0-0	0-1-1	1	0	0	1	1	0	5
Bell	0-3	0-2	0-0	0-1-1	2	0	1	0	1	0	15
Peacock	4-6	0-0	0-0	3-3-6	4	8	0	0	1	0	17
Aminu	2-2	0-0	0-0	1-2-3	2	4	0	2	0	0	14
TEAM				1-0-1							
Totals	32-62	10-22	10-15	13-22-35	28	84	19	16	5	9	200
Pct.	.516	.455	.667	DB: 2							

FG: (1st half: 21-34, .618; 2nd half: 11-28, .393)
3FG: (1st half: 6-10, .600; 2nd half: 4-12, .333)
FT: (1st half: 1-3, .333; 2nd half: 9-12, .750)

Officials: Tony Greene, Curtis Shaw, Bryan Kersey
Attendance: 9,191 • **Technical Fouls:** none

Score by Periods	1st	2nd	Total
North Carolina	42	35	77
Georgia Tech	49	35	84

Lucas: Handle With Care

March 1, 2007

ATLANTA—You go to Marcus Ginyard because it is habit.

You walk into a whisper-quiet Carolina locker room after an 84–77 loss to Georgia Tech. There have been times this year when hanging with the Tar Heels after games has been a joy. Think back to the game at Cameron Indoor Stadium—How long ago was that? A month? A year?—and there was Bobby Frasor beat-boxing in the corner. Really, he was. Danny Green and Deon Thompson and Alex Stepheson were providing the sound effects and Frasor was trying, with limited success, to lay a beat down over the top of it. It was silly and it was crazy and it was something else:

Fun. Remember that, the fun?

That was not happening on Thursday night. Everyone dressed in their own bubble, everyone thinking about passes they threw away, shots they missed, plays they didn't make.

In times like this, quotes are understandably sparse. When you have a bad day at work, do you want to rehash every second of the day? Sure, this is supposed to be play, not work. But right now, in that locker room, for these few minutes, it feels like work. Roy Williams usually tells his teams to enjoy wins until midnight. Losses linger later than midnight. Losses settle like smog over the team plane. Losses are heavy.

So you go to Ginyard. It is both his blessing and his curse to be eloquent in times like this. A blessing because he has a unique way of dissecting games that makes him a great quote. A curse because the Tar Heels just lost a 7-point game, he is standing at his locker half-dressed, and there are a crowd of men with tape recorders standing around him in a semicircle.

But when you get there, you find something stunning. You find him pausing before every answer. You find him saying, "What's the word I'm looking for here?" as he attempts to describe what has caused this two-game losing streak.

This is not Ginyard. But it is the perfect microcosm of this team. The Tar Heels are 24–6 and ranked in the nation's top ten.

But right this minute, they are as fragile as your grandmother's antique vase. On the court, you watch them think, not play. Where do I go? What do I do? Is this right?

When they play, they are fun to watch. Ty Lawson didn't start Thursday's game after a terrible practice on Wednesday. The stat sheet says he had 8 assists and 3 turnovers. Forget about all that.

For the last six minutes of the game, he played defense like he hasn't played all year. He got down in a stance and he moved his feet and he denied the ball and he harassed the ball-handler and he *competed*. For six minutes, he made life very difficult on the perimeter for the Yellow Jackets. He took a Carolina team that had been forced to go to the much-despised zone just to slow the Tech onslaught in the first half and turned them into a bunch of defensive demons.

"That stretch was probably the best defense I have played all year," Lawson said. "We were down, it was late, and we needed something to change. We needed a stop. So I wanted to pressure the ball as much as I could. We needed urgency."

So he gets it. Kind of. Yes, the Tar Heels needed urgency. Here's the next step: find that same desperation before falling behind. Find it in the first half. Find it before tip-off. Find it in the tunnel before taking the floor.

"This has been the toughest stretch of my career," Lawson said. "Of course. We're losing, so things aren't good. The last couple of days we've been trying to figure things out. We're losing so many games."

So many games. Six, total, this year.

"What have we lost?" Lawson asked. "Three in a row now?"

Well, two.

"I don't think we've been on a two-game win streak in a month. We win one, then we lose one."

Tell the truth. How long do you really think it's been since Carolina won two in a row? Go ahead, guess.

It seems like a long time, right?

It was last week. One week ago today the Tar Heels were coming off a big road win over Boston College and a home victory over NC State. They were talking ACC regular season title, ACC Tournament title, and NCAA Tournament.

Now they are talking about getting some help to win the regular season crown and avoiding dreaded Thursday games in Tampa.

So that explains why Marcus Ginyard is choosing his words so carefully. When things aren't going well, everything is magnified. You want to know what's really going on with Carolina basketball?

On Tuesday, Ginyard told a handful of writers he thought last year's team could beat this year's squad. He had his reasons—and, perhaps to the chagrin of some Tar Heels, he elaborated on them. That eventually prompted a clear-the-air team meeting.

Tuesday night, Tyler Hansbrough spent the entire night throwing up. On Wednesday he was hospitalized until 3 p.m. and narrowly made the team plane to Atlanta. That same day, Lawson went through perhaps the worst practice of his Carolina career. Then they played a game, dropping a second straight ACC contest. Thursday night, Hansbrough was so spooked by the prospect of a potentially bumpy flight home that he elected to make the 6-hour bus ride with Dave Harder rather than take the team plane. In doing so, he avoided perhaps the worst team flight of all time, one that ended with Roy Williams pronouncing, "Tyler Hansbrough is the smartest person of all of us," when the aircraft mercifully came to a stop at RDU. At that moment, at least one Tar Heel was getting sick in the back of the plane.

Now, are you sure you really want to know?

"I felt like I stirred up a little too much the other day," Ginyard said. "I felt like I might have had something to do with the attitudes, because some guys might have gotten mad at what I said. I was disappointed in myself. I've got to be more careful."

He shrugged, as if the wisdom everyone was waiting for was not forthcoming. Right now, with only senior day left before the postseason, the platitudes were exhausted.

"We've got to get this team back on track," he said. "We've got to."

I had 13 people on my ticket list for Senior Day against Duke. Normally I'm pretty low-key on the day before a game. I like to stick to myself. But this time I had all my good friends and my girlfriend in town. We went to a big dinner the night before the game, and then we went to the Smith Center and watched the game between the Carolina managers and Duke managers. A bunch of my teammates were at the game, and unfortunately we watched our managers get a pretty good butt-kicking. Duke doesn't have a JV team, so in most cases guys who don't make the team as walk-ons end up as managers. They've got a good squad.

After the game, I got some shots up at the Smith Center with all my friends. It was a different kind of routine, but it was also beneficial. It made me realize how special the Duke game was. To have all those people come to Chapel Hill showed me how important it was to them.

I was in my normal pregame routine until the first time I ran out of the tunnel. As I was doing that, I thought, "Wow, I will only do this a couple more times and then it's over." As we were coming across the floor, I looked at Reyshawn and said, "Wow, four years went by fast, didn't it?"

He said, "I'm trying not to get choked up." That was exactly what I was thinking, and as he said it I could feel myself getting emotional.

Coach Williams has made Senior Day a very big deal since he came back to Carolina. He has never lost on a Senior Day as a head coach, so it's an important day for him. Before the game, they call each senior's name over the PA and we get a rose to give to our mother. Last year, I remember standing on the court as they called David Noel's name and I thought, "I can't believe that's going to be me next year." It always seemed so far away, right up until they called my name and I had to walk over to get the rose. Even then, it didn't seem real.

It was tough not to shed a tear when I gave the flower to my mom. And my dad completely shocked me. Since he retired five years ago, I don't know how many times I've seen him in a sport coat. That was the first shock. But then he opened it up and the lining had interlocking NC's on it. That lightened the mood a little. It stunned me so much I almost gave him the rose by accident. Anyone who knows my dad understands that for him to wear something Carolina is a big deal. He's pulled for me and for our team without question these last four years, but it hasn't been easy. For him to wear that Carolina blazer was a big deal.

After all three of the seniors were introduced, we went to midcourt and acknowledged the crowd. Then we looked at each other and said, "OK, it's time to play a game now. It's time to focus on Duke." It was amazing how I went from almost tipping over emotionally to focused right back on the game. I'm not usually a turn-it-on, turn-it-off kind of person, but in that situation it happened. The ACC championship was on the line and I was absolutely ready to play.

I had to be ready from the start because another senior tradition at Carolina is that seniors always start their last home game. I've started plenty of games in my career. I've played lots of big minutes in big games. But starting at point guard in that kind of game, I almost felt out of place. I played some point guard when Bobby and Quentin were hurt this year, but I hadn't done it in a while. Right before tipoff, I was focused on getting us into our offense, making the easy play, and playing tough defense. The only difference from my usual thought pattern was a little more emphasis on getting us into our offense. Of course, I didn't need much more incentive than seeing those guys in Duke jerseys across the floor. If I was 85 years old and barely able to walk I'd still get down and play defense if I saw Duke across the court.

Our relationship with them has changed during my career. Just before I got here, I think there was more interaction. When I arrived, there were several guys on our team who didn't want anything to do with Duke and there were some who were friends with them. For the most part, we stayed separate over the next couple years.

This year, though, there are some interesting friendships. Wayne Ellington and Gerald Henderson are best friends. Quentin Thomas and DeMarcus Nelson are friends. After those two pairs, it's still separate. It's not like you have to worry about a fight if you see them on the street; we just don't have much occasion to interact. In the ACC, there's a common respect for anyone else who plays on this level. I saw Greg Paulus at an NBA exhibition game and we were courteous. I have respect for him because we've played against each other. But we didn't go out to dinner after the game. As far as I know there aren't a lot of Duke-Carolina friendships other than the two I mentioned. When we play, all the commentators play up the fact that we're eight miles apart and make it sound like we're running into each other every day. It's not like that. They might as well be a hundred miles away because there is very limited interaction.

Outside of basketball, I'm sure the Duke players are good guys. Players from both teams are highly recruited, and that means they're going to know each other from the summer circuit. It's not like they get to school and all of a sudden there are strangers across town. I knew J.J. Redick in high school a little bit, and I ran into him on Franklin Street occasionally. He seemed fine. But he plays for Duke and I play for Carolina. We are arch-rivals. We are in competition, and because both programs are so good, it's not just a local competition, it's a national competition. It's tough to be friends with someone you want to beat so badly between the lines. My perception would be that it becomes tougher for the guys who enter school as friends to maintain that friendship as the years progress.

If someone would have told me I was going to play well in the opening minutes, I would have thought it would be defensively or making a big three-pointer. Who would have known it would be a couple assists driving the lane? That's the most bizarre scenario ever considering my career. I'm not exactly a penetrator.

On the first assist, Duke had just scored their first basket of the game. I've heard Coach yell, "Run!" so much that it rings in my head as soon as the other team scores. As soon as they scored, I took off. Paulus was so close to me that I was by him with one dribble. The lane area was open, so I shielded Paulus with my body and suddenly it was just Brandan, his defender, and me. I decided it might be a good idea to get the ball to Brandan near the basket and let him do something. It was exactly what Coach always talks about: making the easy play.

The second assist was very similar. I went to the basket and made a simple bounce pass. It was mostly just being in the right place at the right time. It felt good in my senior game to contribute offensively in a different way.

Duke has always played me very tight, because that's their style of defense. They face guard me on the wing and don't help off me at all, so it's very difficult to get a good look. Last year at home, I hit a couple three-pointers against them, including one where I came off a ball screen and Shelden Williams was guarding me. I popped it over him from deep—it wasn't a great shot, but it went in. It's one of those shots I will always remember. I ended up in a very similar situation in the first half this year. I came to the top of the key and Josh McRoberts was in front of me. It felt exactly like it felt last year . . . but it didn't go in. It was instinctive, but it wasn't a good shot at all.

Coach was not happy with that shot. I heard him yelling at me on the floor, and he mentioned it again when we came out for second half warm-ups. As unhappy as he was, I think Coach Holladay was even more upset. It was an uncharacteristic shot for me. And I definitely got the message that unless I was planning to make all of them, the coaches didn't want it to become characteristic.

We had an 18–4 run late that broke the game open. I thought it was going to be a routine win. I left the game for the last time and was really pleased. We had swept Duke, I had just come out of the game in the Smith Center for the last time ever, and I was trying to soak in the moment.

Then, out of nowhere, Tyler goes down on a very hard foul by Gerald Henderson.

My first thought was, "Is Tyler OK?" My next impulse was to restrain myself from jumping over that line and going after Henderson. I think most competitors would have had the same reaction. You see your best player and your team-mate go down, and the adrenaline starts flowing. It's hard to stay confined to the bench because you feel helpless. But in the four years I've been here, the coaches have been very clear that if something happens on the court, we stay on the bench. Coach Robinson and Jonas were in the vicinity and I wasn't going through either one of those guys.

The next ten minutes were surreal. The officials were watching the play on video, but we couldn't see it. I was really curious what it looked like. I knew there were just 14 seconds left and it was such an unnecessary play. Then I started thinking about the long-term ramifications. There hadn't been an incident like this in several years in the Duke-Carolina rivalry. Television was going to replay this as fuel for a long time, and Gerald Henderson has three more years left at Duke.

In many ways, I was glad there were just 14 seconds left. If there had been five minutes left, I'm afraid the game would have deteriorated. There's not much time for rational thinking in that situation. The dominant emotion is anger, and I wouldn't have wanted it to play out that way. After the game, I wanted to be the bigger man. I wanted to shake their hands and tell them, "Good game." Henderson had already left the court and I tried to remember there was still a team full of players not responsible for that play.

I don't know how that play will impact the rivalry going forward. We all thought it was a little cheap. It's also an injury that will negatively impact Tyler's play for the next couple weeks, and that's a big deal at this time of the year. One thing is for sure: when Carolina and Duke play next year, that play will get more air time than a Mike Krzyzewski credit card commercial.

Another senior tradition instituted by Coach Williams is the postgame senior speech. For the last four years, ever since I found out about it, I've been nervous about speaking to the Smith Center crowd. I'm not the greatest public speaker. I've become decent at giving media interviews, but that's a crowd of 15 or 20. Talking in front of 100 people or more has never been my strong suit, and now I'd have to talk in front of 20,000.

Dewey spent this week typing some ideas on his computer. I never got comfortable with that, because I was thinking too much about Duke. I knew if we lost no one would care what I said. So I never planned my speech or gave much thought to it. Then the Tyler thing happened and that took over my thoughts.

And suddenly the final buzzer went off and I realized, "Uh-oh, I've got to give a speech in front of all these people. And I'm really nervous."

I gave Coach Williams a big hug. He said, "Thank you," and said he loved me. I told him I loved him, too. That's the thing about Coach—it's not just words or fake actions. He really does care about everyone. Basically, I've been here since he got here. Reyshawn and I are the only two guys who have seen everything he's seen at Carolina. That's important to me. In a way, I feel like a charter member of a special club.

Game 31

No. 14/14 Duke 72
#8/8 North Carolina 86
March 4, 2007 • Smith Center, Chapel Hill

DU	FG	3FG	FT	REB	PF	TP	A	TO	B	S	Min
McClure*	0-3	0-0	0-0	2-0-2	0	0	0	0	0	1	16
McRoberts*	3-7	0-0	3-6	6-4-10	5	9	2	6	1	0	36
Scheyer*	3-8	2-5	2-3	1-3-4	4	10	2	1	0	2	35
Nelson*	5-15	2-7	2-2	1-2-3	2	14	2	1	0	1	35
Paulus*	7-14	3-8	4-4	0-5-5	5	21	4	4	0	1	31
Henderson	8-14	0-3	0-1	1-5-6	3	16	1	2	0	1	30
Thomas	1-2	0-0	0-0	1-0-1	3	2	0	0	0	0	6
Pocius	0-1	0-0	0-0	0-0-0	0	0	0	0	0	0	3
Zoubek	0-0	0-0	0-0	0-2-2	2	0	0	1	1	0	6
Johnson	0-0	0-0	0-0	0-0-0	0	0	0	0	0	0	1
Davidson	0-0	0-0	0-0	0-0-0	0	0	0	0	0	0	1
TEAM				1-1-2							
Totals	27-64	7-23	11-16	13-22-35	24	72	11	15	2	6	200
Pct.	.422	.304	.688	DB: 3							

FG: (1st half: 12-34, .353; 2nd half: 15-30, .500)
3FG: (1st half: 3-11, .273; 2nd half: 4-12, .333)
FT: (1st half: 2-5, .400; 2nd half: 9-11, .818)

UNC	FG	3FG	FT	REB	PF	TP	A	TO	B	S	Min
Terry*	4-8	1-3	6-6	1-7-8	1	15	1	4	1	2	29
Hansbrough*	10-18	0-0	6-9	9-8-17	2	26	0	1	0	1	30
Wright*	5-6	0-0	0-0	0-5-5	3	10	1	2	3	0	30
Burke*	0-1	0-1	0-0	0-0-0	0	0	0	0	0	0	3
Miller*	0-1	0-1	0-0	0-0-0	0	0	4	0	0	0	10
Lawson	4-8	0-1	4-5	0-1-1	5	12	5	1	0	1	29
Thompson	1-4	0-0	0-0	0-2-2	1	2	0	0	0	1	13
Green	1-2	0-0	0-0	0-0-0	2	2	1	0	0	0	10
Ellington	1-5	0-2	1-1	0-2-2	2	3	2	1	0	0	15
Stepheson	0-1	0-0	0-0	0-0-0	0	0	0	0	1	0	4
Ginyard	4-6	1-1	4-4	1-2-3	2	13	2	1	0	1	20
Frasor	1-2	0-0	1-2	0-0-0	2	3	2	1	0	0	9
Copeland	0-0	0-0	0-0	0-0-0	0	0	0	0	0	0	1
TEAM				0-0-0							
Totals	31-62	2-9	22-27	11-27-38	20	86	18	11	5	8	200
Pct.	.500	.222	.815	DB: 2							

FG: (1st half: 17-31, .548; 2nd half: 14-31, .452)
3FG: (1st half: 1-4, .250; 2nd half: 1-5, .200)
FT: (1st half: 3-3, 1.000; 2nd half: 19-24, .792)

Officials: Karl Hess, Jamie Luckie, Les Jones
Attendance: 21,750 • **Technical Fouls:** none

Score by Periods	1st	2nd	Total
Duke	29	43	72
North Carolina	38	48	86

I thought my speech went OK. As far as I know, I didn't forget anyone who was expecting to be thanked. Mostly, I was glad I didn't say any really bad jokes. Bobby and Dewey kept saying I was going to let a bad joke slip, but I didn't. I got some good laughs and I told some people how important they are to me. That's all I could have wished for.

Now the speeches are over. It's time for the most important month of the year.

LUCAS: SEEING RED

MARCH 4, 2007

This will be comforting.

With the Smith Center's foundation shaking and referees huddling and the blood vessels on your temple popping and Roy Williams and Mike Krzyzewski meeting at midcourt and what had been a bit of a ho-hum finish exploding, Tyler Hansbrough said exactly what you thought he would say.

He was standing in the Smith Center training room with his father, trainer Marc Davis, a dentist, and sports information honcho Matt Bowers. The first move was to have him cough into a trash can, which send blood streaming. Finally, the blood stopped streaming from his nose. The front of his jersey, from the neck to the waist, was covered in bright red blood. Hansbrough's blood. And this is what he said:

"I want to go back out there. Like this."

Imagine if that had happened. Imagine if Hansbrough had walked back onto the Smith Center court with his jersey covered in blood, a plug in each nostril, and a menacing glare.

They could have retired his jersey—not the one he wore Sunday afternoon, because that one has already been washed—right on the spot. A man gets 26 points and 17 rebounds against Duke, that's banner-worthy. A man gets 26 points, 17 rebounds, and supplants Eric Montross as the all-time image of a bloody Tar Heel against the Blue Devils, that's something that needs a statue. He'd already had a memorable game. But as soon as he stood up after the foul, it became legendary.

Montross can tell you this is true: for the rest of his life, strangers will approach Hansbrough and say the following words:

"Do you remember that time you were all bloody against Duke?"

Montross is asked about his bloody incident twice as often as his 1993 national championship or his decade in the NBA. Carolina fans remember images. And the image of a scarlet liquid covering the familiar argyle is indelible. You know it's true, because right now you're picturing the big seven-footer shooting free throws against Duke with blood trickling down his cheek.

Fifteen years from now, we'll have the exact same image of Hansbrough—blood covering his face, muscles clenched, eyes popping, mouth guard about to fall out of his mouth, and Dewey Burke holding him back.

Oh yes, senior Dewey Burke. Listed at 6-foot-0, 185 pounds. Often called one of the hardest workers on the team, and now we have verifiable proof that it's true, because without years in the weight room there's no way he restrains Hansbrough.

"I was trying," Burke said with a smile. "I was

in his ear telling him to breathe and relax a little bit. He was pretty fired up."

You think?

"He saw the blood and that's what freaked him out," Burke continued. "He jumped up and I just wanted to bear hug him and tell him to try to breathe until we got him off the court. I was just looking out for my guy."

There's a gift more valuable than a basket of Bojangle's biscuits. By looking out for his guy, Burke prevented any further ugliness. Instead of remembering the game as one where Hansbrough —who was unable to speak to the media because talking made his teeth hurt, but initial reports are that his nose is not broken—lost his composure, we're able to remember it for his Sean May-like effort.

Really, the whole thing was Hansbrough's fault in the first place. With your team shooting free throws, 18.7 seconds left, and an 83–72 lead, you're supposed to give up. After all, the game was over.

"The game was over before (the foul)," Duke's Mike Krzyzewski said. "The outcome of the game, let's put it that way. It's unfortunate those people were in the game."

So the Blue Devils had given up. That's why, when Bobby Frasor toed the free throw line with 18.7 seconds remaining, Duke had Gerald Henderson, Josh McRoberts, DeMarcus Nelson, and Jon Scheyer still on the floor. Greg Paulus had just left after fouling out.

Frasor made the first and missed the second, which sent the ball bounding high off the rim.

At that point, Hansbrough's instincts kicked in and he did what he'd been doing all day—outfought McRoberts for the rebound. It's encoded in Hansbrough's DNA: ball in air, launch self towards ball. Who would you rather be—the guy who hits Hansbrough in the face or the guy who tells him to stop giving maximum effort on the court?

It will be a minor footnote in history that it was Hansbrough's offensive rebound that led to the foul that put him on the free throw line with 17.5 seconds left. But it tells you everything about his game. He might not have more physical gifts than everyone else on the court. But he has more intensity.

That's why Roy Williams was certain of his stardom before the Poplar Bluff product ever wore a Carolina jersey. At the annual gathering of the Tar Heel coaching tree in the early fall of 2005, Williams described his strategy for the upcoming season. Much of it revolved around Hansbrough. Jeff Lebo, now the head coach at Auburn, remembers being a little skeptical of all the plans for a raw freshman. A few months later, he left Williams a voice mail:

"Coach, you were right. Hansbrough is everything you said he was."

Which is to say that he's obsessed with playing hard. After missing his first free throw and then missing the second with 17.5 seconds remaining, he could've just hung around the free throw line with his hands on his hips, or perhaps rolled his eyes at his charity stripe misfortune. He had played 30 minutes and—as would later be noted—the game was in hand. But he wanted to keep playing, keep trying, keep competing.

So he simply got the offensive rebound and went—where else?—back toward the basket. Mayhem ensued (Hansbrough had actually predicted the carnage two months earlier when he said the only on-court contact that could make him lose his cool was a hit in the face).

"I thought it was something out of a movie," Bobby Frasor said. "It was something I'd never seen before. Blood was all over his jersey, his shoes, the floor. Just that passion and that ferocity."

When Hansbrough eventually returned—just in time to enjoy the senior speeches by Burke, Wes Miller, and Reyshawn Terry—it was Frasor whom he asked, "Does my nose look normal?"

Hansbrough asked this while dried blood remained on his face and two plugs were sticking out of his nostrils like a walrus's tusks. Even the deadpan Frasor couldn't resist a small smile.

"Yeah, Tyler," he said. "You look really normal."

ACC TOURNAMENT

I'D LIKE TO FILE an official complaint about the ACC Tournament. Explain this to me: how can they move the ACC Tournament to Tampa, have a four-day event, and put one of the teams in a hotel where they can't watch the opening round games?

Because we beat Duke, we didn't have to play on Thursday. But while four other ACC games were going on, we couldn't see them because our hotel didn't get ESPN2. There should be a league rule against that. If you are going to host a participating team, you have to get ESPN2.

Bobby and I were roommates on the Tampa trip, and both of us are basketball junkies so the lack of the appropriate channel was a big blow. It was the first time we've roomed together this year. I hosted him when he was on his official recruiting visit. It was probably the most boring recruiting trip of all time, and he constantly gives me a hard time about it.

He had already committed to Carolina and came down for Late Night. He showed up with this Polo shirt on and he had his collar popped, very impressive. The first night we had Late Night and practice early the next morning, so I was trying to get focused for practice. I take it very seriously. Meanwhile Bobby is wondering if anyone in Chapel Hill ever has a good time.

You have to remember that Bobby is a little quirky. He's one of the funniest guys on the team, but no one tells him that because it helps his ego. We give him a hard time about his clothes because most of the time it looks like he hasn't washed his shirt in three or four days. I know he does laundry, because he's done it at my house before, but his shirts are always wrinkly and the collars are always messed up. We used to call him Robert Dirtsky or Dirtsky for short. That's another Jonas Sahratian nickname. We still bring out Dirtsky from time to time, but he has cleaned up over the last two years. I think his adjustment to college from a sanitation standpoint was difficult.

We give him a hard time because of his weird sense of humor, but what I like most about him is his knowledge of the game. He's the son of a coach and he has a very high basketball IQ. When we sit on the bench next to each other, we usually say similar things. It's fun to watch games with him and see what he's noticing about a game. Which makes it even more ridiculous that we couldn't watch the ACC Tournament in the same city in which it was being played.

Our Thursday was low-key. We practiced at a local high school—Jesuit High School, but Reyshawn pronounced it "Jay-soot," which was funny. Then we had some free time, went over the scouting report, and went to dinner at Ruth's Chris. One of the best things about the postseason is that we usually eat very well.

Game 32											

Florida State 58
#8/8 North Carolina 73
March 9, 2007 • St. Pete Times Forum, Tampa, Fla.
ACC Tournament Quarterfinal

FSU	FG	3FG	FT	REB	PF	TP	A	TO	B	S	Min
Thornton*	4-13	1-3	3-4	3-3-6	5	12	0	1	0	4	26
Echefu*	2-7	1-2	4-5	2-6-8	3	9	0	2	2	3	37
Swann*	2-7	2-6	0-0	1-1-2	3	6	1	4	0	1	23
Douglas*	2-12	0-4	6-7	1-2-3	4	10	5	4	0	1	30
Rich*	3-6	0-1	2-2	3-2-5	3	8	1	3	1	0	33
Soto	0-0	0-0	0-0	0-0-0	0	0	0	0	0	0	1
Mims	0-2	0-0	0-0	0-3-3	0	0	0	1	0	0	12
Allen	3-6	2-4	2-2	0-2-2	2	10	1	2	1	1	23
Breeden	1-2	1-1	0-0	0-0-0	2	3	0	0	0	0	12
Reid	0-0	0-0	0-0	0-0-0	0	0	1	0	0	0	3
TEAM				0-2-2	1						
Totals	**17-55**	**7-21**	**17-20**	**10-21-31**	**23**	**58**	**9**	**17**	**4**	**12**	**200**
Pct.	.309	.333	.850	DB: 3							

FG: (1st half: 8-25, .320; 2nd half: 9-30, .300)
3FG: (1st half: 2-7, .286; 2nd half: 5-14, .357)
FT: (1st half: 8-8, 1.000; 2nd half: 9-12, .850)

UNC	FG	3FG	FT	REB	PF	TP	A	TO	B	S	Min
Terry*	4-6	1-2	1-6	0-9-9	1	10	1	0	0	1	27
Wright*	5-9	0-0	1-3	0-2-2	2	11	1	3	3	0	28
Hansbrough*	3-7	0-0	0-2	1-3-4	5	6	1	4	0	1	27
Ellington*	6-12	2-5	4-4	3-0-3	0	18	0	1	0	2	26
Lawson*	4-8	0-2	6-6	0-4-4	1	14	8	2	0	3	29
Ginyard	1-2	0-0	0-0	2-2-4	1	2	1	3	1	0	17
Frasor	1-1	1-1	0-0	0-0-0	1	3	0	0	0	0	7
Thomas	0-0	0-0	0-0	0-2-2	3	0	1	1	0	0	4
Green	1-3	1-2	0-0	0-3-3	0	3	0	0	1	0	7
Burke	0-0	0-0	0-0	0-0-0	0	0	0	1	0	0	1
Thompson	1-1	0-0	0-2	2-1-3	4	2	1	3	0	0	14
Miller	1-2	1-2	0-0	0-1-1	0	3	0	1	0	0	8
Stepheson	0-0	0-0	0-0	0-0-0	1	0	0	0	0	0	4
Copeland	0-0	0-0	1-2	0-0-0	0	1	0	0	0	0	1
TEAM				0-2-2							
Totals	**27-51**	**6-14**	**13-25**	**8-29-37**	**19**	**73**	**14**	**19**	**5**	**7**	**200**
Pct.	.529	.429	.520	DB: 6							

FG: (1st half: 13-28, .464; 2nd half: 14-23, .609)
3FG: (1st half: 4-10, .400; 2nd half: 2-4, .500)
FT: (1st half: 6-14, .429; 2nd half: 7-11, .636)

Officials: Mike Wood, Les Jones, Roger Ayers
Attendance: 22,269 • **Technical Fouls:** FSU bench

Score by Periods	1st	2nd	Total
Florida State	26	32	58
North Carolina	36	37	73

Our quarterfinal was against Florida State. We never trailed and Brandan Wright and Deon Thompson teamed up to do a great job defensively on Al Thornton. We played the early game, so we went out to eat again—this time at Maggiano's. As if we need more incentive to keep winning, the longer we stay in Tampa the longer we know we'll be eating well every night. Play well, eat well. It's pretty simple.

I was able to catch some of the other quarterfinals, and the lower seed won both games, including State beating Duke. It made me think back to ten years ago. I was at the ACC Tournament in Greensboro when State was the eighth seed and made it to the championship game against Carolina. Justin Gainey played every minute of the Tournament, all four games, and I liked the way he played. Friday night was the first time I thought they might make a similar run.

Everyone was excited about getting another chance at Boston College. You might not like guys like Jared Dudley and Sean Marshall, but there's no question they force you to compete. When we lost to them twice, we never took them out of what they wanted to do offensively. We played their pace and allowed them to slow it down.

This year, both times we've played them we have forced the tempo. We started running and getting easy buckets and they eventually couldn't keep pace. One thing about their emotion: it works both ways. It really works for them when they are playing well and works against them when they are down. It wasn't long before we noticed they were starting to chirp at each other. That's when we knew we had a big advantage.

Game 33

Boston College 56
#8/8 North Carolina 71
March 10, 2007 • St. Pete Times Forum, Tampa, Fla.
ACC Tournament Semifinal

BC	FG	3FG	FT	REB	PF	TP	A	TO	B	S	Min
Dudley*	7-18	2-4	4-6	3-3-6	3	20	2	1	0	1	39
Roche*	1-2	0-1	0-0	1-0-1	1	2	0	0	0	1	19
Oates*	1-4	0-2	2-2	0-8-8	1	4	1	1	0	0	34
Rice*	1-9	1-5	2-2	0-2-2	2	5	4	0	0	0	39
Marshall*	8-14	4-5	3-4	1-2-3	2	23	0	5	0	2	36
Haynes	0-1	0-0	0-0	0-0-0	0	0	0	0	0	0	1
Kaba	0-0	0-0	0-0	0-0-0	0	0	0	0	0	0	1
Neville	0-0	0-0	0-0	0-0-0	0	0	0	0	0	0	1
Spears	0-2	0-0	0-2	1-0-1	0	0	1	0	0	0	10
Blair	1-5	0-0	0-0	3-1-4	4	2	0	0	3	0	20
TEAM				2-0-2							
Totals	19-55	7-17	11-16	11-16-27	13	56	8	7	3	4	200
Pct.	.345	.412	.688	DB: 3							

FG: (1st half: 7-29, .241; 2nd half: 12-26, .462)
3FG: (1st half: 3-8, .375; 2nd half: 4-9, .444)
FT: (1st half: 6-10, .600; 2nd half: 5-6, .833)

UNC	FG	3FG	FT	REB	PF	TP	A	TO	B	S	Min
Terry*	3-7	1-2	0-0	0-4-4	2	7	2	0	0	0	22
Wright*	10-12	0-0	0-2	2-3-5	2	20	1	1	2	1	30
Hansbrough*	4-10	0-0	1-1	4-9-13	2	9	1	3	1	0	33
Ellington*	2-9	2-4	4-4	0-3-3	3	10	2	0	0	0	22
Lawson*	4-9	0-3	2-2	2-2-4	1	10	8	1	0	1	31
Ginyard	2-3	0-0	0-0	3-1-4	1	4	2	2	0	1	13
Frasor	2-4	1-1	0-0	1-0-1	1	5	0	1	0	0	8
Thomas	0-0	0-0	0-0	0-0-0	0	0	0	0	0	0	1
Green	2-4	0-2	0-0	0-1-1	1	4	1	0	0	0	17
Burke	0-0	0-0	0-0	0-1-1	0	0	0	0	0	0	1
Thompson	1-1	0-0	0-0	2-0-2	2	2	0	0	0	0	10
Miller	0-1	0-1	0-0	0-0-0	0	0	1	0	0	1	5
Wood	0-0	0-0	0-0	0-0-0	0	0	0	0	0	0	1
Stepheson	0-2	0-0	0-0	1-1-2	0	0	0	0	0	0	5
Copeland	0-0	0-0	0-0	0-0-0	0	0	0	0	0	0	1
TEAM				1-0-1			1				
Totals	30-62	4-13	7-9	16-25-41	15	71	18	9	3	4	200
Pct.	.484	.308	.778	DB: 4							

FG: (1st half: 15-30, .500; 2nd half: 15-32, .469)
3FG: (1st half: 1-4, .250; 2nd half: 3-9, .333)
FT: (1st half: 7-9, .778; 2nd half: 0-0, .000)

Officials: Les Jones, Jamie Luckie, Mike Eades
Attendance: 22,269 • **Technical Fouls:** none

Score by Periods	1st	2nd	Total
Boston College	23	33	56
North Carolina	38	33	71

I'm very excited to be in the ACC championship game. I've experienced a lot of positives during my Carolina career, but I've never won an ACC Tournament championship. It's a special event to me, because I grew up attending the Tournament. Even when I couldn't get out of school for the Friday games, I'd tell my teacher I was going to the bathroom. Then I'd go down the hall and sneak into the weight room so I could turn on the TV and watch with no one around. Ever since I've been aware of the Tournament, I've been enamored by it.

Being able to go to several Tournaments as a kid was a big deal. Now that I think about it, I don't know if my friends were my friends because they liked me or because they hoped I would take them to the ACC Tournament. Probably some of both. My dad and I would call it the marathon: our goal was to watch every minute of every ACC Tournament game. This is going to hurt the Carolina fans, but one of my favorites was the 1995 Tournament, when Randolph Childress went crazy. It was a double-overtime championship game and it was a terrific atmosphere in Greensboro. That's the level of play that inspired me to want to play in the ACC.

LUCAS: GETTING IT

MARCH 10, 2007

TAMPA—Marcus Ginyard's smiles on the basketball court come in a variety of flavors.

There's the "Celebrating a big play" smile. There's the "Can't believe that was called" smile. There's the "Dewey just drained another three" smile.

"I'm having fun out there," he's explained in the past. "A lot of guys try to be all hard when they're on the court. But I'm having fun and I don't mind showing it. I don't see any reason to be different on the court than I am off of it."

Never before, though, has there been a smile like the one he flashed early in the first half of Saturday's win over Boston College.

Maybe you saw it. With about 10 minutes left in the first half, Ginyard was guarding Sean Marshall.

He swiped at the ball, forced a turnover, hesitated just a second, and then sprinted off to gather the ball and deposit a layup that put the Tar Heels up 19–9.

But why was he smiling during the play? Let's turn on the audio for just a second.

With Ginyard in front of him, Marshall ripped the ball through. Carolina's defensive ace pecked at the ball.

"You're not going to get the ball," Marshall told him.

At that exact second, karma landed directly on Marshall's head. As he turned and prepared to make his next move, a split second after the words had left his lips, Ginyard *did* take the ball away.

"He turned his back a little bit and I poked it away," Ginyard said. "He looked at the ref for a second and I looked at the ball. It was still out there, so I went and got it and laid it up."

Ginyard is not particularly a talker on the court. But this was an occasion he could not resist. So he looked at Marshall and said the only perfect thing he could say. The only thing left to say, really:

"Hey, man, I got it."

And there you have Carolina's 71–56 ACC Tournament semifinal win in a nutshell. This was, by far, the best game the Tar Heels have played against BC since the Eagles joined the league.

Boston College is a team built to bruise you. Every player on their roster fits their system perfectly. They have a swagger that suggests they are well aware they're going to wear you down, that they're content to plug along until you give up.

Even their offense, a tight version of the flex that is ideally run with everyone inside the paint, is built to eliminate any room to breathe.

Last year in the Smith Center, that worked. Last year in the ACC Tournament semifinals, that worked. The day's theme was simple, and it was reiterated by the Tar Heel coaching staff during pregame preparation:

Soft was not an option. Soft would result in someone getting embarrassed.

"They're a very mentally tough team," Danny Green said. "They play physical and try to get in your head. It's attack or be attacked. And I think today we attacked them and played up to their level of intensity."

Everyone wearing argyle did. Forget about Ty Lawson's 8 assists—his most impressive contribution might have been holding Tyrese Rice to 1-of-9 from the floor. A series of Tar Heels limited Jared Dudley to 7-of-18. Carolina held a mammoth 16-rebound edge.

Thirteen of those rebounds came from Tyler Hansbrough, his third double-digit rebounding effort in the past four games. He holds the mask he's forced to wear because of a big hit in the Duke game in approximately the same regard as he holds the dance skits during Late Night: there's nothing good about them, but they're required.

"I'm not happy with the mask," he said. "I don't think I will get happy with it. It cuts my vision . . . If I'm not going to be able to see to shoot the ball, I have to do something to help this team. So I wanted to get every rebound."

Did you hear that? *Every* rebound. The Tar Heels dealt exclusively in those types of absolutes on Saturday. They defended on every possession. They boxed out on every shot. And they ran constantly.

At times, it looked like a game of red rover, with five white shirts already back on defense as five burgundy shirts walked down the court on offense. When you play for Roy Williams and you see that walking, you know exactly what it means.

"They want to try to use the clock for 35 seconds on offense," Reyshawn Terry. "And we know that with our tempo of game, by the time they've worked it on offense, they might not be aware of us pushing the ball back the other way. So we tried to take advantage of it."

So Carolina earned a slot in Sunday's title game. They earned their 27th win of the season. And they earned something that's been even tougher to find over the last couple of years—Boston College's respect.

That's why, later in the first half after Ginyard had gone out of the game, Marshall had one last thing to say. As he crossed the court and found himself in front of his nemesis, now seated on the Tar Heel bench, he had only two words left:

"Nice defense."

Relative to other teams, I don't think we spend a lot of time preparing for opponents. We have an in-depth scouting report and Coach Williams usually has a big folder with lots of paper on the opponent. But the coaches don't want to overwhelm us with information, so we get a one-sheet scouting report the day before the game.

The routine stays the same. After pregame meal, there's a board with the opposing roster. We have a TV that plays the clip tape we watched the day before in practice. Coach tells us to put our scouting reports away, and then he calls on everyone. He might say, "Ty, tell me about Engin Atsur." Ty has to answer with the information about Atsur that's on the scouting report.

It's a serious atmosphere. Coach takes it very seriously. His theory is that the coaches are limiting the information they give us, so they expect us to know it. After we've gone through all the opposing players, each scouting report has three keys to the game at the bottom. If you haven't been called on regarding an opposing player, you're probably going to be called on to provide the keys to the game.

We had already played two tough games with State before the championship game, so we knew they were a good team. We also knew we had better depth than them and they had been forced to play an extra game because of their seeding.

Our seniors made big contributions against State. I was able to hit a couple big three-pointers in the first half. As a substitute, Coach emphasizes he wants us to keep the level of play the same or even raise it a little. I'm the type of person who always wants to raise it, so I was glad I was able to hit a couple of shots. This is the time of year to have extreme confidence in your play, and I'm at a stage where I feel like it's going in every time I shoot it.

One of our other seniors, Reyshawn, came up huge in the second half. I like to sit near the coaches on the bench because I like to hear what they talk about. I could tell Coach was upset with Reyshawn in the first half. Finally, in the second half he took him out of the game and it was obvious Reyshawn was upset. Coach left him on the bench and let it be known that he wasn't happy with Reyshawn's attitude. Reyshawn responded well immediately, and that earned him another chance to go back in the game.

Everyone makes mistakes. It's how you respond to those mistakes that define who you are, and for Reyshawn to come back in and make the game's biggest plays shows the kind of person he is. A couple of years ago, he would have hung his head. It's also true that Coach wouldn't have had the same amount of confidence in him a couple years ago, and he probably wouldn't have gone back in the game.

It's funny, because Reyshawn and I have been here for four years together. He gets along great with everyone. But off the floor I don't feel like I know him that well. He's more reserved, and it's difficult to crack that shell. But when you sit down with him, you realize how intelligent he is. He has a very interesting perspective on his time at Carolina.

It's indescribable to be able to celebrate an ACC Tournament championship with your teammates. To throw on those hats and hold the trophy is one of the greatest feelings imaginable. It's so rewarding. At the same time, it wasn't very long before we started thinking about the NCAA Tournament.

We watched the selection show as a team, and some of the usual characters were having fun with it when we were announced as a number-one seed. Coach didn't say much until we flew back to Chapel Hill and the bus arrived at the Smith Center.

"Congratulations," he told us. "Winning the ACC Tournament is a great accomplishment. We had a very good weekend.

"And we still have some work left to do."

Game 34

NC State 80
#8/8 North Carolina 89
March 11, 2007 • St. Pete Times Forum, Tampa, Fla.
ACC Tournament Final

NCSU	FG	3FG	FT	REB	PF	TP	A	TO	B	S	Min
Grant*	3-6	0-1	4-5	1-3-4	4	10	1	7	0	0	32
Costner*	10-20	3-5	5-7	0-3-3	3	28	0	4	1	2	38
McCauley*	6-10	0-0	0-0	4-3-7	4	12	1	1	0	1	35
Fells*	5-9	2-5	6-6	1-5-6	3	18	3	0	0	1	36
Atsur*	1-3	1-2	0-0	1-0-1	1	3	5	3	0	1	32
Nieman	0-1	0-1	0-0	1-0-1	2	0	1	0	0	0	13
Horner	4-4	0-0	1-1	0-0-0	1	9	0	0	0	0	14
TEAM				0-2-2							
Totals	29-53	6-14	16-19	8-16-24	18	80	11	15	1	5	200
Pct.	.547	.429	.842	DB: 1							

FG: (1st half: 13-26, .500; 2nd half: 16-27, .593)
3FG: (1st half: 5-9, .556; 2nd half: 1-5, .200)
FT: (1st half: 3-4, .750; 2nd half: 13-15, .867)

UNC	FG	3FG	FT	REB	PF	TP	A	TO	B	S	Min
Terry*	4-7	2-3	3-3	2-2-4	3	13	3	2	0	1	24
Wright*	7-11	0-0	2-2	0-4-4	1	16	0	0	1	0	31
Hansbrough*	2-6	0-0	11-11	0-3-3	4	15	1	3	0	4	29
Ellington*	6-8	2-3	2-2	1-2-3	1	16	1	1	0	1	28
Lawson*	5-10	0-1	3-4	1-3-4	2	13	4	1	0	1	30
Ginyard	0-3	0-1	2-2	1-0-1	2	2	0	0	0	0	13
Frasor	0-0	0-0	0-0	0-2-2	0	0	2	2	0	0	10
Green	2-3	0-0	0-0	0-0-0	3	4	1	0	0	1	13
Thompson	2-2	0-0	0-0	0-2-2	1	4	0	1	0	1	14
Miller	2-2	2-2	0-0	0-0-0	2	6	0	0	0	0	4
Stepheson	0-0	0-0	0-0	0-0-0	0	0	0	0	0	0	4
TEAM				1-0-1							
Totals	30-52	6-10	23-24	6-18-24	19	89	12	10	1	9	200
Pct.	.577	.600	.958	DB: 1							

FG: (1st half: 17-28, .607; 2nd half: 13-24, .542)
3FG: (1st half: 4-7, .571; 2nd half: 2-3, .667)
FT: (1st half: 4-4, 1.000; 2nd half: 19-20, .950)

Officials: Karl Hess, Bryan Kersey, Gary Maxwell
Attendance: 22,269 • **Technical Fouls:** none

Score by Periods	1st	2nd	Total
NC State	34	46	80
North Carolina	42	47	89

LUCAS: WHAT IT MEANS

MARCH 11, 2007

TAMPA—What does it mean to you, Reyshawn? Sometimes it's hard to tell. Carolina's lone starting senior is the master of the poker face. On the court, you might catch him exulting in a big play, but those moments are rare.

When you think about it, not knowing him is the way you know him. Consider this: have you ever felt less knowledgeable about a four-year Tar Heel who played critical minutes as a junior and senior? What does Terry's mother look like? What are his hobbies? Ever seen his girlfriend?

For four years, he's kept it all inside. He has a lighter side, but even his teammates don't always see it.

"Honestly, he's got that same straight face with us that he has with everyone else," freshman Deon Thompson said. "When he shows a lot of emotion, I'm surprised."

Picture a room. It's the day after Carolina's loss at Georgia Tech and popular opinion has it that the wheels are falling off the Tar Heel bus. Shots aren't falling, players are chirping, and Terry is . . . hurting?

And showing it.

Several players addressed their teammates on that Friday after practice. They had chosen that time with a specific intent—they knew everyone would be there, no one would be late, everyone would be thinking about basketball. And when it came to Terry's turn to speak, he did something entirely unexpected:

He cried.

The Winston-Salem native was trying to explain what his senior season at Carolina meant to him.

First, he tried words. "It's so important to me," he said.

The words made an impression, of course. But his tears meant more. Here was the stoic senior, the man whose previous biggest outburst had probably been one of his typical rapid-fire doses of trash talk during a pickup game, and he was simply overwhelmed.

A lot of things were said that day as Friday afternoon turned into Friday evening. None of them made as big an impact as Terry's emotions.

"I was surprised," Ty Lawson said. "Reyshawn is a tough guy. You never see him show anything. When he started crying, I realized how much it meant to him. He felt like we had so much talent and we were losing it. We weren't using what we had to the best of our abilities."

It's always about ability with Terry, isn't it? You've probably said it yourself.

He's got all the ability in the world . . .

What I wouldn't give to have that ability . . .

If he ever harnesses that ability . . .

His first two years, his teammates saw it more than we did. It would come in flashes—a streak of 3-pointers for the Blue team during practice, a particularly vicious dunk during a summer game. What if those flashes—that ability—could happen during a game that meant something?

Sunday, it did.

Understand this: for all the chirping about Tampa as a bad ACC Tournament site, the St. Pete Times Forum turned into a piece of Tobacco Road in the final minutes of the championship game. For just a moment, you forgot the arena on the water and the palm trees and the hotel breakfast area packed with more spring training fans than basketball fans.

It was Carolina and it was State and it felt like every ACC championship game you've seen before. You were standing and you were chewing your nails and you were starting to wonder what kind of horseshoe Sidney Lowe kept in that red jacket pocket.

By the time the Wolfpack closed to 70–69 on the shoulders of a phenomenal effort from Brandon Costner, there were echoes of the Cardiac Pack throughout the arena. There was 1983 and there was 1987, both a long time ago but both also recent enough to sting.

It is into this moment that Terry suddenly introduced himself. He'd watched an extended stretch of the game from the bench. For what reason?

"Um . . ." Terry said after the game.

"He doesn't have to answer that," Roy Williams quickly interjected. "That's between us."

No matter. What mattered was that the relationship between Terry and Williams has progressed to the point that once the senior made an error, he was allowed to go back in the game and redeem himself. That is a good measure of how far he has come. There was a time when one mistake ended his day.

Not Sunday. Williams has been remarkably patient with his senior. It is a relationship perhaps unlike any the head coach has ever had. Sometimes, this is what makes being a coach worth it.

You push and you prod and you wait and you coax and then . . .

This.

Terry with a jumper. Not the best shot in the world, but it is all net. Have you ever noticed that about Terry's shots? When they are true, they never touch the rim, just rip straight through.

Terry inside. Terry twisting, drawing the foul, and scoring.

Now, he is feeling it. So it is easy to fire a 3-pointer from in front of the Tar Heel bench with Engin Atsur all over him. It swishes. Of course.

"Engin was all over him on that shot," Sidney Lowe said. "All *over* him."

It was 8 straight points for Terry, a reigniting of the Tar Heels that eventually led to an ACC title.

This is how he exulted in it:

"When I got back in the game, I felt like I had to give the team a spark," he said. "The opportunity came and I was able to take it."

From his words, it was hard to tell exactly what it meant. He met the media at the podium with a hat pulled low over his face, obscuring his expressive eyes. Wes Miller's hat was backwards, giving a perfect view of how much it meant for a player who came to the Tournament just like you and me—as a fan—for so many years.

Terry was expressionless. What did it mean to him? It was hard to tell.

Not for his teammates. They already knew.

Because he had showed them. In words, in actions, and when it mattered the most.

NCAA FIRST AND SECOND ROUNDS

UNTIL YOU PLAY in the NCAA Tournament, it's impossible to understand what a precision operation it is. I'm not talking about the way we prepare or the actual games. I'm talking about the details of the event itself.

The NCAA doesn't just host regionals. They take over buildings. At every NCAA Tournament event, you find the same blue carpet. Walk from the locker room to the arena? Blue carpet. On the way to the media room? Blue carpet. I really wonder what the line item in the NCAA budget is for blue carpet. It seems like such a silly detail, but it's their way of making sure every single venue is handled the exact same way. And in a way, it's comforting as a player because you always know what to expect.

Just like the way they interpret their rules, everything with the NCAA Tournament is strict and by the book. Everyone has to have an ID to get in the building. If you don't have an ID, you're not coming in. In Winston-Salem this year, they wouldn't let Coach Williams's wife come in with the team. She had to go around to the general public's entrance. Does that make any sense? What was it going to hurt to let Mrs. Williams in the team gate? Nothing, probably, but they don't make any exceptions at all, even at a place like Winston where most of the workers know us because we're there once per season anyway.

There is a practice pin for every practice. You have to wear your pin. There's a game pin for every game. Everyone on the bench has to have that pin. The goal is to get 12 of them by the end of the Tournament—that means you've had six practices and six games. But they're not just trinkets, even though they do make a cool memento. If you don't have your pin on, you're not getting access. It could be a practice day and you could be wearing your team warm-ups, your team basketball shoes, bouncing a basketball walking next to Roy Williams, and if you don't have your pin on, all the staffers start shouting, "Put your pin on! You can't walk back here without your pin on!"

Actually, you couldn't bounce a basketball. That's one of their craziest rules. There's an allotted time for each practice. Balls are sitting on a rack at midcourt when every team gets to the gym. You can't touch the balls on the rack until the clock starts for your practice. They do not joke about this at all. If you even get close to touching the ball, two or three people will yell at you. It turns into a big joke. Before our first practice in Winston, we arrived at the gym ten minutes early. The NCAA people told us, "You can go on the court but you can't touch a basketball." So I was running around on the court pretending to play basketball, but I didn't have an actual basketball. And you better make sure that when the clock expires, all the basketballs are on the rack. Don't even try to squeeze out an extra shot. They'll roll you up in the blue carpet and take you out of there.

I think the open practices are cool. It's 40 minutes when the general public who might not otherwise be able to see us gets a chance to watch a Carolina practice. And we really do practice. Some teams go out there and have dunk contests. Not at North Carolina. It's as much like clockwork as our regular practices. Coach leaves a few minutes at the end for dunking and other things the fans like to see, but I'm sure that if we didn't go hard during the regular part of practice, he'd eliminate the dunking and we'd spend that time working on defensive slides.

Open practices are especially good when you're not in the regular playing rotation. Some of my best individual memories from the 2005 championship run came during open practices. I'll never forget that I hit six or seven three-pointers during a 5-on-5 drill in Charlotte before the first round that year. The whole crowd was cheering for me and I was in a zone.

Of course, I never look forward to the dunking at the end of each practice. I usually throw up a couple of three-pointers from midcourt. That's the best I have to offer. I leave the dunking for the other guys.

The other big part of the NCAA Tournament is increased media attention. No high schooler is prepared for the kind of media attention we get at North Carolina. A lot of guys get attention in high school, but it's nothing like here. Steve

Kirschner, our sports information director, and Matt Bowers, our assistant sports information director, do a great job explaining how to handle the media. Some people think they tell us what to say, but I can honestly say they've never once told me what to say in response to a question.

My first year, I did media training with Justin Bohlander and Reyshawn. Scott Pryzwansky, who has worked in the media, does our media training. He does mock interviews and explains the goal of reporters and what they're trying to accomplish by talking to us. He also tells us some habits that can get us in trouble when we're talking to the media and how to have a good camera presence. We even do an on-camera interview and then review the tape so we can see ourselves in action and see what needs to be improved. Both in media training and in talking to Steve and Matt, they always give one main tip: be honest. They do a good job of letting us know what the topics for the day might be, because as college students sometimes we don't read every edition of the paper or know every quote that's been said about Carolina. So they will give us a heads-up if there's a certain issue that is likely to be a big deal.

The main thing I try to remember about the media is they have a job to do, and that job is to get a story. In many cases, I can tell exactly what a reporter is going to write by the questions they ask. They'll frame it in a certain way that makes it obvious what theme they're going to follow. This year, we've gotten a lot of questions about chemistry. I've heard every chemistry question possible. There's a big difference between, "What kind of chemistry does this team have?" and "How have you handled the inevitable chemistry problems this year?"

Young guys have to learn that if a reporter won't let something go, it's best to be honest. There have been times this year when we've had to say, "Look, we have great chemistry. Let's move on to something else."

Another part of learning to deal with the media is realizing you're not going to understand every question. That sounds really basic, but it's true. The reporter might use a word I don't know or ramble on with his question and I'll lose track of his point. The temptation is to guess what they're asking and come up with an answer that fits. But the safer strategy is to simply say, "Can you repeat that?" When there are 15 people standing around asking questions, it's important to take time to listen to what they're asking. When you zone out, that's when you get in trouble. I had an advantage because my first two years, no one wanted to talk to me. By the time I was a junior, I had two years of observation and preparation.

It's such a catch-22 with the media. After games, everyone wants to shower and go see their family. But if the media wants to talk to you, that means you're making a contribution to the team. Everyone deals with it differently. Some guys love it. They enjoy talking and enjoy being in front of the camera. And no one wants to be the guy who no one wants to talk to. It's that simple. You don't want everyone else to be doing an interview while you walk out of the locker room undisturbed. Even if you're in a huge hurry and have a million things to do, you can't help but think, "Hey, I'm a part of this team, too."

We're still with our postseason roommates, which means I'm with Bobby. We both love to watch basketball, so there's no fighting over the TV. Anyone rooming with Marcus quickly finds out he would rather watch MTV or some movie than a basketball game. He's rooming with Danny, so that's a good match since they roomed together as freshmen. I've never known an athlete who cares less about sports than Marcus. During the selection show, we were joking—sort of—with him by trying to explain that there were 65 teams in the field and the champion would have to win six games. He claims he understands, but I'm not sure.

The most interesting roommates are Dewey and Tyler. From what Dewey has told me, it's difficult to watch games with Tyler because Tyler gets mad at the television. If he thinks we're better than the team that's playing and they're doing well, he gets mad. If the officiating is bad, he gets mad. Or if it's being called differently than our games, he gets mad. He'll be sitting there watching TV and jump off the bed yelling. And when Tyler yells, sometimes it's hard to understand him because he's sort of a mumbler, so you've got this huge angry guy yelling strange sounds at the TV.

Dewey has spent a lot of time in our room watching games with Bobby and me.

We spent a lot of time in our room on Thursday, because our game wasn't scheduled to start until almost 10 p.m. That makes for a very, very long day. We didn't have the team breakfast until 11 a.m. It's very difficult to sit in the hotel and watch everyone else play on television. There's so much excitement around the NCAA Tournament and there's a certain envy watching other players get to be part of it. I was chomping at the bit. It was hard not to get antsy.

As we took the floor for our game, a big roar went up in the coliseum when it was announced that Duke lost to Virginia Commonwealth. That was a very popular upset pick among our team. Several guys called that one.

The crowd certainly seemed to enjoy it. Because of the

proximity of Winston-Salem to Chapel Hill, it was almost a home game for us. Having two games in front of a very friendly crowd is a big advantage in the NCAA Tournament.

It's funny, one of the big things a crowd will respond to in a situation like that is our pregame warmup routine. For some reason, it really gets people fired up. When Coach Williams came to Carolina, it was the day before our first exhibition game and we were going over our pregame on-court routine. He proposed this drill where we chop our feet and then dive on the floor a couple times. I don't even know what to call it—slides, maybe? People love it. It's something we do as a team, so they like that. And I think they like the message that we're ready to get on the floor even before the opening tip.

The win over Eastern Kentucky was a grinder. We were up big early and then they closed our lead to 48–44 in the second half. After the game, I got a lot of questions like, "How worried were you that you'd be the first one seed to lose to a 16 seed?"

Honestly? I wasn't worried at all. No one was in panic mode, and that's why we were able to pull away again. We were disappointed in the way we played in parts of the second half, but we also understood how to turn it around.

Immediately after the game, we went in the locker room and Coach Williams told us his sister had died the day before. From what I understand now, very few people knew about it before the game. I felt so bad for him. We have a family here and we want to support him. When someone goes through something like that, we are all affected by it.

To his credit, none of us had any idea that was going on until he told us. He has such complete devotion to the team that even in a terrible time for his family, we never felt we were cheated out of his attention. He showed amazing spirit in concentrating on the game while also, I'm sure, being worried about his family.

```
                              Game 35
Eastern Kentucky 65
#4/4 North Carolina 86
March 15, 2007 • Lawrence Joel Coliseum, Winston-Salem, N.C.
NCAA Tournament East Regional First Round
```

EKU	FG	3FG	FT	REB	PF	TP	A	TO	B	S	Min
Brock*	3-8	0-1	0-0	2-2-4	1	6	3	3	0	1	29
Dialls*	8-9	1-1	0-0	1-3-4	2	17	2	1	1	1	27
Leonard*	5-12	2-8	2-2	0-2-2	1	14	1	4	0	3	35
Rose*	5-13	3-8	0-0	1-0-1	1	13	2	1	0	2	34
Mascoll*	6-8	0-2	0-0	0-1-1	3	12	2	2	0	2	29
Mestdagh	0-0	0-0	0-0	0-0-0	0	0	1	0	0	0	2
Brown	0-4	0-0	0-0	1-1-2	2	0	0	2	0	0	14
Daniel	0-1	0-0	1-4	0-0-0	1	1	0	0	0	1	6
Taylor	0-2	0-2	0-0	0-0-0	0	0	1	1	0	0	11
Douglas	1-2	0-0	0-0	1-1-2	2	2	2	2	0	2	13
TEAM				0-0-0							
Totals	28-59	6-22	3-6	6-10-16	13	65	14	16	1	12	200
Pct.	.475	.273	.500	DB: 2							

FG: (1st half: 14-29, .483; 2nd half: 14-30, .467)
3FG: (1st half: 4-13, .308; 2nd half: 2-9, .222)
FT: (1st half: 3-6, .500; 2nd half: 0-0, .000)

UNC	FG	3FG	FT	REB	PF	TP	A	TO	B	S	Min
Terry*	8-9	2-3	0-0	0-5-5	1	18	1	6	0	0	24
Wright*	6-11	0-0	1-2	3-3-6	1	13	1	2	5	3	33
Hansbrough*	9-11	0-0	3-5	4-6-10	0	21	3	2	1	0	35
Ellington*	4-8	2-5	2-2	2-4-6	4	12	5	2	0	1	24
Lawson*	5-9	2-2	0-1	0-4-4	2	12	7	2	0	1	23
Ginyard	1-2	0-0	0-0	1-2-3	0	2	4	1	0	2	14
Frasor	1-2	0-1	0-0	0-0-0	0	2	1	2	0	0	8
Thomas	0-0	0-0	0-0	0-0-0	0	0	2	1	0	0	9
Green	1-2	0-1	0-1	0-0-0	0	2	0	2	0	0	9
Burke	0-1	0-1	0-0	0-0-0	0	0	0	0	0	0	1
Thompson	2-2	0-0	0-0	0-0-0	0	4	0	0	0	0	5
Miller	0-0	0-0	0-0	0-0-0	0	0	0	1	0	0	7
Wood	0-0	0-0	0-0	1-1-2	0	0	0	1	0	0	1
Stepheson	0-0	0-0	0-0	0-1-1	0	0	0	0	0	0	6
Copeland	0-0	0-0	0-0	0-0-0	0	0	0	0	0	0	1
TEAM				0-1-1							
Totals	37-57	6-13	6-11	11-27-38	8	86	24	22	6	7	200
Pct.	.577	.600	.958	DB: 3							

FG: (1st half: 20-30, .667; 2nd half: 17-27, .630)
3FG: (1st half: 4-8, .500; 2nd half: 2-5, .400)
FT: (1st half: 3-6, .500; 2nd half: 3-5, .600)

Officials: Verne Harris, Bruce Hicks, Steve Welmer
Attendance: 14,148 • **Technical Fouls:** none

Score by Periods	1st	2nd	Total
Eastern Kentucky	35	30	65
North Carolina	47	39	86

LUCAS: THROUGH THE LOOKING GLASS

MARCH 15, 2007

There was a time when the NCAA Tournament seemed endless.

Remember that? The first two rounds were an unofficial holiday. Four whole days of nothing but college basketball. Four whole days! Forts could be built and knocked down in that length of time. Friendships could be made and lost.

And memories could be made. It was simple: get off the bus and run home on Thursday. Sit on the floor in the den, bracket spread out next to you, watching games. There was no internet. You had to make your own bracket busters and Cinderellas. For three weeks, the coffee table books were off the table and replaced with brackets for everyone in the family, winning picks highlighted in yellow. And when Dad got home, you'd meet him in the garage with breathless news of the day's upsets.

"Georgetown almost lost!" you'd say. "And you'll never believe what happened to UNLV!"

The best part: there were still three and a half days left, including the rest of the evening . . . which occasionally stretched until after midnight. There was nothing cooler than walking into school the next day and torturing the kids who had to go to bed early with your analysis of the late game in the West region. It seemed like sports at its most pure: the underdog, win or go home, clutch performances.

These are the memories that come rolling back during a Thursday spent waiting for a Carolina tip time that ended up being after 10 p.m. Eastern. Don't fret for the Tar Heels—players love late tips because it means they can sleep in. Remember, they're college students in addition to being phenomenal athletes, so "sleeping in" means something different to them than it means to you and me. To them, it means at least past 10 a.m. They roll out of bed, hit the team meal, go to shootaround, and then they're ready for—what else?—a nap.

Schedules are different in the sports world. Nights are days and days are nights. Weekends are the work week. Mondays are off days. Thursday was my son's second birthday. It was spent not by tucking him in with his blue satin pillow and his "ball game" pajamas, but by telling him goodnight over the telephone while watching two teams from hundreds of miles away battle for the right to spend two more days in Winston-Salem. There are times when it feels like you're standing with Alice peering through the looking glass.

That's why this scenario made perfect sense: on Wednesday, a Tar Heel team manager hauled a duffel bag into Carolina's open practice at the Lawrence Joel Veterans Memorial Coliseum. Inside the bag were three Diet Sprites intended for the coaching staff.

"You'll have to leave those drinks outside," an NCAA representative told the manager after inspecting the bag.

"They're Coke products," the manager replied. Coke, as we all know, is a "corporate champion" for the NCAA, which is a fancy way of saying they pay the NCAA a bunch of money.

"Doesn't matter," the rep replied. "Leave them out here."

Inside, the arena was plastered with Coke logos, including one for . . . Diet Sprite.

That may not make sense to you. If not, you need to spend more time around the NCAA Tournament. Eventually, after a few hours of exposure, things like telling head coaches what kind of cup to use to drink their postgame beverage almost sounds rational. The closer you get to it, the less pure it seems.

Until the games start. No matter how complicated they make it in the concourse or in the press room or even in the locker room, even the most ridiculous of rules can't ruin the NCAA Tournament.

Here was North Carolina: big, bad Carolina. Top seed in the region. Conqueror of titans.

And here was Eastern Kentucky: 16th seed in the region. Conqueror of Tennessee-Martin, Eastern Illinois, and Austin Peay.

Whoops, wait a minute—they lost (twice) to Austin Peay.

And here's the great thing: with 16 minutes left in the game, the Colonels had the Tar Heels scared witless. They stripped the game down to the absolute basics—spread the offense out, open the passing lanes, and dash backdoor. For about a dozen minutes, Carolina simply could not defend this play.

"The help side wasn't there," Brandan Wright

said. "We weren't getting out in the passing lanes, planting, and staying with our guy. It was pretty simple. Sometimes you get the urge to make big plays all the time, and you try to go for steals or overruns. You have to stick to fundamentals of defensive principles."

All this money, all these commercials, all these officially sponsored cups, and it all comes down to sticking to defensive principles. No one ever filled an arena to watch a corporate champion. We come to watch David against Goliath. We come to watch moments—shining ones, even.

That's why despite the overbearing way it's presented to those involved, the NCAA Tournament still works. Higher seeds still fall. Defense is still played. The happiness of tens of thousands still rests on the whims of a leather ball. After biting our fingernails and screaming at the TV and covering our eyes, all we really want is one simple favor: to be granted the opportunity to play one more time. That's all we ask. One more game. Please.

In the Carolina locker room, in plain black marker, the number "32" was written in the upper right corner of the white board. After Friday night, that's how many teams out of 336 will still have a chance to win the national championship.

One of those teams is North Carolina.

And that's why they play. And why we can't stop watching.

Coach Williams usually tells us to enjoy a win until midnight. But the Eastern Kentucky game didn't end until after midnight, so there wasn't much time to enjoy it. We had two more long days ahead of us before the Michigan State game, because it was scheduled for another late tip on Saturday. Friday was another sleep-in day.

Saturday was another long day. This one was different, though. Before the Eastern Kentucky game there was a sense of the unknown because we didn't know a ton about them. But most of us knew Michigan State. I've watched them a lot this year and knew how impressive they were. They have some key traits—they're tough, physical, good rebounders, and solid defenders—that make them a very difficult Tournament matchup. There are very few teams in the ACC that play the same way Michigan State plays.

As I watched games this year, I grew to really appreciate Drew Neitzel's game. He seems like a total gym rat. I have a lot of respect for anyone who went from a pass-first, set-up guy to being his team's go-to offensive threat. He's had some great games this year and hit some big shots.

I knew it would be a big challenge to guard him. It's exciting to defend a good player, especially when you know a majority of their offense is geared towards getting him a shot. Not necessarily a good shot, but a shot. Every time they ran a set, they were setting screens for Neitzel. It reminded me of playing against J.J. Redick. Every time I guarded J.J., I felt if I stopped him, I was stopping Duke's offense. That's not totally true, but when one player is such a big part of a team's offense, stopping him makes it very difficult for them.

He scored 26 points and made six three-pointers, but I honestly felt we did a good job on him defensively. He seemed a little tired at the end.

<table>
<tr><td colspan="12" align="center">Game 36</td></tr>
</table>

Michigan State 67
#4/4 North Carolina 81
March 17, 2007 • Lawrence Joel Coliseum, Winston-Salem, N.C.
NCAA Tournament East Regional Second Round

MSU	FG	3FG	FT	REB	PF	TP	A	TO	B	S	Min
Morgan*	4-12	1-1	10-11	3-2-5	3	19	0	4	0	1	35
Gray*	4-6	0-0	3-3	3-4-7	5	11	1	0	0	0	19
Naymick*	0-1	0-0	0-0	2-0-2	3	0	0	0	0	0	27
Walton*	0-2	0-0	0-1	0-2-2	5	0	5	1	0	1	32
Neitzel*	9-27	6-17	2-2	0-1-1	3	26	5	4	0	2	38
Darnton	0-0	0-0	0-0	0-0-0	0	0	0	0	0	0	0+
Tibaldi	0-0	0-0	0-0	0-0-0	0	0	0	0	0	0	0+
Curry	0-0	0-0	0-0	0-0-0	0	0	0	0	0	0	0+
Suton	3-7	0-0	0-0	3-5-8	4	6	4	1	0	1	23
Ducre	0-1	0-1	0-0	0-0-0	0	0	0	0	0	0	0+
Dahlman	0-0	0-0	0-0	0-0-0	0	0	0	0	0	0	1
Joseph	1-2	1-1	0-0	0-1-1	1	3	0	0	0	0	16
Hannon	1-1	0-0	0-0	0-1-1	3	2	0	0	0	0	9
TEAM				0-2-2							
Totals	22-59	8-20	15-17	11-18-29	27	67	15	10	0	5	200
Pct.	.373	.400	.882	DB: 2							

FG: (1st half: 12-29, .414; 2nd half: 10-30, .333)
3FG: (1st half: 5-10, .500; 2nd half: 3-10, .300)
FT: (1st half: 4-5, .800; 2nd half: 11-12, .917)

UNC	FG	3FG	FT	REB	PF	TP	A	TO	B	S	Min
Terry*	4-10	2-7	4-6	0-2-2	3	14	1	1	1	0	27
Wright*	1-5	0-0	1-2	3-4-7	4	3	1	3	1	1	23
Hansbrough*	10-17	0-0	13-17	2-7-9	2	33	1	1	1	1	38
Ellington*	1-4	1-3	2-3	0-3-3	0	5	1	1	0	1	22
Lawson*	6-10	3-5	5-6	2-3-5	2	20	8	1	0	1	36
Ginyard	1-1	0-0	0-0	2-1-3	4	2	0	1	0	2	17
Frasor	0-0	0-0	0-0	0-0-0	0	0	0	0	0	0	2
Thomas	0-0	0-0	0-0	0-1-1	0	0	0	0	0	0	2
Green	0-1	0-1	0-0	1-2-3	0	0	1	0	0	0	8
Burke	0-0	0-0	0-0	0-0-0	0	0	0	0	0	0	0+
Thompson	2-4	0-0	0-0	3-0-3	2	4	0	0	0	0	13
Miller	0-0	0-0	0-0	0-0-0	0	0	0	0	0	0	7
Wood	0-0	0-0	0-0	0-0-0	0	0	0	0	0	0	0+
Stepheson	0-0	0-0	0-0	0-1-1	0	0	0	1	0	0	5
Copeland	0-0	0-0	0-0	0-0-0	0	0	0	0	0	0	0+
TEAM				1-2-3							
Totals	25-52	6-16	25-34	14-26-40	17	81	12	10	3	6	200
Pct.	.481	.375	.735	DB: 4							

FG: (1st half: 15-32, .469; 2nd half: 10-20, .500)
3FG: (1st half: 3-9, .333; 2nd half: 3-7, .429)
FT: (1st half: 8-11, .727; 2nd half: 17-23, .739)

Officials: Randy McCall, Patrick Driscoll, L. Douglas Sirmons
Attendance: 14,148 • **Technical Fouls:** none

Score by Periods	1st	2nd	Total
Michigan State	33	34	67
North Carolina	41	40	81

I thought our locker room was a little subdued considering we had advanced to the Sweet 16. Part of that was probably because everyone was tired. It was a very physical game. But I wanted to make sure everyone understood what a big deal it was to be one of 16 teams still playing. I've been here four years and it was just the second time I've been that far.

The other time, we won the national championship. Still having the chance to do that when there are 320 other teams who want to be in your shoes is a very nice feeling.

LUCAS: TRUE GRIT

MARCH 17, 2007

WINSTON-SALEM—In the wake of Saturday night's victory over Michigan State, Reyshawn Terry was looking for the right words to describe the Spartans. He pondered for just a second, and then he said this: "That is a tough team. The toughest team we've played all year long."

Tough is one of a basketball player's biggest compliments.

Sometimes, it is a synonym for dirty. Not on Saturday. On Saturday, tough meant tough.

"The big thing I noticed about them is their intensity and how hard they go through their offense," Marcus Ginyard said. "They really run through their sets hard and execute."

"They set great screens," said Wes Miller, who saw plenty of those screens first-hand while he was chasing Drew Neitzel. "You have to really make a commitment to getting through those screens or around those screens. That's the only way to play against them."

In most places, the story of the game will be Tyler Hansbrough's mask-less 33 points. Or maybe it will be Terry's now customary late game heroics. Or perhaps Ty Lawson's sheer domination of the game's tempo and his 20 points.

Not here. Here the story is something different.

Here it is something that is not immediately evident on the stat sheet, unless perhaps you locate the 40–29 rebounding advantage against a team that entered the game fifth in the country in rebounding margin.

On the very first possession of the game, Lawson ripped the ball away from 6-foot-8, 235-pound Marquise Gray. With 8 minutes left in the half, Miller hurled himself on top of a loose ball near midcourt. On the sidelines, with the crowd roaring and the game in the balance late in the second half, Roy Williams was down in his fighting stance, pleading for just one stop.

This was a second-round game? That's not how it felt. And it's not how it looked on the court.

Something has happened to these Tar Heels over the last two weeks. And even they're not sure they know exactly what it might be. Watch this group. Really watch them. Not just the player with the ball but all five Tar Heels on the court. For that matter, not just the ones on the court. Watch the bench, too. They've stopped talking about toughness and togetherness and they've started *doing* it. For the first six months of the season, they were happy to be pretty. Now, all of a sudden, they're gritty.

"It's hard to put your finger on," Ginyard said. "You come in the locker room and there's that feeling in the locker room. There's that excitement coming from everybody for the game. The bench gets into the games even more. You're starting to see those chest bumps again after good plays. At timeouts, the guys on the court are getting met at midcourt with high fives. The heart of this team is really starting to show."

You think it makes you happy to hear that? Imagine how it makes the coaching staff feel. Maybe that's why Roy Williams punctuated his customary writing of "16" on the white board in the locker room—to signify the teams left in the NCAA field—with a little dance shimmy lifted from Mike Copeland.

They do not award points for midcourt high fives, of course. But it pays off somewhere, somehow. A fragile team—and although this seems like ancient history right now, this team seemed fragile just two weeks ago—would have been ground into dust by Michigan State.

Here is what Michigan State does: they do exactly what they want. Every time. Carolina knew Neitzel was their primary offensive threat, knew he'd carry the bulk of the offensive load. And still he found 27 shots, admitting afterward that he'd never had that many shots in a game at any level. The Spartans ran him around screens. They chipped, they double-stacked, and on one particularly devious first-half play, they ran him around a double screen, took advantage of Carolina's overpursuit, and then sent him backdoor for a layup.

Four different Tar Heels—Ginyard, Miller, Lawson, and Quentin Thomas—took a turn on Neitzel. Finally, worn down by additional ball-handling duties caused by Travis Walton's foul trouble, the fatigue began to show. Neitzel bent over, his hands on his knees. When he stood, he put his hands on his hips, mouth open, trying to suck in a fresh breath of air.

"I wanted to be there every time," Ginyard said. "I wanted him to look for me every time he caught the ball."

Years from now, we'll probably remember Neitzel's 26 points and six 3-pointers. Lost only to history—and to the Carolina coaches—will be the fact that he only shot 33 percent from the field, and he had to hoist 17 trifectas in order to make six.

The Tar Heel offense will get the headlines on Sunday. The defense? It'll stay comfortably in the background.

"When you're on defense, you have to be thinking only about defense," Miller said. "The fact of the matter is, if you play defense, play with five guys moving together and finish it with a box-out and a rebound, you have a chance to beat anybody in any game."

And you have a chance to do something else, something that no one might have expected at the beginning of this month.

You have a chance to be tough.

SWEET SIXTEEN AND ELITE EIGHT

WE HAD OUR EASIEST PRACTICE of the year on the Monday after we beat Michigan State. Besides pre-practice and the usual fast break drills, we didn't do anything live. We did some shooting drills, a shooting competition, and a dribbling relay race. We broke into four teams of four for the relay. It was made up of very simple drills with a very simple reward—the team that won didn't have to run at the end of practice. We've done something similar once or twice over the last couple years, and it's a good way to break a sweat, stay competitive, but not kill everyone's legs.

Even when it's just basic drills an elementary school camper would do, it still turns heated when it involves people as competitive as college basketball players. My team included Will Graves, Brandan, and Tyler. That might not be the strongest group for a dribbling relay, but we did OK in that leg. We made up a lot of ground in the passing relay and eventually won the drill.

As soon as the Michigan State game was over, the media started asking us questions about playing Texas. The Texas-Southern Cal game wasn't until the next day, but we were already being asked about Kevin Durant and facing Rick Barnes and all the Texas storylines. It was one of those later-round matchups everyone anticipated when the brackets were released. I had watched Texas play several times this year and knew they were a good team.

But I'd also watched Southern Cal, and I remembered how well they played last year when they beat us. In some ways, once they advanced it was an advantage that they had beaten us the previous season, because everyone who played in that game knew it would require complete focus to beat them this time.

The next round was played at the Meadowlands, which sent us back to New York. This time, though, we didn't stay in New York City. We stayed in Teaneck, New Jersey. On clear days, we could just barely see the Manhattan skyline from our hotel. I'm not sure it's possible to be any closer to New York and feel so far away. Teaneck—at least the area where we stayed—is not the most active area in the country. There may be an actual town of Teaneck with actual houses and people, but I never saw it. I saw the Jersey Turnpike. We might as well have been in Eastern North Carolina on the side of I-40 with nothing around for miles.

Bobby and I were roommates again, of course. Dirtsky did a good job keeping his side of the room clean during the postseason. Maybe "clean" isn't the word. But it wasn't a disaster, so that was an improvement.

One night, we couldn't sleep so we ordered a movie. We got Casino Royale, a Bond movie. Bobby had seen it, and I told him before it started I was getting tired and would probably fall asleep while it was playing. He told me it was so good I wouldn't fall asleep.

What happens? Five minutes into the movie I started falling asleep. And he kept getting angry at me for falling asleep. Every ten minutes he would wake me up and tell me I had to watch a really cool action scene. Does anyone want to wake up from their sleep to watch an action scene in a movie they haven't even been following? I doubt it. But for some reason he thought that was exactly what I wanted to do. I could probably tell you more about the global warming movie I watched with Brandan back in November than Casino Royale.

In the postseason, we see a lot of the same faces in the hotel lobby. The same people tend to travel with the Rams Club and they're always at our hotel. Carolina fans are usually easygoing. They might want to say hello but it's unusual for them to really bother us. They just want to tell us, "Congratulations," or something equally nice. Having those folks around adds to the excitement of the postseason.

The people that do bother us are the eBay guys. They're easy to spot—they sit in the lobby all day waiting for autographs and they don't know very much about the team. They make it hard to go to the lobby, because they always walk up with a handful of basketballs for us to sign. I enjoy signing for kids or for a true fan who has one ball that it's obvious they're going to cherish. But honestly, what is a 40-year-old man going to do with six basketballs and five 8 by 10 photos? We all know those items are going straight to eBay.

It's a tricky situation, because I never want to turn down any autograph request. I've always been honored by any request. But somehow it feels different when I know the item I'm signing is going straight for profit. The eBay guys wear on Coach Williams, too. We had an incident at Boston College this year where we were in a hurry to get on the bus and Tyler didn't have time to sign an autograph for one of the eBay guys. The guy called Tyler something unprintable, and Coach got very fired up. I've never heard him say this, but I think he feels like those people cheapen the experience for everyone else. He values college basketball and North Carolina so much that he hates to see someone ruining it for everyone else. We could sign autographs for kids all day long if we didn't have those four or five people standing there with a backpack full of items.

I've never looked on eBay to see what the going rate is for my autograph. I've been in the locker room when other guys have looked, and I've been told one item I signed was up to 90 cents. I probably won't be retiring on autograph proceeds.

I have been asked to sign some crazy items. Body parts are usually the most awkward moments. Female chests are a more frequent request than you might think. One time I was asked to sign that body part with her husband standing right next to her. I've never understood the idea of signing a body part. What are they going to do with the signature? Won't it come off the next time they're in the shower? It seems to defeat the purpose of creating a memento.

The deeper you get in the Tournament, the more anticipation exists. When it starts, there are 64 teams and it's hard to comprehend that many teams at one time. By this weekend, though, we're down to 16. It's easy to list every team that's left and you know the national champion will be one of those 16 teams. Every team in the country started with the same goal in October and now only those 16 have a chance.

As usual, Bobby and I watched some games to pass the time. We knew Southern Cal would be a challenge, and we also knew Reyshawn, at best, was going to be limited. At practice the day before the game, Coach Williams called me over.

"How would the guys feel about Reyshawn not practicing today but then playing tomorrow?" he said. "Would it impact our team?"

We knew two things: we knew Reyshawn was strong enough to deal with it and we knew we needed him to win basketball games. We know the general rule is if you don't practice, you don't play. But we also know he's a key cog. The problem was that without him practicing all week, no one was certain what we would get out of him. In my opinion, that's why he didn't start against Southern Cal and that's why his minutes were limited. In a one-and-done situation, it's hard to take a chance when you're not sure of someone's health.

I'm as big a stretcher as anyone on the team other than Tyler. But in the NCAA Tournament, I never feel like I have to stretch. We were in our locker room while Vanderbilt was playing Georgetown in the other Sweet 16 game. There's a game clock in the locker room but no TV, so all we knew was how much time was left, and then we'd try to combine that with the crowd noise to figure out what was happening. Some guys went out to the tunnel to watch and some guys were stretching. But there's so much energy in an NCAA Tournament building that my body always feels loose as soon as I walk in the door.

Because it's one-and-done, it hits you during every NCAA Tournament game that this could be the end of the season. It's a flash that enters your brain and then it's gone, and it happens at the strangest times. That's what gives every Tournament game a sense of urgency. That's why it is so emotional—at any second, it can be over. I hear a lot of talk about Game Seven in the NBA. I'm sure they are a big deal, but every postseason game is Game Seven in college basketball.

Game 37

Southern California 64
#4/4 North Carolina 74
March 23, 2007 • Continental Airlines Arena, East Rutherford, N.J.
NCAA Tournament East Regional Semifinal

USC	FG	3FG	FT	REB	PF	TP	A	TO	B	S	Min
Young*	6-13	1-5	2-2	1-6-7	4	15	0	6	0	0	36
Gibson*	7-12	0-0	2-3	3-9-12	5	16	4	4	0	0	34
Stewart*	6-15	3-7	0-0	0-4-4	1	15	2	2	1	0	36
Hackett*	2-4	0-0	1-2	0-1-1	1	5	3	3	0	0	29
Pruitt*	5-15	1-6	2-2	2-2-4	3	13	7	2	1	5	38
Lewis	0-2	0-0	0-0	0-1-1	1	0	1	1	0	0	10
N'Diaye	0-0	0-0	0-0	0-0-0	0	0	0	0	0	0	0+
Wilkinson	0-0	0-0	0-0	0-1-1	2	0	0	0	1	0	14
Cromwell	0-0	0-0	0-0	1-0-1	2	0	0	0	0	0	3
TEAM				3-5-8							
Totals	26-61	5-18	7-9	10-29-39	19	64	13	18	7	5	200
Pct.	.426	.278	.778	DB: 1							

FG: (1st half: 17-34, .500; 2nd half: 9-27, .333)
3FG: (1st half: 3-7, .429; 2nd half: 2-11, .182)
FT: (1st half: 5-7, .714; 2nd half: 2-2, 1.000)

UNC	FG	3FG	FT	REB	PF	TP	A	TO	B	S	Min
Wright*	9-15	0-0	3-4	5-4-9	0	21	1	2	1	0	35
Hansbrough*	1-6	0-0	3-4	2-2-4	3	5	0	1	0	0	29
Ginyard*	3-9	0-1	4-5	4-5-9	2	10	0	1	0	0	26
Ellington*	6-16	0-2	0-0	2-2-4	1	12	0	1	0	1	28
Lawson*	2-10	0-3	0-1	2-5-7	2	4	4	1	1	3	32
Terry	4-6	1-2	0-1	0-0-0	0	9	1	0	0	0	5
Frasor	0-0	0-0	0-0	0-1-1	1	0	0	1	0	1	5
Thomas	0-0	0-0	0-0	0-0-0	0	0	1	0	0	0	3
Green	3-7	0-2	2-2	3-5-8	2	8	4	1	1	1	18
Thompson	1-4	0-0	0-0	1-1-2	2	2	0	0	1	0	9
Miller	1-4	1-4	0-0	0-1-1	1	3	0	0	0	0	9
Stepheson	0-0	0-0	0-0	0-0-0	0	0	0	0	0	0	1
TEAM				1-0-1				1			
Totals	30-77	2-14	12-17	20-26-46	14	74	11	9	4	6	200
Pct.	.390	.143	.706	DB: 3							

FG: (1st half: 15-40, .375; 2nd half: 15-37, .405)
3FG: (1st half: 2-12, .167; 2nd half: 0-2, .000)
FT: (1st half: 1-3, .333; 2nd half: 11-14, .786)

Officials: Tom Lopes, Mike Sanzere, Michael Roberts
Attendance: 19,557 • **Technical Fouls:** USC bench

Score by Periods	1st	2nd	Total
Southern California	42	22	64
North Carolina	33	41	74

That realization that this could be the end of my career came to me when Southern Cal was up 49–33 with 18 minutes left. I knew we had a very short amount of time to turn it around. It wasn't a panic, but it was an extreme sense of urgency. As usual, the turnaround started with defense. We got a couple of stops and Marcus provided some important offensive energy. Before you knew it, we were right back in the game.

Once we won, Coach did his traditional thing where he writes the number of teams left on the board in our locker room. This time it was a big "8." That's when it hit me how close we were to the Final Four. We were one of eight teams left in America.

LUCAS: DO WHAT YOU DO

MARCH 23, 2007

EAST RUTHERFORD, N.J.—Ty Lawson was gassed.

You might not have seen it, but he was. There were four minutes and eight seconds left in the East Regional semifinal and his hands were on his hips, his mouth was wide open, and he was gasping for air.

Brandan Wright was shooting free throws, so Lawson took the opportunity to sidle over to the Carolina bench.

"Man, I'm tired," he told Roy Williams.

That is point guard speak for, "I need a rest."

Another time, another game, Williams would have looked down his bench and pointed his finger at Bobby Frasor or Quentin Thomas. "Get Ty," he would have said, and Lawson would have taken a seat beside Joe Holladay.

Not on Friday. Not in the middle of what was—according to sports information as of 2 a.m.—Carolina's best NCAA Tournament comeback.

"You've got eight more seconds until the timeout," Williams told his droopy point guard.

"OK," Lawson said. "I'm staying in."

Of course he is.

Four minutes left, round of 16, there is no other choice. This is the time that you do what you do. Lawson plays. We pray.

Wes Miller, for example. As Carolina stretched the improbable lead from three points to five points, the entire Tar Heel bench was standing—some of them, these 6-foot-6 trees, were standing on their tiptoes.

Not Miller. The shortest Tar Heel was crouched down, his hands on the floor. Asked what he was thinking right at that moment, right as he watched Danny Green coax a turnover out of Southern Cal, he said exactly what you were thinking and exactly what I was thinking:

"Whew. I was thinking I couldn't take it."

It's harder to watch than it is to play. Not physically. Physically it is not that difficult to sit in your recliner and watch the Tar Heels, rising only to protest the latest blown call or exchange a high five.

But mentally, it is harder. On the court, there is no time to think about what is happening. Just run down the court, run the offense, see the ball, crash the boards. That is why Green didn't have time to consider the ramifications of his enormous play that gave the Tar Heels the lead for the first time.

You remember it. Green got a steal out of a media timeout. He fired ahead, and it looked like Wayne Ellington was going to coast in for an easy dunk.

Except he missed it.

It wasn't quite Brian Reese's missed dunk against Cincinnati in 1993 in this same arena, but it was close enough to be painful. All this comeback, all this work, and now a dunk was bouncing off the back of the rim. There would be no one there to rebound it. This could be a comeback-snuffer. Surely Green would not have bothered to waste the energy to run down the floor and follow the play.

Right?

"No, no, no," said Green, who was playing in front of a sizable chunk of family and friends. "I wanted to chase it. I had to chase it. I thought he might get cut off and need to pass it back, so I wanted to be there for that. Luckily, Brandan and I were there to follow it up."

Yeah, that was pretty lucky. Or maybe it has to do with all those practices in an empty Smith Center, all those afternoons with Williams screaming, "Run!" at his team as they go through another 2-hour session.

Oh, about Williams. You were doing what you do. You changed seats or wore your lucky shoes or sat completely still lest you disturb the comeback mojo. And what did he do?

Exactly what he always does—let his team work through their problems.

He watched a 42–33 halftime deficit balloon to 49–33 with 17:43 remaining. There were no time-outs called. The lone timeout he used all game came with 0.8 seconds left in the first half, when the Tar Heels diagrammed a terrific play that gave Wayne Ellington a perfect look at a three-pointer, but it didn't fall.

How do you let your team fall behind by 16 points without calling timeout? Go ahead, admit it, you were saying that in your living room or in your seat at the Meadowlands. Call timeout, Roy! You don't get to take them home with you after the game!

How do you let that happen?

You trust your team. And they reward you.

"We look over at Coach Williams, and he's not calling a timeout," Marcus Ginyard said. "He's just telling us to get the ball up the floor and continue to play. All the players can feel the confidence Coach has in this team. It's really hard to say how important that is for a player, for a coach to feel that confident about his team and the way he knew we'd be able to come back."

Hey Coach, how about a favor? Next time, if you know it, can you flash us a little sign or something? Scratch your nose or cross your eyes or whatever it takes. Maybe then these games won't be quite so exhausting. How can a basketball game sap every ounce of your energy and at the same time wire you to the point that you can't sleep for hours?

There's bad news for Williams, too. At some point during the comeback, the Tar Heel bench turned into a melee. It was at about that point that Dewey Burke clocked his head coach in the jaw with a misplaced forearm. Burke later claimed that

Wes Miller had initiated the contact that led to the collision. Williams wasn't having any of it.

"How many plus points does Dewey have?" he asked in a happy Carolina locker room. "I think we've got to take some away for that."

Well, OK. But just be aware it might be necessary to repeat the performance on Sunday. This is the NCAA Tournament and there are eight teams left. This is no time to take a chance. Ty and Brandan and Marcus and Danny and you other guys in argyle, you were important. But don't forget about the fan in Gastonia leaving the room, the diehard in Richmond changing into his lucky t-shirt, the slightly obsessive Tar Heel in Swansboro laying her hands on her team poster, and even William Graves and his magical shiny belt buckle (seriously, check it out).

"You know what I think the turning point of the game might have been?" Woody Durham asked after the Tar Heel Sports Network went off the air. "I think it was when I said, `Go where you go and do what you do.'"

Everyone nodded. It made perfect sense. Probably, he was right. It made as much sense as anything, because how else do you explain recovering from a 16-point second-half deficit in the NCAA Tournament?

Doing what you do—no matter who you are or what it is that you do, from the head coach right on down to whoever holds up the bottom end of the Tar Heel totem pole—did it. This was an acceptable explanation for what had just transpired. At some point, life will return to normal and you can drive to work on a different route or use a different toothpaste or wash your shirt.

Yes, it is irrational and it is silly.

Just keep doing it.

❧

I came out of the game soon after we went up 10 points against Georgetown. I sat on the bench, looked at the score, and thought, "If we get a couple more baskets, we might be there. Just push the lead out a little more and we might be in good shape."

We were ahead 75–65 with less than seven minutes left. That's how close we were.

At that point, stops were paramount. A couple stops might have broken Georgetown's will. Each time they came down the floor, I thought, "OK, let's get a stop here." But they kept piling up the points. And soon when we got the ball I started thinking, "We need a basket on this possession," because it seemed like a long scoring drought.

They run a very dynamic offense and they have a counter for every defensive strategy. They're always moving and cutting and they're always looking to go backdoor. In the last five minutes, they started getting some offensive rebounds and beating us on the glass. In past games this year, that's been because we lost focus or weren't competing. That wasn't the case this time. This was two teams at maximum effort.

We have to give them credit. They made some enormous shots. Jonathan Wallace hit a huge three-pointer to tie the game. There were 31 seconds left.

When we started practicing back in mid-October, I would

have been very excited if someone had told me we'd have one possession with a chance to make a basket and go to the Final Four. Anyone involved with basketball would tell you that's a good proposition. We had the ball in the hands of Ty Lawson, a point guard who constantly makes plays. And we had Wayne Ellington, a good shooter, taking a good shot. What can you do? It would almost be easier if something obvious had gone wrong because then there would be something easy to blame. It was the first loss this year where I felt like we left everything on the floor. For some reason, we came up empty. I don't know if I'll ever understand why.

It's easier to be on the court in those do-or-die situations than on the bench. I had to do breathing exercises at the close of regulation because it was killing me to watch it. I felt that way to a certain extent in 2005, but I felt it even more this year because I was a bigger part of the team. It was my last chance. When we broke the huddle with 24 seconds left in regulation, I remember thinking, "Is this really happening?"

It became obvious early in overtime that Georgetown had the momentum. We missed some good shots and they made a couple of tough ones. With about a minute left, I realized it was over. It was a surreal experience and I still haven't come to grips with it even today. It felt like everything was shaking around me. On the floor, I couldn't believe it. Once I got in the locker room, it hit me.

The last locker room of the season is always bad unless you win the national title, and only one team gets to do that. Playing college basketball consumed my life. It was a large part of my identity. It's stunning to have it end so quickly. It's shockingly awful.

The only benefit to the George Mason loss in 2006 was

that I could immediately start looking forward to the next year. I used it as motivation. I can't use the Georgetown game as motivation. I'll never have another chance. Looking around our locker room, I was jealous of the guys who get to do it again. That was the only time this year that I consciously thought I might be hurting more than someone else. It did cross my mind that it probably hurt Reyshawn and Dewey and me more than the younger guys.

Game 38

#9/8 Georgetown 96
#4/4 North Carolina 84
March 25, 2007 • Continental Airlines Arena, East Rutherford, N.J.
NCAA Tournament East Regional Final

GU	FG	3FG	FT	REB	PF	TP	A	TO	B	S	Min
Summers*	7-10	2-3	4-4	0-6-6	1	20	0	3	2	1	35
Green*	10-17	1-1	1-3	0-9-9	1	22	3	1	1	2	42
Hibbert*	6-10	0-0	1-1	5-6-11	4	13	4	1	6	1	31
Wallace*	7-11	3-4	2-2	2-1-3	1	19	7	1	0	0	38
Sapp*	5-9	2-4	3-5	2-2-4	3	15	8	2	0	0	36
Macklin	1-3	0-0	0-1	1-0-1	3	2	0	0	0	0	9
Rivers	0-1	0-0	1-2	0-1-1	1	1	2	2	1	0	17
Ewing Jr.	2-5	0-2	0-0	0-2-2	4	4	2	0	1	0	17
TEAM				1-0-1							
Totals	38-66	8-14	12-18	11-27-38	18	96	26	10	11	4	225
Pct.	.576	.571	.667	DB: 1							

FG: (1st half: 19-32, .594; 2nd half: 15-27, .556; OT: 4-7, .571)
3FG: (1st half: 4-6, .667; 2nd half: 4-7, .571; OT: 0-1, .000)
FT: (1st half: 2-5, .400; 2nd half: 3-4, .750; OT: 7-9, .778)

UNC	FG	3FG	FT	REB	PF	TP	A	TO	B	S	Min
Wright*	4-8	0-0	6-6	3-3-6	4	14	0	0	1	0	26
Hansbrough*	6-15	0-0	14-16	6-5-11	4	26	3	1	0	0	32
Ginyard*	0-0	0-0	2-2	0-3-3	0	2	2	1	0	0	18
Ellington*	2-11	1-6	0-0	1-1-2	2	5	0	1	0	0	24
Lawson*	2-9	1-4	0-0	0-0-0	3	5	6	5	0	0	40
Terry	4-13	2-5	0-0	2-4-6	2	10	0	0	0	1	29
Frasor	0-0	0-0	0-0	0-0-0	0	0	1	0	0	0	2
Thomas	0-0	0-0	0-0	0-0-0	0	0	2	0	0	0	2
Green	0-6	0-4	3-4	1-0-1	2	3	0	0	1	2	9
Thompson	6-7	0-0	2-2	4-2-6	1	14	0	1	2	1	21
Miller	1-1	1-1	0-0	0-0-0	0	3	1	0	0	0	14
Stepheson	0-1	0-0	2-4	3-3-6	1	2	0	0	0	0	8
TEAM				1-1-2							
Totals	25-71	5-20	29-34	21-22-43	19	84	15	9	4	5	225
Pct.	.352	.250	.853	DB: 3							

FG: (1st half: 15-31, .484; 2nd half: 9-27, .333; OT: 1-13, .077)
3FG: (1st half: 3-4, .750; 2nd half: 1-8, .125; OT: 1-8, .125)
FT: (1st half: 17-20, .850; 2nd half: 12-12, .1.000; OT: 0-2, .000)

Officials: Curtis Shaw, Mike Scyphers, John Higgins
Attendance: 19,557 • **Technical Fouls:** Georgetown bench

Score by Periods	1st	2nd	OT	Total
Georgetown	44	37	15	96
North Carolina	50	31	3	84

The worst part is the pain never goes away. Some people think you go in the locker room, you cry, and the next day you feel better. It's not like that. I'm not crying anymore, but it still hurts. I don't anticipate it will ever go away. Since the summer after my eighth grade year, all I ever wanted to do was play basketball in the ACC. It's like my life to this point is over. Now I have to start over, and that's scary.

LUCAS: 102 STEPS

MARCH 25, 2007

EAST RUTHERFORD, N.J.—This hallway is much too long.

And this hallway is much too short.

This hallway is a back corridor of the Meadowlands in New Jersey, which opened in 1981 but seems much older. NCAA Tournament postgames work this way: the head coach and two players answer questions at the podium in front of the assembled media. Some media never leave the podium area. Others make the walk down the hall to the locker room to get quotes from players not called to the podium.

After Sunday's loss—really, "loss" doesn't do it justice, does it?—you stop at the podium area first. Mostly, in truth, just to have a place to sit. You sat at courtside for as long as you could, watching Roy Hibbert grin and Jeff Green point to the "Georgetown" on the front of his jersey and every Hoya wearing dark blue get a hug from John Thompson Sr.

It is hard to believe. With what seemed like just moments left in the second half, you looked at the clock and it still said 7 minutes and 51 seconds remained. Was this clock ever moving? It was going . . . so . . . slow. So close to the Final Four but not wanting to think about it but you couldn't help letting it creep into your brain and then you shooed it away before anyone could notice.

Then the clock rushed. It cascaded. It snow-balled. Then shots weren't falling and three-pointers were being jacked up and a 10-point lead was gone, just like that. Some will say Carolina couldn't stop Georgetown in overtime. That's not true. Carolina couldn't stop them beginning at tipoff. The Hoyas shot 59.4% in the first half, 55.6% in the second half, and 57.1% in overtime.

Ugh.

Which brings us to this hallway. You can only sit in the podium area for so long without wondering what's happening in the locker room. People pay thousands of dollars for the privilege of getting one sneak peek into the Tar Heel locker room. And right now, there's nowhere less appealing.

The NCAA brings the same blue carpet to every tournament venue. It was the same in Winston-Salem and the same in East Rutherford and it'll be the same in Atlanta, not that you care enough to watch and find out.

Right now, you're staring down at that carpet and pondering a long walk to the locker room. This is the exact definition of "trudging." Just get in there, get the feel of the room, and get out. Don't linger. Keep your head down between here and there. No eye contact. Maybe it'll be deserted back here.

Thirty-eight steps later, here comes Joe Holladay. He's got a Midwestern sense of humor that is delightful. Right now, there are very few people you want to see less. It is nothing against him. It's just that, well, right now there is not much to say. Any suggestions? "Good game, Coach," doesn't seem appropriate. "Sorry" doesn't either. The answer to, "How are you doing?" is obvious.

So you look up, give a little shake of your head, and pat him on the back. He doesn't say anything. There is nothing to say.

Eighteen steps later, here is the Georgetown band. They are hollering and high-fiving.

Twenty steps later, C.B. McGrath and Jerod Haase are standing against a wall. College roommates, fast friends, their wives even gave birth within a couple months of each other. It is almost impossible to be in a room with them and not hear words bouncing off the walls, the rapid-fire easy chatter of best friends.

They're not saying anything now. They're just standing there, looking down at this blue carpet.

Five steps later, you go around a corner and come upon some very tall individuals. It's every single Georgetown player, and they're laughing and hopping to their locker room. Hibbert has a piece of net stuck behind his ear. They're wearing championship t-shirts. Somewhere, there is a box of Carolina championship t-shirts. Probably, someone moved them closer to the court with 6 minutes left. That way they'd be closer to the court for the celebration. Now we'll never see them.

The Georgetown band spots the players and merriment ensues. It is festive. It is joyous. And it sounds exactly like fingernails on a chalkboard.

Twenty-one more steps, and you're in the locker room. This is, without question, a losing locker room. Some years there is a chance to prepare. You know it's coming. This year, it felt like things were just falling into place. It still felt that way less than an hour ago.

Now there are hotel room keys tossed on the floor. Dewey Burke is in full uniform, just sitting there. It's quiet, strangely quiet considering how many individuals are crammed into this space. Players answer questions in hushed tones, and there is none of the usual back-and-forth between players as they get dressed.

Something is out of place: it's the jerseys. Usually, they're tossed in the laundry to be washed for the next game. Now there is no next game. So Danny Green's familiar number-14, still blindingly white, is hung on a peg behind him. Surry Wood's is folded neatly on top of his travel bag. It's hard to explain why this is so jarring. It's the official confirmation that there's nothing left in this season. These jerseys won't be needed again.

That's the most striking sight. To Green's left, in another part of the room, is the most striking sound. It sounds like this: *sniff clickclickclickclick.*

It's Tyler Hansbrough, and he's trying not to cry but the tears are coming. This is like chum in the water for photographers, who press their lenses right up to his face to get the shot. One photographer goes high, the other crouches down and shoots the sitting Hansbrough from below. For effect, you know. My words aren't good enough to explain how uncomfortable this should be, intruding on a moment like this. These particular individuals—not photographers as a whole, but these individuals—don't seem bothered by it.

There are a total of 102 steps between the podium area and the locker room. That sounds like it's a lot, but it's not enough.

People wonder why Roy Williams cries at the end of almost every season. Looking around this room, it's completely obvious. This room is broken. Every single team except one ends the season this way. At this particular moment, the BCS sounds like a good idea in college basketball . . . except that you know how good it feels to be that one team that ends the season with a win. That's what keeps you playing. That's what keeps you dreaming. That's what will get most of these players back in the gym later this week.

Like Wayne Ellington. He knows the magnitude of the shot he missed at the end of regulation. He's taken it thousands of times in his driveway and thousands of times in practice. Even took it a handful of times at the end of high school games.

"Most of them went in," he says, and he shrugs a little.

This one didn't. Now he has to figure out what to do next.

"I want to get some rest, but I want to get back in the gym," he says. "You're so upset that you want to work on things. It depends on how I feel physically, but I'm ready to get back to it."

It took 102 steps to get here.

The first step of 2008 is on the other side of the locker room door.

The hardest part about the aftermath of the Georgetown game was waking up and not knowing what to do. For the first time in a long time, there was no scheduled workout. For four years, I've woken up and thought, "How can I play better basketball for the University of North Carolina?" Now that opportunity is finished.

For my whole life, I might not have known where I was going to college or which school would recruit me. But I knew I would be playing basketball somewhere. Now I'm not sure, and for the first time in almost 10 years I'm facing the unknown.

It took me about a week to be ready to shoot again. I didn't touch a basketball for a week, which has never happened before. I went down to the Final Four to meet some people. I have some friends who are getting into coaching, and since I'd like to follow that path I thought I should network.

For a long time, I've known I want to coach. I know in my heart I have a passion for basketball and I want to be around it. At the same time, I'd love to keep playing the game. When I met with Coach Williams after the season, I told him I don't want to do anything that would hamper my coaching future.

If going overseas would hurt me at all, I don't want to do it. He thought playing overseas would help me, and I'll put all my trust in him.

We're at the point in our relationship that if he told me the best way to become a coach was to jump off a cliff, I'd jump without hesitation. He's going to help me. That's just what he does. He'd do it for any of his players. I don't know what the next step is, but I have a feeling he probably does.

I've heard him say before that his relationship with players changes when they graduate. It becomes less player-coach and more friendship. But I can't imagine he'll ever be anything other than "Coach" to me. And the opportunity to play for him, and to play for the University of North Carolina, will always be one of the highlights of my life.

EPILOGUE

I'M NO LONGER A Carolina basketball player. That's been a very difficult adjustment.

I'm not a college student, either. Reyshawn, Dewey, and I graduated in May. Our commencement speaker was Madeleine Albright, the former secretary of state. But we also had another special guest at our ceremony: Dean Smith received an honorary doctor of laws degree. It had been kept fairly quiet that he was going to be there, and when his name was announced at Kenan Stadium—where graduation was held—the crowd went crazy.

The coolest part of the day was that our senior class had our picture made with Coach Smith and the chancellor, James Moeser. That's a picture I will treasure forever.

Since then, I've spent my time traveling and trying to get my camps started. We've had a great response to them and it's been a great learning experience.

I know most of the response is because right now people still think of me as Wes Miller, Tar Heel basketball player. And one day in July I got my last chance to play that role. A handful of Duke players came over to Chapel Hill to play some pickup games. It was the end of the second session, so many of the current players were at home or working camps. Ty, Bobby, and Q were all out of town, and we really needed a point guard—fortunately, I hadn't forgotten too much of what Coach Williams taught me since the season ended.

My team included David Noel, Jawad Williams, Tyler Hansbrough, and Marcus Ginyard. Seeing the Duke guys walk into the gym with their royal blue shirts and shorts, it was hard not to feel that same burst of adrenaline. We played in the practice gym, so the total attendance was probably about eight. That's a big difference from almost 22,000.

But it was still electric. Tyler still screamed when he made a big play. Marcus still hit the glass. And I was still able, thankfully, to hit a few big three-pointers.

Formal statistics aren't kept in pickup games, of course. But I don't mind saying that our team lost just once out of eight games that we played. I felt it was an appropriate swansong for my Carolina basketball career. It was hard to remember that I was now one of the "old" guys, not one of the current players.

I'm no longer a Carolina basketball player.

But I'll always be a Tar Heel.

ACKNOWLEDGMENTS

I WISH I COULD SAY that this book was my own original idea. Unfortunately, it was not. At some point during my redshirt season four years ago I discovered that Coach Jerod Haase had written a book while he was a player at Kansas. I read the book and was glued to the pages. Going into this season it occurred to me that it would be interesting to embark on a similar project. I want to give a special thanks to Coach Haase for his advice and willingness to help me copy his idea. I have always looked up to Coach Haase as both a coach and a friend and although this book could never compare to Floor Burns, I hope he is proud that his thoughts and work have inspired another.

Adam Lucas is someone else who I can't possibly give enough credit. Throughout this season Adam and I met for a couple hours every week to work on this book. What started as a talented writer helping a player keep a journal, turned into a friendship and a meeting that I looked forward to each week. I want to thank Adam for helping me write this book, for always finding a way to point out something positive and insightful in every one of his columns and for becoming a good friend.

As always a special thanks goes out to Coach Williams. I approached him prior to the season and asked his permission to write this book. He told me that would be just fine. I then asked him if he wanted to give me any guidelines or rules as to what I should or should not write about. His only response was, "Wes, I trust you." First, I want to thank Coach for allowing me to discuss what goes on behind the scenes with Carolina Basketball. I want to thank him for giving me the opportunity to be a part of the Carolina Basketball family, for believing in me, and for helping me become a better basketball player and person. Wherever life takes me I will always be able to look back and realize that I am better human being for having played basketball for Coach Williams.

I want to thank the rest of my coaches: Steve Robinson, Joe Holladay and C.B. McGrath. I learned so much from each of them throughout my career. Our strength coach, Jonas Sahratian, and trainer, Marc Davis, are also key parts of the program.

An extra special thanks goes out to each one of my teammates: Marc Campbell, Will Graves, Wayne Ellington, Tywon Lawson, Deon Thompson, Alex Stepheson, Brandan Wright, Bobby Frasor, Marcus Ginyard, Mike Copeland, Danny Green, Tyler Hansbrough, Quentin Thomas, Surry Wood, Dewey Burke and Reyshawn Terry. I want to thank these guys for letting me share our stories and for their dedication, support and friendship. They are all truly brothers.

Acknowledgments

Thank you to all of the basketball office staff: Jenn Holbrook, Armin Dastur, Cynthia Somers, Kay Thomas, Ryan Zurawel, and Meredith Jones. Thanks to all of our managers, Bobby Cooper, Sean Stout, Matthew Fletcher, Brandon Rhodes, and Lauren Ripley. To our head manager, my roommate and good friend Preston Puckett: thanks for keeping our team on track.

Thanks to our Video Coordinator Eric Hoots. Amazingly enough, he was able to put up with me as a roommate and best friend for the last 3 years. He was also a big part in helping me recount what was going on with our team and keeping my journals updated while I wrote the book. Steve Kirschner and Matt Bowers helped me cross into the media world and served as great proofreaders.

I want to thank my former teammates and every one of the former Carolina players who have come back to Chapel Hill to interact and support our team during my career. It is an honor to be part of the Carolina Basketball family.

I want to thank all of my good friends for all of their support. A special thanks to Ashley Love, who was my girlfriend during the past two seasons. I know it wasn't easy putting up with me and having to be in a relationship with both me and Carolina Basketball. Thanks for all of her love and support.

Finally I want to thank my family for their unwavering love and support of anything I try to do: my parents, Ken and Susan; my brothers and sister, Matthew, Bo, Walker and Lauren. Without you guys I would not have been able to pursue any of my dreams, much less write this book.

—W.M.

The Road to Blue Heaven

EVER SINCE I WAS LITTLE, I've been hoping someone would write this book. I grew up obsessed with Carolina Basketball, and I always wondered what the real life of a player might be like. What went on in those player meetings? What was the pregame routine? What was being said in the locker room?

It just so happened that Wes Miller was the perfect player to write it. He has a Tobacco Road native's sense of perspective on ACC and Carolina hoops, and he's willing to recognize that he lived a dream in Chapel Hill.

For letting me tag along on that dream for a year, I'm very grateful. Because of his grit and skill set, Wes is the player I wished I was when I was shooting baskets in the driveway as a kid. Now, he's something even more than that—he's a friend.

All the other 2006–07 Tar Heels—Dewey Burke, Marc Campbell, Mike Copeland, Wayne Ellington, Bobby Frasor, Marcus Ginyard, William Graves, Danny Green, Tyler Hansbrough, Ty Lawson, Alex Stepheson, Reyshawn Terry, Quentin Thomas, Deon Thompson, Surry Wood, and Brandan Wright—played an important role in this book. The Tar Heel coaches—Roy Williams, Joe Holladay, Steve Robinson, Jerod Haase, and C.B. McGrath—were willing to have the curtain pulled back on their season and were always extremely cooperative. Jennifer Holbrook, Cynthia Somers, Kaye Chase, Ryan Zurawel, and Meredith Jones make the basketball office a well-oiled machine, even when idiots on the radio were giving out false information about signed basketballs.

Eric Hoots deserves his own paragraph. In addition to being another Carolina fan living a dream, he had the unenviable task of keeping Wes on time (more or less) throughout his senior season. He also contributed several of the funniest stories in this book.

Woody Durham, Jones Angell, Eric Montross, Ken Cleary, Ben Alexander, John Lyon, Steve Kirschner, and Matt Bowers frequently make being *around* the game as much fun as going *to* the game—even when we pick up unexpected passengers on the way home. Eric, of course, is still amazed that Wendy's now has a new flavor of Frosty—chocolate! Billy Puryear and Ray Gaskins get us back home safely and quickly, even on the unforgettable Atlanta-to-Raleigh flight. Lauren Brownlow was an essential resource for this book and is an invaluable *Tar Heel Monthly* editor/contributor.

As great as that crew might be, there's an even greater group: my family. I appreciate my parents, Jim and Dubba Lucas, for allowing me to grow up thinking I might play for Carolina and never breaking the news that I was not, in fact, very good at basketball. They are also responsible for one of the best pieces of advice I ever received—do what you love. That's what this job requires every day.

One day I'll give that same advice to my children, McKay and Asher. They are the only people who could drag me out of bed with a smile at 7 a.m. after I stayed up until 2:30 covering the latest 9 p.m. Tar Heel start.

And my wife, Stephanie, has somehow been married to me—and Carolina sports—for over six years. She is someone even more valuable than a dominant post scorer or a versatile shooting guard. She is the best wife and mother I know.

—A.L.